FINDING *Your* FAMILY HISTORY *in* NORTHEAST OHIO

Vicki Blum Vigil

Gray & Company, Publishers • *Cleveland*

This book is dedicated to the Early Settlers Association and to the many historical and genealogical societies in Northeast Ohio. By valuing the past, they enhance the present, which, ultimately, will enrich the future.

Gray & Company, Publishers
1588 E. 40th St.
Cleveland, OH 44103
(216) 431-2665
www.grayco.com

Library of Congress Cataloging-in-Publication Data

Vigil, Vicki Blum,
Finding your family history in northeast Ohio / Vicki Blum Vigil.
p. cm.
1. Ohio—Genealogy—Handbooks, manuals, etc. I. Title.
F490.V54 2003   2003022510

This guide was prepared on the basis of the author's best knowledge at the time of publication. However, because of constantly changing conditions beyond the author's control, the author disclaims any responsibility for the accuracy and completeness of the information in this guide. Users of this guide are cautioned not to place undue reliance upon the validity of the information contained herein and to use this guide at their own risk.

ISBN 1-886228-69-8

Printed in the United States of America

First Printing

Contents

Introduction

Does the world really need another genealogy book? Well, the world may not need one, but you may if you live in or near Northeast Ohio or if some of your family is from in the area. This book is comprised of three key significant elements to help guide you along on your family history research adventure:

Resources and facilities

You'll see that the chapters are arranged by research topic and area facilities. Chapters on the repositories go into extensive detail to explain where to find helpful resources and how to use them. Alas, what good is it to go to look at a gazetteer at the Cleveland Public Library if you don't know what to look up in it once you have it in hand? Or why go to Fairview Park Regional Library to look at the microfilm of the Cleveland News if you're not sure what to look for in that newspaper. This book will walk you through each facility so that even first time visitors will be prepared and comfortable, and veteran researchers may discover areas they've missed on previous visits.

Personal stories

Because I believe most people learn best by hands-on instruction, I've included personal stories contributed by other family history researchers just like you. Their stories are interesting and instructional, and with the accompanying graphics, provide the closest thing to hands-on I could present within the format of a book. By sharing the frustration and joy in these genealogy tales, you'll get a better sense of the intricacies involved in research, as well as the role that fate or luck can play.

Famous Families of Northeast Ohio

You'll also find vignettes of well known families in Greater Cleveland interspersed throughout the book. It's interesting to see how important family was to some of the movers and shakers in Northeast Ohio, and how they tried to pass on their particular take on family history. These stories are meant to inform and inspire readers. For example, many readers may have no idea that Murphy's Oil Soap was born and raised in Cleveland, or that Garrett Morgan, an African-American inventor who lived and worked in Cleveland, overcame incredible odds just to get his life-saving inventions put to use.

Whether you choose to read this book from cover to cover, use it off and on as a reference for your research, or just read the stories and vignettes, I hope it makes a significant contribution to your understanding and appreciation of family history and to your accomplishment of personal goals. And in that vein, I add these words attributed to Edmund Burke as encouragement: "People will not look forward to posterity who never look backward to their ancestors."

Author's note: All prices, hours, and websites addresses were current as of August 2003.

1 The Ultimate Time Travel: Your Own Family History

Genealogy has been described as puzzle-solving, mystery-unraveling, link-finding work. And it is. It is also a journey, actually a set of trips—back in time.

Yet unlike those fantasy trips from old television shows, you won't be strapping yourself into a time machine. You'll be immersing yourself in history. Those time machines have always been unpredictable, dropping people into the middle of international conflicts they suddenly had to solve. Your family history may take you to other nations and centuries, but instead of resolving someone else's problems, you'll be putting together the pieces of your own family story. This will be much more interesting to you, and probably less dangerous.

Like all trips, you start from home and make plans. Here are some things you will likely be doing:

Looking at maps. Maps and genealogy go hand in hand. Perhaps you'll need to find a map of the town where your great-grandfather lived. When he was born, the town was in Poland. By the time he died, the town was part of Russia. This is the sort of information you'll need to know when requesting vital records.

Gathering information about the destination. Whether you are going to a library or a cemetery, you'll need to know: What hours is the library open? Can you park near the cemetery?

Asking friends about their travels. Poll your friends, neighbors, and relatives who have done some genealogical research already. Ask them for any tips on who the knowledgeable volunteers are at certain facilities. What have they found is the best time to visit the library?

Researching some history. What did it mean to volunteer in the Civil War? Was the only economic depression in the U.S. during the 1930s? This information will have an impact on how you understand your ancestors.

Packing your bags. You will need a research log, a copy of your four-generation chart, plenty of change for parking and copy machines, a magnifying glass, and a well-thought-out to-do list. (These items will be discussed in detail in Chapter 2.)

Setting an itinerary. On this trip you might think you can plan out the itinerary, but you won't exactly be in charge of it. Your ancestors will continually interrupt your travel and take you in a different direction. And that's the fun and challenge of this trip back in time.

So, strap yourself in—a seat at the kitchen table or on the sofa might be most comfortable—and let's begin the journey.

tle Advice to Get You Started

ecting and researching your family history is a process. It cannot be accom-
d in one day, or one sitting (you knew that already). Like all worthwhile
it takes time and patience. The good thing is that as such a large task, re-
hing your family history can easily be divided into stages.

y one all-encompassing piece of advice to you along this journey is to docu-
t each time you do even the smallest amount of research. Write down where
've been (Aunt Irene's house); when (30 November 2002); and what you found
re (letters from Paul Stein, made copy, returned original to Aunt Irene). Include
well any letters you wrote (to Lucy Grasser in Santiago, Chile), what you asked
r, when the letter was sent and to what address, and if and when you received a
eply.

This way, if you don't do any further research for weeks or even months, you
have a written record to get you back on track when you do pick it up again.

Pitfalls

The trip, I'm sure you know, is not without its pitfalls. Time will be a major
issue. You will need to decide how much time you want to devote to researching
your family history, because the time starts to add up very quickly. You will need
information and details from other family members, and this will require their
time as well. Some family members you need to talk to may not have much time
left, so there can be a sense of urgency to gathering information also.

Don't be too disappointed in the lack of cooperation from some people. This
may be due to a total lack of interest in genealogy, or even out of fear that you
may discover or bring up an incident previously considered untouchable territory.

Pitfalls may be foisted upon you when you discover what some may consider un-
savory information: the aunt and uncle who never legally married; a relative who
was incarcerated; or someone whose death certificate lists syphilis as the cause of
death. Even if the individuals directly involved are no longer alive, the ownership
that a family feels for loved ones stretches back further than we may realize.

There is also the issue of writing down or documenting information about living
members of your family—how much to ask, and what to do about "different sides
of the story." You will have to handle each situation differently and probably with
ambassadorial diplomacy. However, a general suggestion is to not say or write
things that can be hurtful and destroy relationships between living family members. You can still put information in the family history and simply choose to not
have it released to others until after a certain time period.

But of course the fun part is to focus on the satisfying benefits of time travel
through your family history.

Finding a Focus

"Why are you interested in family history all of a sudden?" your friends ask
you. And what do you expect from it? Although no explanations are really necessary, I think it's a good idea to set some goals—which can be changed or altered,
of course. Here are some possible ways to define your endeavor:

The challenge—see how far back in time you can trace your family, how many
names you can find, and how completely you can fill in your pedigree chart.

The legacy—leave something for others to see and learn from. You may want to
write a biography about one family member or group. Or you could write a family
narrative including as many generations as possible, with the addition of other

No Parting in the Kingdom

When Cleveland resident Sarah Sanders passed away 23 October 2002, she left behind one brother, one son, five daughters, 26 grandchildren, 36 great-grandchildren, four great-great-grandchildren, family history records dating back over 200 years, and a heritage of family reunions starting in 1963.

Sarah Bowman Sanders had long been in love with history, so it was not surprising that some 35 years ago she became interested in researching her own family's history. Eventually Mrs. Sanders was able to trace the family back to 1797 when 12 brothers arrived in North Carolina from Africa and were sold into slavery.

Sanders's grandmother, Maggie Boswell, was a young girl when slavery was abolished and often told stories about life both before and after slavery. As a child, Maggie witnessed her father being sold to another man—brazenly taken away from his wife and child. When Harrison Boswell left he was singing, "There Will Be No Parting in the Kingdom." This hymn is sung at every Sanders family reunion.

Sanders was not the first in the family to be bit by the genealogy bug. In fact, her cousin Fred Boswell passed his research on to her before he died. And Mrs. Sanders's records have been passed on to her son, James Williams. However, it is the biannual family reunion that allows all members of the family to learn about, pass on, enjoy, and contribute to their family history.

The first reunion was held in Pine Level, Alabama, the site Harrison and his brother called home after becoming the property of Rev. John Boswell in 1852. Since then, reunions have been held in Birmingham, AL; Montgomery, AL; Chicago, IL; Cleveland; Youngstown; Saginaw, MI; and Washington, DC.

While each family reunion has something different, they are all organized and planned over a year in advance. Attendees receive a reunion booklet containing the weekend's itinerary, a summary of the Boswell family history, a list of descendants, and a directory of attendees.

And at each reunion the Boswell family tree is displayed. At the base of the tree is the motto, "Deep Roots, Strong Branches"—this was the theme that the Cleveland reunion committee came up with for the 2002 reunion. "We always pray," explains Cheryl Marone, Ms. Sanders's youngest daughter. "My mother was our prayer warrior/chaplain and sergeant of arms."

Figure 1-1: Mrs. Sanders, her first husband, and their children. *Courtesy of Cheryl J. Marone*

items such as pictures, copies of wills, birth certificates, marriage licenses, etc. Writing out your history is a good way to pass it on to future generations.

The learning—understand your past. Piecing together a history helps you understand family relationships and gives a voice to the silent. By delving into your history you may be able to identify people and names with their families and stories; learn about hereditary diseases; answer previously unanswered questions; perhaps even solve mysteries. The more we know and understand our past, the better we know and understand ourselves.

The pride—know and appreciate your family's heritage and keep it alive. Historical events take on a personal meaning when one of "our family" was affected

Family Reunions

Though family reunions seem to be experiencing a resurgence in popularity, they are nothing new. The booklet shown here details the Ehrett family reunion from 1894.

Figure 1-1: Family reunions are not a 20th-century fad. The twelve page history of the Ehrett family was given to all in attendance at the August 19, 1894, reunion held at Luna Lake (Stark county) Ohio.
Courtesy of Mary Ananea

by them. We don't want to lose our past, our uniqueness, our place in the world. It is a life-affirming act to make connections—to join a lineage association, to connect with our past and history. Ancestors then become "real people" as they are immortalized with family stories.

The reality—capture stories before they are lost through death. People are getting older and we don't want to lose the information, stories, and wisdom they can share with us. Finding out more about your family history can spur you to put together a family reunion, or make the next one better. To learn about your past is to recognize that life, for us, did not begin with our birth.

Written Family Histories as Idea Generators

Take the time to think about what you want your finished history to be, as this may help you shape your research. The best way to generate ideas is to look at published family histories to see what others have done. There is a wide range of these projects. Not all libraries keep family histories. I looked at several that I found on the open stacks toward the back of the Western Reserve Historical Society library, where they are arranged alphabetically by surname. I also did a computer search on the library's computer using the subject "Family History."

One of the books I found is a volume about the Kelley family: "A Genealogical History of the Kelley Family Descended from Joseph Kelley of Norwich, Connecticut with Much Biographical Matter Concerning the First Four Generations, and Notes of Inflowing Female Lines"; it was compiled by Hermon Alfred Kelley and privately printed in Cleveland in 1897 (it can be found on the open shelves at the WRHS library). By skimming through this volume I learned that Kelleys Island was once called Cunningham's Island. Mr. Cunningham was a French trader who supposedly settled on the island in 1808 to barter with the Indians and was badly wounded in 1812. The book has an index, follows each generation, and contains many portraits and illustrations.

The book *Tori in Amerika, The Story of Theodor Kundiz* was actually shelved in the WRHS library under "Cleveland" because it is more about Cleveland than just this individual and his family. Yet included is much information about Kundiz, the cabinetwork for which he was famous, his extended family, and his mansion in Lakewood. Interestingly, the author of this family history, as well as another one mentioned later, is Christopher Eiben. I guessed that Eiben was a professional researcher hired by families to either research the family lines or take the research already done by others and put it into book form. However, I was wrong. I called Mr. Eiben and learned that these two books were, as he put it, "a labor of love." Kundiz had brought over Eiben's great-grandfather from Europe. And Eiben married one of the great-granddaughters of Theodor Kundiz.

Another book by Eiben is *The Red Hand Forever: The Hugh M. O'Neill Family of Cleveland, Ohio*. This one is about an Irish family that can trace its roots back several generations. In 1897 O'Neill was a member of the Cleveland Mounted Police. The book recounts several legends, including one about a boat race to settle the rule of Ulster.

According to this legend, it was agreed that the first person to touch the far shore would win the race. The O'Neill family member was the better sailor and favored to win. Although O'Neill was in the lead for the greater part of the race, as it got down to the end it seemed he would lose. That's when he performed the act for which this book is titled, which won him reign over Ulster. Desperate to win the contest, and clearly behind his opponent, O'Neill reached for his sword, cut off his left hand at the wrist, and threw it onto the shore before his opponent

Dear Diary

Pat's family was from North Kingsville in Ashtabula County. In the mid-1970s, Pat's aunt gave her a diary from 1878. Her aunt "inherited" the diary after the deaths of her husband and sister-in-law, who was Pat's mother. Although she skimmed the handwritten volume when she received it, all Pat remembered was that it was written by her great-great-grandmother. A few years ago Pat sat down in earnest to read the diary.

The diary was in very good condition and documented the writer's everyday life, including "doing the work, baking pies . . . sewing, corresponding, taking care of the family." Suddenly Pat was seeing names and places she knew very little about.

Pat got on the Internet and found the website for the Ashtabula Genealogical Society. She wrote and received in return birth, death, and marriage information.

"What made it so exciting, and I must admit very emotional at times, was that my mother's family claimed to know only that my grandfather left the family when he and his brother and sister (both prominent figures in the diary) were quite small. My grandmother died and, not being interested in family history at the time, I never questioned her. My mother's sister died at 92 last year and steadfastly denied any knowledge of her father's lineage.

"Now after several intense readings of the diary, fitting dates, names, and places together with information gleaned from sources in Ohio, I am able to trace the diarist's origins to 1818. It may sound overly trite, but at times while reading the diary, I almost feel as if my great-great-grandmother was looking over my shoulder and 'pointing the way' to some clue. With the help of a Rand McNally road atlas, I have been able to find some of the towns mentioned. My quest for my mother's family history is so fascinating I wish I had more time to devote to it. The diary has been a wealth of information. I feel a special closeness to this woman, who very carefully inscribed her name on the inside: Harriaett Z. Palmer, N. Kingsville, Ohio. She's been gone a long time, but she's certainly not forgotten.

could touch land. Thus the O'Neills claimed victory and we learn the meaning of "the red hand forever."

These are just a few examples of the many books you can use to inspire you along the way.

How to Use This Book

This book is expressly designed for family history researchers who either are conducting research from Northeast Ohio or are researching family members who at one time resided here. Detailed information about libraries, courthouse records, and other local resources makes this book unique and essential for Northeast Ohio research. The attention to detail should allow your research to proceed more smoothly and be most productive.

Clearly, this book places a strong emphasis on Greater Cleveland—and not without reason. Due to its wealth of genealogical resources and its central location, Cleveland is an ideal place for family history research focused in Northeast Ohio. Whether you live in the area or come here to visit and conduct research, you will be satisfied with the depth and diversity of what we have available on this subject. And by using this book, you will know how to access the information and services available at many public and private institutions within this relatively tight geographical area.

This book is arranged to be useful to both the novice and experienced researcher. To that end, each chapter is meant to stand alone so that if, for example, you are at a point in your research where you need to get across the pond and find out how and when your ancestors first arrived in the U.S., you can go immediately to Chapter 15, "Immigrant Ancestors."

Meanwhile, the person new to genealogy would definitely want to go directly to Chapter 2, "Beginning Your Own Research," and begin filling out the family group sheets and then looking for the "at home" resources.

But Chapter 2 is not strictly for the genealogy "newbie." As all who have been involved in this endeavor know only too well, looking at "old" information for the third, fourth, or nineteenth time, or checking the attic or basement once more, often leads even veteran researchers to new material and over some of those "brick walls" only too common in genealogy research.

Many readers never check out such ordinarily dry sections as the appendix. In this book the appendix provides an in-depth description of local resources, and tips on precisely where to look, and how to use the materials. This can save you time and trouble by orienting you to the collections, the layout of the facilities, and what is and is not available.

Just hearing the words "court records" or "property research" is enough to bring fear and trembling to the most august family historian. But as Chapters 11 ("The Courts") and 12 ("Land and Property Records") will show you, these can be reservoirs of great information. By missing them, you may be missing your ancestors—or at least an important part of their lives.

And of course, when you get tired of the work, or maybe a tad frustrated, delve into some of the real-life stories included throughout the book. These may spur you on, give you that extra push, or even provide a new lead.

Interspersed throughout the book are vignettes about "famous families." You may be familiar with some of their names, and others may be new to you. I include their stories as illustration of the appeal of family history research, to underscore the fact that all people both great and small have similar interests and worthwhile stories, and as a way to acknowledge some of the area's long-standing leaders.

Now that you've been properly introduced to the entire book—let's continue on.

With so many ancestors to investigate, you may be wondering where to begin. Well, the fundamental rule in genealogy is to begin with yourself and work backwards. That way you will be starting with what you know. Sounds overly simple, but it's where all searches begin—figuring out what you know and then how to find out what you don't know.

2 Beginning Your Own Research

Ancestor Chart

You can plunge right in and accomplish something immediately by filling in a chart called an ancestor chart—also called a pedigree chart (see appendix for the form).

Charts can be confusing until you are familiar with them. On this chart males are always even numbers, females are odd numbers. Let's start filling it out. The first name to write in is yours—you are number 1 on your chart (gender doesn't matter here). Put down your full name, where you were born and when, and other information in the space provided. Write your surname (and all surnames) in ALL CAPS. This makes it easier for you and others to read and follow "lines of descent."

Your father is number 2, his father (your paternal grandfather) is number 4; your mother is number 3; her father is 6 (your maternal grandfather). Wives are always their husband's number plus 1. This seems tricky until you've plugged in a few names, then you get the hang of it.

Use pencil on the charts, at least at first. (Many people use pencil for information that is not yet proven and ink for that for which they have documented evidence.)

Use the full birth name of each person; always list the woman's maiden name for her surname.

Use what I call the "European method" for dates, writing first the day, then the month, and then the entire four digits of the year. Thus, September 11, 1875, is written: 11/9/1875.

List all places from smallest locale to largest: Cleveland (city); Cuyahoga Co. (county); OH (state). Country is understood here as U.S., but if it is a foreign country then write: Tampico, Veracruz, Mexico.

Begin with yourself and work backwards. Again, this is the fundamental rule in genealogy. We begin with the known and work toward finding out the unknown. But don't accept something as fact unless it can be proven with a document. This doesn't mean you can't put that information down on the chart, just that you still have to prove it. (As mentioned above, this is where pencil versus ink comes in handy, pencil being questionable information, and ink being proven.)

If you know where your parent was born, you know where your grandparents were living at that time. This may be the hometown/home country of the previous generation as well.

Next write the names of your parent and their parents—filling in the same information. Do you have everything you need, or are there gaps already? Don't feel badly that you don't know the birthplace of your maternal grandmother, or the

---

❗ Research Strategy

Research one family line, and in the beginning one person, at a time. Males are usually easier to trace, as their surnames don't change.

❗ Unmarried Couples

Filling out a chart and including significant others who are not married—what to do? Try using "partner" for spouse and "met" for date married.

Family Legends—Beware!

Almost every family has a story of lost treasure or a love affair between a commoner and royalty that is intriguing and, usually, vague. Do not let this be your point of departure. Always begin with yourself and the present and work back. If the path takes you to the "famous countess," you will already have substantial documented information from which to continue the serious search. Everyone likes to hear and pass on these family stories. Your job is to investigate the story, see if you can get facts and details, and analyze the factual information you obtain to check for the truth.

birth date of your paternal grandfather. Now the search, the work, and the fun begin! Just remember that the more information you have, the better. Once you have a city and state (better yet, a street address), you will be able to check records at local venues such as churches or synagogues, courts, schools, funeral homes, historical and genealogical societies, libraries, and cemeteries, all of which are discussed in later chapters.

Look in Your Own Home

Start your research in your home. Most of us actually have more information close at hand than we realize. Either we never looked for it, forgot we had it, or

Keep Asking

Cindy followed up on a query in her genealogy society's newsletter. The query led to her connecting with a relative in Australia. "We were having a family reunion in Atlanta, Georgia, so I invited him to attend. He accepted and all the cousins had lots of fun sharing pictures and stories. Then a local cousin of my dad's produced two family photos she'd never told me about.

"She had a portrait of my great-great-grandparents and their sons, and a photo of the family store on St. Clair Avenue in Cleveland. And I thought she had shown me everything she had!"

Make sure you ask and keep asking if the relatives have anything else!

Figure 2-1: Another forgotten picture, this one of Cindy's great-great-grandparents' Brandt and Sons Grocery Store on St. Clair comes out of hiding when visitor arrives from "down under." *Courtesy of Lucinda Brandt Newton*

Figure 2-2: Her cousin never thought of showing Cindy this picture until a relative from Australia visited. The existence of that relative was unknown until Cindy answered a query in her Cleveland-area genealogical society newsletter. *Courtesy of Lucinda Brandt Newton*

didn't ask the questions. Now it's time to find and look through that box of papers your sister asked you to store when she moved. Also check old scrapbooks, photo albums, baby books, and even those piles of papers you've been meaning to sort. Remember to look on the back of pictures or other papers for those little notes folks sometimes jot down.

Let's say you've found an envelope with the out-of-town address of a possible relative or close family friend, but it's probably 20 years old. What should you do? Make contact. Even after 40 or 50 years people have been located in this manner. Address the letter to the "Family of Johann Smith" (because Johann may no longer be alive).

Also, include a self-addressed stamped envelope (SASE; the glossary at the back has many more terms that will be used throughout this book). That way, if the family has moved but the current resident has some information, they can easily respond to you.

Many researchers recommend a handwritten letter, or at least something that does not look like just another personalized advertisement. You certainly wouldn't want your letter tossed in the circular file unopened.

Phone the Relatives

Start calling your relatives in town and out of town. Don't overwhelm them, just let them know you are interested in putting together the family history and would appreciate their help. What you want is to ask them two things: first, could they look around their house and see what information they have (of course you'll offer to help if they live nearby), and second, could they answer a few questions.

Most people won't keep this information in an orderly manner. It will be in cardboard boxes and old suitcases located in attics, basements, and crawl spaces. Get out the gloves and old blue jeans.

A complete list of what to look for is included on the checklist titled "Have You Checked These Sources?" (see appendix). But to begin with, ask about written documents such as birth certificates, baptismal papers, marriage certificates, and obituaries or death notices. A scrapbook or old photo album may provide more clues as well.

Boxes in the Basement

When I began researching my family history I found two cardboard boxes in the basement. (Why is it that genealogical data are almost always stored—whether at home or in public places—at the very bottom of the building, or the very top of the shelf?) My parents asked if they could store these boxes with me when they moved to Florida about 18 years ago. I totally forgot I had these. In the bottom of one box was my mother's diary as well as letters she and my father had written to each other when she worked in Washington, D.C., before they were married. This gave me a fair amount of family gossip and also included last names of distant cousins, some interesting details of my mother's work at the Justice Department, and the address my dad lived at in Solon. Prior to this, all we knew was that he had stayed in Solon, but now I had an address.

Tape-Recorded Visits

Carl Johnson writes, "Many of my relatives have wonderful stories to tell but have never thought about writing them down. When I visit these folks, I take a small recorder, turn it on, and let the conversation flow. Sometimes directional questions are helpful. I once asked my mother to tell me about my father's employment history. The result was a lengthy story about where we lived, Dad's jobs, events such as illnesses, births, etc., that occurred during that time, and the result was wonderful. At the end, she looked at me and said, 'Is that damned thing still on?'"

Then start with questions such as where someone was born, or why Charlie was in France. Remember that not everyone is as interested in family history as you are, and perhaps they didn't even know you cared about it until just now—so go slowly. You can call again, or write, e-mail, or visit.

Have your list of questions in front of you when you call (see the list of suggested questions below). If the person seems receptive, begin with some open-ended questions—ones that require more than a yes/no answer. For example: Whom did you play with as a child? What was dinner like? What school did you go to and how did you get there? What did you do in the summer? How did you celebrate holidays? What do you know about where your parents were born? Where were they married? Where did they come from? Does your name mean anything? Who were you named after? What do you know about that person? Why did your parents move to this place? Did anyone serve in the military? Why not?

If the person is not very talkative, just let them know you will contact them again once they've had time to think about some of these things.

Be sure to include everyone in the family—half brothers, stepsisters, and foster parents—firstly because they are truly a part of your family, and secondly because often there are family ties involved in these arrangements. Leaving someone out of the family tree may weaken all the other links, whereas including them may help you find more.

The follow-up to these visits may be a second round of appointments with some relatives, to either go through papers or talk to them about some new information you've uncovered. Perhaps sharing the new information will remind them of something they knew but forgot the last time you spoke.

Family members, particularly elderly ones, may not immediately recall anything about someone they haven't heard about in a long time. When you, the researcher, mention a surname, or a little bit of information about an individual, this may jog their memory and produce new and significant information. Just because cousin Joan said she didn't know anything about Uncle Oscar in the first interview doesn't mean she won't have something to say about him a month or two later.

After this visit, and any visit you make, be sure to record it. Simply type up your notes, make a copy that you give to a family member living elsewhere, and keep your copy in a file with your other important papers—not the attic (too hot) or the basement (too damp) please. If you make it a habit to document your visit immediately you will avoid problems such as deciphering your notes, remembering certain details, and repeating the same research.

Personal Interview Questions

- Be sure to ask how to spell all proper names.
- Ask about people in photographs—photos can serve to stimulate further memories, even vignettes.
- What is this heirloom? Where did it come from? Who owned it? Used it? Brought it?
- What memories do you have of your grandparents?
- What do you know about your grandparent? (details of life-cycle events, job training/military service)
- What was the house like that you grew up in? Your grandparents' house? Did you go there often?
- Where were people born? christened? married? buried?
- What are the names of your parents? your siblings? Did any other people live with your family?
- List all the places you lived.
- Were any foreign languages spoken at home?
- What was dinnertime like?

❗ Add a Picture To The Voice: Video Recording

Take Carl's advice one step further and use a video camera to capture a few of these conversations.

- What were favorite games you played at home? with friends? in the car?
- Did you take vacations, go places as a family? have a car? have an allowance? have chores? have family rules?
- Were your parents strict? Were they involved in clubs or organizations?
- What advice or philosophy did your parents pass on to you? What advice did you give to your children? Would you change that now?
- Did you ever do anything out of character? What?
- Did you have any major illnesses?
- Do you remember what your school looked like, any of your teachers, the school routines?
- Were you in any protests or demonstrations?
- What historical events did you live through and how did they affect you?
- How and where did you celebrate holidays?
- Were you ever discriminated against? Ever in jail? Ever interviewed on TV or radio, or in the newspaper?
- When was the first time you saw TV? A computer? Took a plane ride? Held a job?
- What was the first car you owned or drove?
- What was your schooling/occupational training/military involvement?
- Whom did you marry? Can you give information about your spouse?
- What details can you give about your children—birth, christening, marriage, etc.?
- How is each of your children different?
- Do you have any old pictures, postcards, albums, newspaper clippings, or souvenirs we could see?
- What religion were you? Others in your family?
- Any family customs or rituals?

The Family Bible

Looking for the family Bible? It usually travels with female members of the family.

Family Group Record

Now you can begin filling in a family group record (see appendix; you will want to make several blank copies of these to work from). These sheets help you view people as members of a family, not just through lines of descent. It is also how we include aunts, uncles, and cousins.

Start with yourself. You are a child on the family group sheet of your parents. If married, you are a spouse on another family group sheet. Eventually you'll want to complete a family group sheet for everyone who gets married.

At this point you probably have some blank spaces on your ancestor chart or family group record. You know your grandparents, or you know about them, but do not have all the information you need, such as maiden name and exact date and place of birth. Plus, even if you "know" these, every date has to be proven through a record or document.

The most important information to know is the "where," as in where the family was living at different times that events occurred. Then, not only can you locate birth and marriage certificates, you can find land and probate records as well. These will help you pinpoint people to a specific place on an exact date, and may also help fill in biographical details of a person or group. Such records may help you to distinguish between persons with similar names. Often, first and middle names were interchanged, so be careful in looking at records to determine if the person mentioned in the record is indeed the person you believe he or she is.

It's best to begin by accumulating or looking at vital records, family bibles, and other materials around the home; then look at church records and census records; finally, look at wills and probate files. After these, widen your search by looking for military and pension files, naturalization documents, and material relating to

Reading Faded Documents

When trying to read a document with faded information, try putting a 75-watt black lightbulb in a lamp and direct the light onto the paper.

other family members—the spouse, children, or parents of the person you are researching.

Most beginning researchers want to look immediately at the census. If possible, get the vital records first. They will help place your ancestor in a specific location at a specific time, thereby ensuring your census research will go more smoothly—and quickly. Also, you will then be familiar with new names or relationships and better know what to be on the lookout for.

What to Do with the Information You Find

You may not fully understand why you are putting so many details down on so many different charts and papers. But soon it will pay off. There are excellent books available offering different filing systems for the information family historians collect (see bibliography). If you're just beginning, make sure you keep everything. Make copies of all documents and maintain your records either according to surnames or family groups.

Organize Your Records

Make sure you have an organizational system that can be understood by others. Providing a hard copy of an index to your personal collection is a good idea. And update it yearly, or more frequently.

Possible filing methods are:

- according to document type (birth certificates in one file; marriage records in another)
- by surname, or by family group
- by the source (came from attic; from historical society; from probate file)

I use the family surname method and then place all documents behind the family group sheet within that surname file.

No doubt one document will often relate to several persons. In instances such as these, you can make multiple copies of that document to place in each person's file. Or, write on a separate sheet of paper the name of each of the people referred to and note in whose file the document is placed; then place these sheets in the files of the individuals.

Preserve Your Records

Next, be sure to preserve and maintain your records so they can be saved for future generations. Here are some helpful tips.

- Use photographic viewing sheets for copies of pictures.
- Use archival acid-free materials for photo albums.
- Store negatives away from the picture.
- Do not laminate originals, nor should you tint an original black-and-white photograph.

However there are some modern-day techniques you can use to spruce up and/or preserve copies of pictures or photos. These include using an air spray to clean dust from slides, prints, or negatives; digital tinting or retouching from a professional lab; making black-and-white copies of important color prints; and using archival storage boxes for large items.

Color-Coding

Many people color-code in ink different family groups or lines they are researching. The operative rule is do whatever makes it easier for you to follow.

- Do not fold original documents; buy a box large enough to accommodate the size.
- Do not use sticky notes on important papers—the adhesive has chemicals that will break down over time and may harm your document.

As you accumulate documents, file them under the family group with which they are associated or according to whatever system you have chosen. As your experience grows, but before your files get too large, take a look at the books describing sophisticated record-keeping systems (see bibliography). Use the same size paper all the time. This will make it easy to move material from one file to another. Full-size sheets are less likely to get lost. If you jot down a note on a scrap of paper, transfer it to a full sheet as soon as you can. Put your name on each sheet of paper in your files—in either the upper right- or upper left-hand corner.

Keep everything—and keep it longer than necessary. At the time you find or read some material it may not match up with any of your known family members or collateral lines. Do not discard it—especially if you are a beginner (which I loosely define as having less than one year of active research under your belt). Connections are often made later; names once misspelled or misplaced are later recognized, so this is one time that it's advisable to be a pack rat.

Keep a Research Log

A research log is an accounting of what you accomplish each time you do research: from your computer at home, at a local library or archive, or on a trip to a cemetery. You are going to keep records for three categories:

- What you found
- What you did not find
- Leads you got on something/someone you weren't even researching

Take a look at the research log in the appendix. On the side of the sheet marked "Description of Source," you will list where the research was done, the date of the research, and which sources provided which information. If the information comes from the census, take down all of the data: enumeration district, date completed, page number, line number, and so on. This will save hours of work later when you realize you have conflicting information about an individual and need to justify your choice.

On the right-hand side of the sheet is a column for "Results." This is where you will note not only when you find information, but when you don't find information. This will refresh your memory as to where you've already looked unsuccessfully.

Lastly, write down any lead you get on someone you are not currently researching. State what it is, to whom it refers, and exactly where you found it—the book, the page, and the library or archive it was in.

Save Notes, Make Copies

Make copies of pictures, letters, and documents as you collect them. Do not carry originals with you, whether you're going around the corner or across the country. Make copies and keep them in a file or folder. File copies with the appropriate family and keep them behind or with that family group sheet. Organizational experts advise filing an item immediately. Handling it once instead of several times actually saves you time.

Many people save everything to disk or CD-ROM so the information can be

Helping Others

Those of you who are more experienced—remember what it was like for you at the beginning, and try to help out the new subscribers ("newbies") on your listserve, members of your genealogy society, or those who post queries on message boards. This uninitiated person may eventually lead you to a wealth of information. The personal stories in this book attest to that.

◆

A Royal Canadian Story by Grace Phipps

A couple of years ago I decided it was time to put some order to a lifetime-plus of family pictures. What a job! I ran across a snapshot of a Royal Canadian Mounted Police officer. The picture had been cropped to fit into a small space, but what I could read on the back identified him as follows: "This is Constable Archie Peacock for Grace. He was sent out on a hurry up call to help keep order at Flin Flon, Manitoba." There was a barely visible note that said "he had work [*sic*] his uniform for a month so it was in need of pressing."

Who was this man? I put the picture aside and gave it some thought. I vaguely remembered my mother corresponding with Aunt Rose in Saskatchewan, Canada, many years ago. I knew all of my mother's relatives, so I supposed it to be on my father's side. (My parents divorced when I was three years old and there was little contact with my father and his second family over the years.)

I wrote to the RCMP headquarters in Regina, Saskatchewan, and asked for their help. They responded, "We do not keep records dating back as far as you require for this Division."

Also, they forwarded my letter to the Archives Branch at headquarters in Ottawa. A few weeks later I received a letter from the RCMP Archives Manager in Ottawa stating that the Access to Information and Privacy Act prohibited them giving me what I requested; he photocopied a few newspaper articles that I might find of interest. The articles were (1) a brief synopsis of Archie's service record, (2) a picture of him taken in 1932, (3) an announcement of his marriage with a picture of the bride and groom, and (4) a copy of his obituary from the newspaper in Regina.

Bingo! There were the names of his parents, his brothers and sisters, and the cities they were living in at the time of his death (1971). That was great

Figure 2-3: Photo of Constable Peacock found by Grace when she was doing some organizing.
Courtesy of Grace M. Phipps

news—at least I had some names, but I supposed they were all dead. After all, it was 1999. So, I thought about it for a while (again).

Meanwhile I contacted the Haliburton Highlands Genealogy Group (in Ontario, Canada, where my grandfather was born) for more clues. I was very unlucky there and later decided to see if I could find anything about Archie's brothers on the Internet. Guess what? I found two of them, both living in Saskatchewan. I quickly wrote letters to them.

About a week later I received an e-mail message: "Hi Cuz, my dad wants you to know he received your letter and is making copies of all the family information he has. You'll be hearing from him soon."

Two days later the phone rang and a man said, "Hi Grace! This is your cousin Harvey Peacock. How are you? We've been wondering what happened to you." We chatted for a while (Harvey's mother, Rose, was my grandfather's sister), and his final comment was, "I have a little information about the family that my older brother, Wesley, put together before he passed away. I've put it in the mail . . . "

When the package arrived, it had family pictures, including my grandparents' wedding picture, one of my father and grandfather, a picture of my great-grandfather (who just walked away one day in about 1885 and never was heard from again), one of my great-grandmother, and even one of my great-great-grandparents plus several pictures of Harvey's family. Also included (from England) were the marriage registration of my great-great-grandparents and (from Canada) the marriage registration of my great-grandparents. There was a narrative of all the family events that Wesley knew of concerning the members of the family who had left Ontario and migrated west to Saskatchewan and Alberta. It included a similar narrative (written by a cousin in Ohio) about the family members who left Ontario and moved to Northeast Ohio. What a treasure trove!

Since then Harvey and I continue to correspond and talk on the phone. The other brother, Walter, lives in Regina. I've been invited to visit them in Canada and I hope I'll be able to do so soon.

passed on via the computer. The sophisticated computer genealogist will include scanned images and tape recordings of family members along with the usual ancestral data.

Keep an Eye on the Details

Family history requires attention to details. The place someone was born, the date of an event, variations in spellings of both first and last names—all are necessary pieces of information that may lead to finding more information. As you take notes do more, not less. Don't exclude information just because you are not familiar with it or are sure you know it already. For example, because many records are housed according to county, note not only the city and state of a marriage but the county as well. Always write down where you got your information.

If something doesn't make sense, don't discount it—try to figure it out. If the birth date on one document is different by several years from the birth date on another, you have some evaluating to do. Does the information make sense? Would a 12-year-old girl get married? Would a 70-year-old female give birth? Are both documents referring to the same person? If so, what do you need to do to verify this information?

How to Handle Common Names

When you find someone with a name that's the same as or similar to that of a person you are researching, how do you decide that this is or is not "your person"? Clearly not all individuals with the same name (or a similar one) will be the person you are looking for, but we tend to leave the decision-making process out of our notes—which means that you may end up having to go back later to records you looked at before but didn't consider relevant.

If you have a common surname like Smith, Murphy, or Jones, you have to be more diligent. Keep the best of records on your common-name ancestors. Write down everything you know "for sure" about your ancestor and then look at your paper trail to see which information, if any, from those with the same surname seems to fit with this person. Keep each individual's information separate and make a timeline or attempt to fill in a family group sheet for these other "possible" ancestors. Analyze the information and decide who fits and who doesn't. Also, make a to-do list of what information you need to find in order to make the decision definitive.

For example, instead of looking for the individual named "Kelly," look for a sibling or in-law with a less common name (yet still someone who connects to Kelly).

Search using both given and surnames and search on genealogy websites.

Refine your computer-based search by typing in "Smith AND Philadelphia."

Assume Nothing

Assuming a given ethnicity or religious affiliation can lead to holes in your research. Remember that surnames were often changed, because someone had a desire to be part of the "melting pot," or some official had difficulty understanding the limited English of the immigrant, or because certain groups were discriminated against, and therefore changing "Polansky" to "Mueller" might have made perfect sense to a Polish immigrant in a German area.

Depending upon the size of the area where immigrant ancestors settled, access to the religious denomination of their choice may have been severely limited. There-

You've Made Progress!

Here is a review of the first steps you can take in researching your family history:

- Look around your house for information
- Contact relatives for information
- Get vital records/civil registrations
- Begin with one person
- List the key events for that person and where these events took place
- Write, call, or visit the place where records for that location are kept; request copies or search for them yourself
- Always check alternative spellings
- Organize your research and keep copies of everything

fore, the fact that the family belonged to a Methodist church does not mean they were or had always been Methodists. Religious affiliation may have been affected by marriage. Also, churches change names, merge, and dissolve. So consider contacting other churches in the same neighborhood, or serving the same ethnic group.

By knowing someone's occupation or workplace, you may have another avenue for information. Trade organizations and unions maintain important biographical information. Most people easily think of contacting professional organizations such as medical societies and state nursing boards, but what about guilds? The guilds in Great Britain had records dating back to medieval times. Some of their records can still be found in the country's city archives.

Analyzing Data

Every time we look at a record and the information it contains we should ask ourselves:

- When and why was this document created?
- Was the information contained here provided at the time of the event (birth, death, marriage) or sometime afterward?
- Could the person providing the information have had a reason to alter some of the details (illegitimate births, age, questions of legality of residence, distrust of government officials, difficulty understanding the language, desire to "look better" in the eyes of social peers through, for example, a high-status occupation)?
- Realize that today we place great emphasis and importance on the facts in these documents. Our ancestors may not have cared if someone got their birth date wrong by one day—what difference could that possibly make?

Feeling Stuck?

Folks in genealogy call it "hitting a brick wall"—when you've been following an ancestor and the trail goes cold. It will happen sooner or later, and more than once. When it does happen try the following strategies:

- Look for a cousin or in-law
- Look in a neighboring town or county
- Follow the siblings
- Read a history of the area
- Check out the neighbors. According to the "cluster theory," people do not exist in a vacuum, and often neighbors move with each other; people often marry neighbors. Also, before 1849 people usually migrated in groups because it was safer.

Birth Records

If all else fails, try checking the mother's hometown. Many women returned "home"—where they were raised—to give birth, especially with their first child.

"Fishing Expedition"

Let's say you really don't know where a particular person died. But you do know that at one time he or she was living in the small- or medium-size town of "X." Try telephoning the history department of the library in that city. Ask if there is an index to obituaries and if they could look up a name and what it costs. Many libraries charge a nominal fee ($1 to $2), for which they will then send you a copy of the obituary. Others may refer you to an online index. Libraries that may not have obituaries online may still have a way to be contacted online. Try this website: www.libraryspot.com.

So how does it feel to have finally begun your family history trip? Remember to go at your own pace and try not to take too many side trips along the way. You are probably just beginning to feel comfortable with some of the forms. Let's venture out now on a field trip.

3 Visiting Cemeteries and Funeral Homes

While this book is designed to show you what to look for and where, it's also important for you to begin thinking like an investigator, because as a family history researcher you are investigating your family. So let's begin with death, because death is part of life, and can give us a lot of information about a person's life.

Think of all the information you might want to find out after someone has died:

- Age
- Date and place of birth
- Date and place of death
- Home address
- Cause of death
- Marital status
- Family information (names of spouse, children)
- Occupation
- Where buried
- Favorite pastimes
- Religion
- Fraternal organizations

These are the sources that may provide that information:

- Burial records (found in classified section of newspaper)
- Death registration/certificate
- Funeral record/booklet
- Obituary
- Death notice
- Cemetery records
- Gravestone

So to begin with, let's do some fieldwork.

Cemeteries

A visit to a cemetery can provide a great deal of information that will help in your family research. Before going to the cemetery, do your homework. Look at the information you have uncovered from the search through your home and from relatives, and determine which cemetery to visit.

Call or write the cemetery or look it up online to find out exactly where it is located, when it is open, and when the office is open (the cemetery may be open on Sunday, but if there is no office staff available, your questions may not get answered).

Try to visit when staff will be available—if that is not possible, find out beforehand the exact location of your relative's grave.

Cemetery workers are accustomed to finding their way around the cemetery where they work—that's their job. But in a large, or even medium-sized cemetery, having a section number and even a lot number might still not lead you directly to the grave. And, if the weather is not cooperating, you may not feel like walking up and down row after row of headstones. So "play dumb"—ask for the most specific description possible of the location, including perhaps the presence of a large marker nearby, or ask if the site could be marked for you on a map.

Take Care of Gravestones
Be careful of those gravestones. Don't rub them with chemicals or dirt. Talcum powder or powdered limestone is suggested. Take photos of tombstones and surrounding areas as well—to help locate the site again.

What to Do About "Closed Cemeteries"

If a cemetery has no staff or phone number, it is probably a "closed cemetery." This does not mean you cannot visit, just that you won't get much help. It's not closed in the sense that you cannot go see it; it's closed in the sense that there are no new burials, and likely, no staff available to answer your questions or assist you in locating a grave. In such cases, contact the local historical or genealogical society to see where the records for this cemetery are kept. In some small townships or suburban areas, records may be at the local library or city hall, the city engineer's office, an archive, or a court facility.

Visiting the Cemetery

If possible, call the day before or day of your visit to make sure there's not a funeral at the time you will be arriving, thereby making staff unavailable for your questions. You can politely inquire if coming 30 minutes earlier or later would be helpful.

Take with you:

- Camera
- Paper, pencil, pen
- Clipboard (easier to write on when you are standing up)
- Grass clippers
- Rag or old dish towel—to wipe off grave, clear grass clippings, or kneel on
- Small putty knife—to gently nudge earth away from edges of flat markers
- Small whisk broom and gloves—to clean headstone of lichen and other gifts from nature
- Snow brush or child's broom—helps clean off flat headstones, particularly during fall and winter
- Names, death dates, and other identifying information on the relatives whose burials you are researching.

Wear comfortable clothes. Some areas retain moisture more than others, so even if it's not damp near your house, it may be wet and muddy in the cemetery.

As you enter the cemetery be aware of your surroundings. How are things arranged—are the sections marked with letters or numbers, on the ground or on trees? Do some sections have only flat markers? Is there clearly a veterans' section (lots of government markers and probably a flagpole with the American flag)? Is it clear where the "oldest" section of the cemetery is (older, fading, whitish-gray markers, slanted or leaning, illegible writing, dates from early 1800s)?

Check in at the office even if you know exactly where the plot is. Ask what information they have on the person you are researching. You may be pleasantly sur-

The Lost Key

Bill's story begins with his wife looking for a lost key. During the search, she found the funeral registry book for Bill's grandfather, John Takacs, who had died in 1954. Although Bill had seen the registry book before, somehow he'd missed a page in the front listing relatives who had attended the funeral.

As Bill tells the story:

"My grandfather had four sisters, and I had only been able to account for three of them. My wife spotted two signatures in the book that were not recognizable—other than that, in parentheses, next to the names, was the surname of my grandfather's other sister's married name. One of the

Figure 3-1: Page in the funeral registry book that helped Bill learn the surname of his great-aunt and led him to meeting a second cousin. *Courtesy of Bill Takacs*

names in the book was 'Porter,' the other name was 'Paczelt.' Looking for 'Porter' was like looking for a needle in a haystack. 'Paczelt' was less common and it deserved a try."

Bill used the Cleveland phone book and on the second phone call got lucky. The person he'd called was a relative of the individual who'd signed the funeral registry book. She took Bill's phone number and agreed to notify the individual to see if she was interested in talking to Bill.

An hour later Bill received a phone call and had found a new second cousin. The cousin's husband was also involved in genealogy, and so the newfound relatives continued to share information and were able to add a new family line to their family tree.

---

prised—some cemeteries keep death notices, information from the funeral home, and, because their services must be paid for, may have receipts with names and addresses of other relatives you need. If the staff member is busy, offer to wait, come back at the end of your visit, or call later. These folks are inundated by genealogy requests and most are happy to give you the information, but some days are busier than others.

Find your ancestor's grave. Clean off the marker and surrounding area, if it needs it. Flat markers may need a minute with grass clippers or putty knife so you can read and see everything. Write down the date of your visit as well as everything written on the headstone, exactly as it is written. Look at the front, back, and sides of all markers. Take pictures of the headstone from different angles. Walk around the area where your relative is buried. Some families bought family plots so all their members could "rest in peace" together. By walking down a few rows on either side of your ancestor you may discover a few more peaceful family members.

If you do see a familiar name, or one you are uncertain about that has the same surname, take down that information as well. Then check this out with the sexton or other cemetery staff, as well as other family members you can talk to when you return home.

Whether visiting a cemetery far from home or a few miles away, you might want to try finding out if anyone else has "visited" the same ancestor.

Laminate a note or other identifying information about yourself (this can be done at most copy centers), so people can contact you. (Use your e-mail address or a work phone number, or that of a friend if you do not want to give out your home information.) Leave the laminated note on top of an upright headstone under a rock, or use one of the plastic sticks that accompany floral displays to anchor your note in the ground next to the headstone.

You could also write a "we were here to visit grandma" note and laminate it together with your contact information, securing it to the ground with a modest stake.

When you return home from your cemetery visit, you will likely have new information to add to your charts; note which information you need to verify with official records.

Before you begin writing, calling, and visiting libraries and other official places, you might want to follow up your cemetery visit by contacting some funeral homes.

Funeral Homes

As with the cemetery staff, the funeral home staff has been keeping track of our dead relatives for a long time. Often they can provide us with details and records that will lead to more information. If the funeral home is still in existence, look them up in your telephone book. If it is out of town, try a website such as www.funeralnet.com/index.html (which also lists cemeteries). You can search by funeral home name, or by city, county, and state, or call long-distance information at 1 + area code + 555-1212. These businesses keep records that may include obituaries, family members' addresses, and receipts. The website will have a mailing address, phone and fax numbers, and perhaps even links to related sites.

I suggest calling the funeral home first and explaining that you are looking for "some information about a family member." Depending upon what staff is available, you may be successful on the first call. But remember, you do not simply want verbal verification that they handled the burial, or information on where the person is buried. You want copies of written records. Offer to call back at another time or come in person (if convenient). Some of these places are working with huge handwritten ledgers. And of course the "old" ones are, you guessed it, in the basement. Those fortunate establishments that have computerized their records can access the information on the computer, but they will probably still need to retrieve the documents you want from the original file. Some funeral homes will accept an e-mail inquiry; others require a written inquiry.

The Next Phase of Your Research

Now that you've visited a cemetery or funeral home you probably have new information about one or more of your ancestors. After you've typed up your notes and made copies of them, decide if you would like to continue your detective work. If so, look at the new information and see if you can plug in any more names or dates on your ancestor chart. Does this leave you with more questions for which you would like answers?

It's time to take the next step and build on the information you have—you are ready for library and/or historical society research. In Northeast Ohio, we have a unique group of agencies and institutions available to us for family history research. The next five chapters describe what is available in our own backyard:

- The Cleveland Public Library (CPL)
- Cuyahoga County Archives (CCA)
- The Library of the Western Reserve Historical Society (WRHS)
- Family History Centers (FHC)
- Fairview Park Regional Library

These chapters go into extensive detail to explain the resources of each facility and, more importantly, will teach you how to use them.

GRIES

Famous Families

Many consider Robert Dauby Gries to be a sportsman. Although his father, Robert Hays Gries, was one of the founders of both the Cleveland Browns and the Cleveland Rams, this fifth-generation Clevelander clearly has a more participatory bent to his sports experience. Though he has climbed more than a mountain or two and rides his bike hundreds of miles a week on "vacation," for this man Cleveland and family really tell his story. And Gries is proud that story can be traced back to 1833/34, when a young Bavarian émigré, Simson Thorman, arrived in Cleveland.

Thorman was 17 when he left his hometown of Unsleben, in what was then Bavaria. He was a fur trader who stopped in Cleveland and then continued west in search of more pelts but soon returned to Cleveland to live. Thorman's letters to family and friends in Bavaria encouraged others to join him. When they did, the first Jewish settler in Cleveland had successfully formed the city's Jewish community.

Any time Gries or others want to know about this family, they can go to the Western Reserve Historical Society and look in the manuscript file under "Thorman." This file contains an article from the October 25, 1937, *Cleveland Press* titled "Jews of City Honor Their First Settler." It is, of course, about Simson Thorman, whose daughter married Kaufman Hays. Hays's daughter then married Rabbi Moses Gries—Robert Dauby Gries's grandfather.

Also in the file is a black three-ring notebook with the trunk of a tree on the cover that contains handwritten notes with genealogical questions and comments such as:

"Write to Dauphan and ask the year the property was bought."

"The date Simpson and Regina were buried and died. . . ."

Inside the manuscript is also a letter to Sophia Thorman (who married Harold Thorman) from Robert Hays Gries, dated 22 July 1959, which states: "At long last, the family tree! I hope you have as much fun looking. . . ." The tree was compiled in 1957.

Not in the manuscript file but elsewhere at WRHS is what is known as the Alsbacher Document. This historic paper is addressed to Moses and Yetta Alsbacher, the leaders of a group of 19 Jews who left Germany in July 1839. Dated 5 May 1839, it instructs the group to maintain, practice, and preserve their religion and culture in America. America is described as "a country without compulsory religious education or Jewish law . . . a land of tempting freedom." Simson Thorman met this group when they arrived in New York and convinced 15 of them to join him in Cleveland.

Robert Gries was probably not surprised when his daughter, Peggy Gries Wagar, moved back to Cleveland in 1990, with one of her reasons being to live closer to her father. A few years later, Wagar's studies with the Wexner Heritage Foundation sparked a desire to know more about her greatgrandfather, Rabbi Moses Gries.

Even though Robert Gries has always emphasized and cherished family history, recounting and retelling that history is one thing; seeing it and getting personally involved in it is very different. And so it was that Wagar went to WRHS and looked through the manuscript file to get a sense of who her great-grandfather was. She found articles written by him, copies of his sermons, and details of 19th-century life.

While Bob Gries can trace his family back to prominent Clevelanders Rabbi Moses Gries and Nathan Dauby (owner of the largest retail operation in the city), as well as Simson Thorman, his great-great-grandfather, this is not the primary source of his enthusiasm for family and family history. Gries can trace that back to his parents. He remembers noticing birth and death dates in his father's prayer book. His mother's prayer book contained the same information for her side of the family. He cherishes these books.

Gries has always been interested in history, and family history was just a natural extension of that interest. Gries remembers his father working on the generational chart almost 40 years ago.

"You are remembered by the good that you've done," explains Gries as he recalls a meeting several years ago with Anna Brown, the director of the Cleveland Office on Aging for over 14 years, who died in 1985. Her family was from Rahway, New Jersey, and Gries's grandfather owned a clothing store in Rahway. When Brown's grandfather was accepted into college (probably more than 80 years ago), the entire town knew and was excited about it because he was the first African-American from the town to go to college. Gries's grandfather invited Brown's grandfather to his store and gave him a suit for college. Many years later Anna Brown met Bob Gries, and they realized their connection. That explains Gries's philosophy of giving back to the community—"it lives on and has an impact on life long after."

4 The Cleveland Public Library

As you enter the main building there is an alcove on the right where you can check out and return books. This is also where you'll find the change machine. Guards are posted at the entrance. The General Reference Room is directly ahead, just past the security guard.

General Reference Room

Of the many services available at CPL, general reference is of particular interest to genealogists. Here you'll find books, online catalogs, and CD-ROMs.

Entrance Area

At the entrance to the general reference room are banks of computers. One set of computers offers Internet access; another set, on the right as you enter, offers "Catalog Plus," which permits you to search the various databases within the library system but does not have Internet access. The first five copies printed at these terminals are free. After that copies are $.10 each.

The Cleveland News Index can be accessed from computers throughout the library. On this database you will find obituaries from the *Plain Dealer* from 1983 to the present and obituaries from Cleveland newspapers from 1976 to the present.

To access the database from the computer, first go to the CPL home page. Select "Database," then "Alpha list," then "D," and receive a description of what this database includes.

Obtain the exact date of death and possibly where the person is buried.

Reference Room—East (to your right as you enter the room)

The open shelves in this area house bibliographies, encyclopedias, and biographical indexes as detailed below.

Annals of Cleveland is a set of books that summarizes articles in local newspapers from 1818 to 1876. There are 48 books, and each volume has a name/event index in the back.

Use: Check for names of people who might have been mentioned in the local papers. They did not have to be famous or prominent—the population of the area was small during most of this time, and newspapers often listed tidbits of information about residents in the area.

Cleveland Public Library (CPL)
325 Superior Ave.
Cleveland, OH 44114-1271
216-623-2800
Hours: 9–6, Mon–Sat
1–5 Sun (during the school year)
....
Website: www.cpl.org
Parking: There is limited street parking (meters) around the library as well as commercial lots located in the vicinity. The library is comprised of two buildings—the Main Library and the Louis Stokes Wing. Both have entrances from Superior Avenue with an underground walkway connecting the two buildings.

❗ Introduce Yourself

Upon entering a new library, historical society, or other repository, go to the desk and introduce yourself. State what you are researching at this time and ask, "What resources are here that are not obvious to me?"

Quick Link to Vital Records

The "History" link on the CPL website is a wonderful resource. From the CPL home site, select "History," then "Genealogy," then "Vital Chek." This will give you an address anywhere in the U.S. to write to for vital records.

The Biography Index contains articles in journals and books from January 1946 to 2000. Although it is based on current events and notable people of national interest, there are some Clevelanders included. Listings are alphabetical by subject (i.e., Cold War) and person.

Use: If your ancestor was a notable person, or involved in a noteworthy event, check here for his or her name.

Volumes of the New York Times Index are available from 1851 to the present. The *New York Times* is the only national paper for which the library has an index, as well as having it on microform. Any event or person written about in the *New York Times* will be indexed here. This includes obituaries of well-known national and international figures. Citations include date, page, and column. If you are searching Cleveland papers and there is no index for a particular time frame, it might pay to look in this index.

Use: Look for information on famous or infamous people and events of nationwide interest.

New York Times Biographical Service provides biographical materials, excerpted stories about prominent people (actors, writers, political figures), obituaries, and feature articles from 1974 to the present. It is very thorough and contains the actual articles.

Use: If your ancestor was considered an expert, a noteworthy individual, or an otherwise prominent person, search for him or her here.

The Personal Name Index to the New York Times Index is a set of books that lists alphabetically by last name anyone whose name appeared in the *New York Times* from 1851 to 1974 and 1975 to 1996. The citation next to each name refers to a volume of the New York Times Index, in which you can then find the date and page you need to look for in the New York Times itself.

Use: A great way to look up anyone who might have been written about in the New York Times during this time period.

Reader's Guide to Periodicals Index lists articles in major national magazines by year from 1890 to the present. Articles are indexed according to subject, name, event, and author's name. Citations list title of article, author, publication month, year, and page.

Use: If it is possible your ancestor either wrote an article that was published in a major national magazine, or was written about in a magazine during this time period, look for their name here.

The Reader's Guide is also on Infotrac (a computerized database) on the CPL database but only dates back to the 1980s there. Likewise, the New York Times Index is online but only goes back a few years.

Poole's Index to Periodical Literature, a six-volume set of books, is similar to the Reader's Guide but for an earlier time period—1802 to 1906. The beginning of each volume lists the names of magazines included and a subject index by person.

Use: Look for the name of an ancestor who either authored an article in a major national magazine or was written about in a magazine during this time period.

The Index to Black Newspapers is a set of books listing black newspapers in the U.S. by year from 1979 to the present. Information is listed by subject and person and refers the researcher to a newspaper by month, date, and year. You must then proceed to the microform room to request the corresponding film. If CPL does not have the particular newspaper on microform, a request can be made for an interlibrary loan.

Use: Searching for African-American ancestors who may have been noteworthy enough to be included in any U.S. black newspaper from 1979 to the present.

Index to the London Times, also on the open shelves, covers articles from 1973 to the present. For volumes prior to 1973 patrons need to ask the librarian.

Use: Finding articles that appeared in the London Times covering certain subjects or containing the names of specific individuals.

The Washington Post Index is available in book form from 1972 to the present. It also lists items alphabetically by name, topic, and event. The researcher is then referred to the specific date and page of the newspaper. One must then go to the microform room and request the appropriate newspaper reel, put it in a microform reader, find the article, and print it out if so desired.

Use: Finding articles that appeared in the Washington Post covering certain subjects or containing the names of specific individuals.

Cleveland News Index is available in book form from 1976 to 1994 (also on-line from 1983). Found here are obituaries indexed from the Cleveland Press and Plain Dealer, as well as local and national stories that mention Clevelanders or Ohioans. It is alphabetized by subject and name.

Use: Names and death dates of Cleveland-area residents who died in this time.

The Canadian Periodical Index is a set of books from 1980 to the present listing articles in major Canadian publications, arranged alphabetically.

Use: Look for name of ancestor who was written about or wrote an article.

The Annals of Cleveland: Bibliographical Series contains biographical sketches of Clevelanders that appeared in Cleveland newspapers from 1870 to 1938. However, these were in smaller newspapers (not the Plain Dealer, Cleveland News, or Cleveland Press), such as suburban, business, ethnic, and organizational publications. They are arranged alphabetically, and the reader is referred to the newspaper where the original article appeared. The newspaper can be viewed on microfilm in the adjacent microform room.

Use: Look for an ancestor living in Cleveland during this time who may have been written up in newspapers other than the major dailies.

The Annals of Cleveland Foreign Language Digest is a multivolume set of books covering 1885 to 1939, and the following ethnic groups: Italians, Germans, Hungarian Jews, Lithuanian Jews, Slovenians, Slovaks, Carpathian Russians, Romanians, and Czechs. The citation refers to the newspaper in which the article appeared. To view the original article, write down the citation information and go to the microform room to locate the copy of the original article.

Use: If your family belonged to any of these ethnic groups, perhaps they were written about and you can find their name here.

The Annals of Cleveland Court Records (1837 to 1877) gives topical news abstracts. The table of contents at the front of each volume and the index at the back lead the researcher to an abstract of the original record. Notations at the start of each entry refer the reader to the original document, which in this case is a record from either common pleas court, district court, probate court, or superior court.

Use: Think your ancestor was involved in a court case during this time period? Check here.

Reference Room—Central Area

The librarian's desk is just past the computers as you first enter the reference room. Near the desk are the following resources:

Guide to Ohio Newspapers 1793–1973 is a book kept near the librarians' desks. It lists alphabetically by city the name of the paper and the dates it was published, and which libraries have copies.
Use: Determine which Ohio newspapers are relevant for your area of research.

American Newspapers 1821–1936 similarly provides a listing of U.S. newspapers arranged by state and then by city and lists the dates published. If CPL does not have these newspapers, they can be requested through interlibrary loan. Genealogy researchers often use the interlibrary loan service when looking for obituaries or other information in newspapers around the country. When these papers do not have an index, it can be a time-consuming process to request one roll after another until the information, hopefully, is found.
Use: Determine which U.S. newspaper may have relevant data for your research.

Black Biography is a two-volume index of items written about African-Americans between 1790 and 1950. Organized alphabetically by last name, it gives the individual's date and place of birth, occupation, and religion, and the page on which the biographical citation is found; if there is an illustration it gives the page where that citation is detailed. It then references a microfilm number and page where information about this individual can be found. The purpose of this book was to gather as much data about African-Americans as was available. This can be very useful to genealogists, as it tends not to be limited to prominent people.
Use: Doing research on African-Americans? Look up surnames here.

Reference Room—West (to your left as you enter the room)

The National Union Catalog can be found here. This lists all books in the Library of Congress published before 1956. If your ancestor authored a book in the U.S. prior to 1956, there should be biographical information about him or her in these volumes. Listings are alphabetical by author.
Use: Consult if you are searching for a hard-to-find book or author.

The British National Bibliography, a similar set for British authors.

The National Union Catalog Manuscript Collections lists those manuscripts published from 1959 to 1992/1993.
Use: Consult if searching for a manuscript or if there is the possibility your ancestor wrote one or was written about in one.

Union List of Serials in Libraries of U.S. and Canada is a five-volume set listing those newspapers from other countries that are available on microform between 1948 and 1983.
Use: Consult if interested in events or people in a particular country during this time period.

The Biography & Genealogical Master Index, shelved in the center of the room near the librarian's desk, is a set of books with a collected index of people in various fields and professions. The citation includes name, birth and death dates, and codes for the books or other publications in which the biographical informa-

Slave Research at CPL

Hazel Head had researched her family enough to know they had been slaves owned by Terry Leak. Hazel's own "Leak" family lived in Salem, Tippah County, Mississippi. She shared this information with members of the African-American Genealogical Society of Cleveland. Sandra, an active member of the group, was reviewing the "Records of the Antebellum Southern Plantation from the Revolution to the Civil War" at the Cleveland Public Library for her own family research when she came upon a Leak reference in the book's narrative index. This index lists the names of planters whose records are in the collection, as well as the county and state where the records originated. This Leak family was listed in Salem, Tippah County, Mississippi, as well as in North Carolina.

Sandra remembered the 1880 census showed that Hazel's grandfather was born in Mississippi but his father was born in North Carolina. So the reference to a Leak planter from those two states seemed to fit. Also, the fact that Leak is not a common surname led Sandra to think she was hot on the trail of a real find for a friend—and an unplanned one, at that.

Going through the microfilm roll that accompanies the antebellum book, Hazel and Sandra garnered much new information. The papers of Francis Terry Leak (covering the dates 1839 through 1865) stated that the planter-lawyer migrated from Rockingham in Richmond County, North Carolina, to Salem in Tippah County, Mississippi, bringing with him 32 slaves.

Leak's papers are basically work records of his plantation hands and a combination plantation journal and diary. His notes covering the years through 1863 describe the various tasks performed by individual slaves (by 1850 the number had grown to 110), the rations and clothing meted out to each (with the age and shoe size next to each name), and the everyday events of the plantation. Leak details who was sick, who died, who was born, what new slaves were bought, and what visitors came to call. We learn when Leak first decided to buy a plantation in Arkansas in 1853, and how he transported his slaves back and forth from the Mississippi plantation to work on his Arkansas plantation every year.

Hazel's father, Harvey Leak, was born in Arkansas. His father, James Terry Leak, was born in Tippah County, Mississippi, but her great-grandfather, Harvey Leak, Sr., was born in North Carolina. In the 1880 Benton County (formerly Tippah County), Mississippi, census, James Terry Leak, age 24, is listed as the head of household. Further information from this census states Jim was born in Mississippi, his dad was born in North Carolina, and his mom in Maryland. The seasoned researcher checked the household next door and found Jim Leak's widowed sister, Violet Mason, age 36, who gave the same data. Their widowed mother, Leah, lived with Violet and said her parents were Maryland natives.

The 1870 census for Tippah County, Household No. 176, revealed the makeup of the household of Harvey and Leah Leak (Hazel's great-grandfather and great-grandmother). Living with the 61-year-old farmer were his children: Levin, 20; James, 16; Nancy, 13; John W., 9; B.H., a 5-year-old male, and Roda Leak, an 80-year-old Maryland native thought to be Leah's mother.

By comparing information from these two censuses with the slave lists in Francis Terry Leak's journal, Hazel could confirm family data for her grandfather, great-grandparents, great-aunts and -uncles, and her great-great-grandmother.

In the journal page dated 22 October 1852, Leak stated, "Leah and Harvey's baby died this morning." From the pages titled "Birth of Negro Children," Hazel learned many more specifics regarding Harvey and Leah's children.

On 21 May 1857 the slaveowner noted: "Measles got into our family last week. They are in Harvey's and Uncle John's families." Then on May 29, "Harvey's Tom now lying up with it. . . . Violet and Little Levin sufficiently recovered to go out to work."

Probably the most unique entry was one in which Leak described "a Negro wedding on Saturday night." There was a formal marriage ceremony with seven slave couples standing in a circle; the parties each exchanged vows and Leak himself acted as minister. Neighbors, including slaves from surrounding plantation and from the next county, attended the ceremony and a reception afterwards.

What Is a Microform?

Microforms contain extremely small photographic images that require use of a machine, called a reader, to view. Microforms (and microfiche) allow thousands of pages of material to be condensed and stored easily on small rolls of film. This prevents damage to the original document and possibly loss of data for future users. Information from microform (or microfiche) can be printed for a modest fee—currently $.15 per page (change machines are available in the microform center and in other areas of the library, including the sixth floor in the Stokes wing).

How to Read the Small Type

Those pesky microfilm files are often hard to decipher. Try placing a sheet of yellow paper on the reader machine to improve the contrast and thereby improve the readability of the document. Also, buy a small magnifying glass (some come with a light that runs on batteries) to help you read fading print.

---

tion is found. The notation "port" indicates that a portrait of the individual is in the original source. Once you have the citation information, you can then consult the online catalog to access the specific publication either at CPL or elsewhere. This index is also available online.

Use: If you know or suspect that your ancestor was well known in her profession or field of study, check here for her surname.

Index to Biographical Sketches is a current and retrospective biographical dictionary that helps you determine which publication to view for biographical information. It contains more than 12.7 million sketches indexed by last name.

Use: Consult if there is a possibility your ancestor was important enough or well known enough to merit a biographical sketch.

Microform Center (Microfilm and Microfiche):

The microform center, located to the left as you face the general reference room, is accessible either directly from the reference room or through a separate front entrance off the lobby. This room contains Ohio census records, newspapers, newspaper clipping files, city directories, and city phone books. None of these are hard copies; all are preserved on film.

Necrology files contain information on the date of death and place of burial of persons who died between 1850 and 1975. The information comes from local cemetery records and newspaper death notices from 1833, 1847 to 1848, and 1850 to 1975. They are shelved on the wall behind the reference desk. Also available on-line from CPL's home page.

Use: Obtain exact date of death and possibly cemetery where person is buried.

The Biography Clipping File contains biographical information from approximately 1910 to 1975 about prominent Clevelanders, compiled by library staff. It is indexed by last name; ask for it at the desk. Because newspapers and other print materials were not indexed at the time, inclusion in this file depended upon the judgment of library staff.

Use: An easy, but not comprehensive, way to look up famous or infamous locals.

Census Data Notebook is found in a three-ring notebook at the reference desk in the microform room. It explains census data, detailing what each census contains and how to use the soundex system. For the 1870 census you need to look for the ward where the individual or family lived. It is possible to "guess" the ward according to crude maps in this notebook. But the best ward maps are in the Map Room on the sixth floor of the Stokes Wing (detailed below).

Other items of interest in the microform room are the newspaper collection, city directories from 1837 to 1980, and Cleveland phone directories from 1880 to the present. Also, there is file film of Cuyahoga County soldiers in World War II and Korea, compiled from local papers. And there is the Index to the Official Roster of Ohio Soldiers in the Civil War.

Periodical Center

Located to the right as you face the General Reference Room, the Periodical Center can be reached directly from General Reference or through a separate entrance off the lobby.

Newspapers stay on the open shelves for one week to three months depending upon if they are dailies, weeklies, or monthlies and are then microfilmed. Magazines remain on the shelves for about one year, after which they are bound and then shelved. The copy machine here accepts dollar bills, and copies are $.10 each.

CPL has a huge collection of U.S. daily as well as weekly newspapers. The dailies are kept for three weeks and the weeklies for three months. Some papers (a brochure with more specifics is available) are saved on microform. The library subscribes to various nationality newspapers in the U.S. as well as international newspapers from 28 countries. Their selection of historic Cleveland newspapers is second to none.

Newspapers contain information on births, deaths, marriages, and class reunions.

The Periodical Center contains magazines that may be of interest as well. Some of their holdings for current genealogy magazines are: American Genealogist; Certified Copy; Genealogical Computing; Genealogical Journal; Genealogists' Magazine; Journal of the Afro-American Historical and Genealogical Society; Names; National Genealogical Society Quarterly; New England Historical and Genealogical Register; New York Genealogical and Biographical Records; Prologue; The Journal of the National Archives; Ohio Genealogical Society Newsletter; and Queen City Heritage. Older holdings are bound, are on microfilm, or are stored in remote storage. For specific information about these, check the CPL catalog or call 216-623-2904. You can also search online at www.cpl.org; choose "catalog," then "subject keyword search." Enter "genealogy," and limit the search to journals and magazines.

Government Documents and Patents
(Stokes Wing, Fourth Floor)

The most relevant documents here are the patent files—and then only if your ancestor applied for and received a patent. If so, then this is the place for you.

The patent number is needed in order to retrieve the patent record. Here is the procedure for obtaining this number:

(1) If the patent was registered less than 30 years ago, use "Cassis II," a computer search program available in the library or via computer off-site. You can search Cassis using the individual's name; or, if there was corporate research involved in obtaining the patent, use the company's name. Write down the number of the patent. Then proceed to the open shelves on this floor and look for microfilm boxes that are arranged by patent numbers. Use the available reader machine to find the patent.

(2) Patents registered from 1790 to 1989 are on a CD-ROM that is kept at the reference desk on this floor. If you are searching for patents from 1989 to the present, consult staff. (These are in the process of being converted to CD-ROM and are available on microfilm.)

(3) Very early patents (those from 1790 to 1836) were filed according to a different system. They are known as "X Patents," and a listing of these is in a notebook kept at the reference desk. The U.S. did not start using a numbering system with patents until 1836, thus the need for a separate search for these early ones.

Photograph Collection (Stokes Wing, Fourth Floor)

This collection is kept in a separate room. You are requested to hang up your coat and place personal belongings in a locker (key provided at no charge) and to register with the staff on duty.

!

Check the Backs of Photos

Sometimes the backs of photos have dates, or even copies of an accompanying newspaper article cut out and taped on the back. While this may not be good from a preservation standpoint, for the family history researcher it may be a bonus.

The Photography Department has several different collections, some of which will be of interest to family history researchers. These may provide pictures of the house, church, street, or business of an ancestor. Unfortunately, they are arranged in different collections, each of which must be searched separately. This means you will have to do multiple searches if you're looking for a specific name or item.

Postcards—This collection is stored in the first two drawers of the wide metal filing cabinet and is arranged by subject. There are a few portraits, such as the postcard with a picture of Francis P. Bolton. Apparently at one time postcards were used as publicity in political campaigns. Subjects such as orphanages and parks might be of interest. There are even some postcards from other states and countries, for example one from Brussels in World War I.

Cleveland Picture Collection—This is a collection from Stanley McMichael and includes some portraits as well as other types of photos. Most of these date from the 1890s to the 1940s. They are on microfiche, and originals can then be requested from remote storage. They will arrive at CPL in a few days, and patrons can then look at the original photograph and even make a copy of it. You can make a copy of the microfiche, but requesting the original is recommended. These are arranged alphabetically. Though most of the people in the photos are prominent Clevelanders, there are also pictures of groups such as mail carriers, and even of locations such as bridges, canals, and cemeteries.

Standiford Files—Ethel Standiford-Mehling operated her studio in Cleveland from 1919 to 1936. She was well known for photographing Cleveland's most prominent residents, for which she won numerous prizes. She donated 500 of her autographed photographs to the Cleveland Public Library.

Cleveland Optical Disk File—This file is accessed at the computer in this department. You can type in a subject or address and then view photographs of the desired topic. Because you must type in the name exactly as it is catalogued, a search for Goodwill Industries will not be successful if the final "s" is left off "Industries," or if Goodwill is spelled "Good Will." One strategy is to type in a term beginning with "a," such as "airport," and then use the "end" key to scroll down the entire list. Press "F5" to find out if a negative of that photograph is available. This file contains photographs only for Cleveland proper. Most of these pictures were taken by City Hall staffers in connection with a Cleveland-area crime, housing violation, hazardous condition, or disaster. A few depict restored or cleaned-up properties. Some photos in this file date to the 1800s. Copies can be purchased; ask staff for prices and restrictions for use.

Cleveland Subject Collection Boxed Photographs—This is primarily a collection of photographs and some illustrations that were in local newspapers such as the Cleveland Plain Dealer, Cleveland Press, Call and Post, and Cleveland News. Most of these date from the 1890s to the 1980s, although some may be from as early as the 1860s. They are arranged by topic, and subjects related to Cleveland are separated from those pertaining to the rest of the U.S. and the world. Only staff can retrieve these files. You can use the finding aids mentioned below in your search. Typical search terms are: "residences," buildings," or "courthouse," as well as a specific street or address. Each box has several folders in it. Within each folder the pictures are arranged in no particular order. It is okay to make copies of these for personal use. If someone is writing a family history and wishes to include a picture of a local amusement park, for example, and the book will not be sold, only given out to family members, that is considered "personal use."

African-American Family Collection—This collection consists of photographs donated by several families that can be viewed by the public.

Hispanic Family Collection—This collection is in its initial stages but hopefully will soon grow to include photographs of many families within the Cleveland area.

Finding Aids

Be sure to check these two books that can help you search the various collections.

Cleveland Picture Collection Subject Lists—This is for the microfiche collection. The table of contents lists all the subjects by which the collection is categorized, for example, airports, buses, markets, museums, railroads, settlement house, WPA. Then it lists specifically which microfiche contains those photos.

Guide to Cleveland and Ohio Photographs and Photograph Collection of the Cleveland Public Library—Topics listed here are categories of people and refer to everything from "bank employees" to "nationality groups" and "union members."

Figure 4-1: Patrons and staff wear gloves while handling photos and other archival material. *Courtesy of Michelle Jones*

Copying Photographs

Located in this department is a black-and-white copy machine that is better than most others at CPL. It has both a picture setting and a text setting. Current cost is $.10 a copy. A color copy machine has been requested.

If you find a picture and would like a copy of the negative, this can be done. Cost is usually about $35 to $40.

History Department (Stokes Wing, Fourth Floor)

The History Department offers the following information of interest in family history research: a variety of books on Cleveland's past, covering subjects such as pioneer families, county histories, and passenger lists; PERSI (see glossary); and The Pennsylvania Archives (one volume of this book has names of individuals who took the Oath of Allegiance to the province, and later state, of Pennsylvania from 1727 to 1775; another volume has early Pennsylvania land records from 1685 to 1739; and another has an index to colonial governmental records, baptismal records, and marriage records for Lancaster County from 1752 to 1786).

Although many genealogy researchers use these facilities, remember that staff members are not trained genealogists. Nevertheless, librarians' expertise is in "information retrieval," and that is a great deal of what genealogists need to do.

There are many books on how to do genealogy, how to organize your research, and how to use the Internet for genealogy. They are located in the section behind the reference desk. They can be found listed in the online card catalog as well. CPL does not use the Dewey Decimal System but rather the Library of Congress cataloging system.

While some of the genealogy-related books you may need are reference-only materials, there are many that do circulate, and therefore you can borrow them using your CPL card or the Greater Cleveland Access card.

Ohio County Histories are a set of books shelved alphabetically by county, found behind the reference desk.
Use: Helps with historical facts. Often lists names of early pioneers.

City Directories are in hard copy from 1936 to 1980 and can be located lying flat on the open shelves across from the reference desk. (Directories before 1936 are on microfilm, first floor of the Main Building.)
Use: Helps determine where person resided, and therefore where to find records.

> ## ❗ Finding Aids
> There are easy ways to search many reference materials—they're called "finding aids." The index at the back of a book is considered a finding aid. But there are more sophisticated finding aids, and it pays to ask what finding aids are available anytime you are doing research.

Oh, Give Me a Home— But Where?

Drew wanted to locate the birth records of his immigrant ancestor to confirm the town of birth. His maternal great-grandfather, "Toriskie," arrived in the U.S. in the 1890s. According to his naturalization papers found at federal court (though now available only through the Great Lakes Region/Chicago NARA—National Archives and Records Administration), he was from Livohutta, Austria. Drew went to the map collection at CPL and with the help of the librarian there located the town in a German gazetteer, "Ritters Geographisch Statistisches Lexikon" (1910). The town was in present-day Slovakia. Another reference at CPL had information on all the towns in Slovakia, including alternate names. There he found that the town was now called Livovska Huta. So now, knowing the town of birth, he was able to access original records in Europe.

The Printed Index to the Ohio Census (1820–1880) is located here and gives citations by page number. You must copy the citation and go to the microform room for the correct reel. For censuses from 1900 on, use the index that is in book format. The 1930 census is not soundexed.

Use: Census data includes birthplace, occupation, citizenship, native language, and more.

The Passenger and Immigration Lists Index is a series of books covering 1883 to 1895. Each volume is a separate set, and as the series is a work in progress, the researcher may need to look for surnames in all volumes. The last volume, however, does have a comprehensive index. Names are listed alphabetically in each volume and followed by the citation. If the library owns the source material from which it was cited, the number has been penciled in next to it and refers to the call number of the source material. The next step would be to request the source book cited.

Use: Helps locate the ship's manifest with possible information as to birthplace of immigrant.

Morton Allan Directory of European Passengers is a book used to help determine the name of the ship your immigrant ancestor took. It is arranged by year and lists the steamship company and then the names of the ships alphabetically. It gives dates and departure port as well as the port of arrival.

Use: Helps locate the ship's manifest with possible information as to birthplace of immigrant ancestor.

Germans to America is a multivolume set listing the names of Germans who came to America from 1850 to 1897. It is indexed and lists the boat and where it docked; the researcher can then request the passenger list from the National Archives or Family History Center. Similar books offer the same information for Italian immigrants and for immigrants from many other countries, including Czechoslovakia, Ireland, and Russia.

Use: To locate the ship's manifest and then learn the birthplace of an immigrant ancestor.

Across from the reference desk and next to the microfiche reader is a file cabinet with the following:

- Index to Cleveland and Ohio regional history
- Clipping file (important events that may have impacted your family)
- Biographical clipping file (names of possible family members and biographical information)
- British parish registers (vital records of England)
- Heraldic Register of America (find your coat of arms)—located at the back of the sixth floor, in the furthest part near the restrooms
- PERSI (Periodical Source Index)—back file—located in the section marked "indexes" directly across from the reference desk. PERSI is explained in detail in Chapter 7: Family History Centers.
- Kaiser Index to Black Resources 1948–1986 (for African-American research)

Map Collection (Stokes Wing, Sixth Floor)

The map collection is in a separate room to the left as you exit the elevators on the sixth floor. CPL has an extensive collection of maps, atlases, and gazetteers that are easily available and accessible to the public.

Maps show boundaries and jurisdictions—which help the researcher determine which governmental agency to contact regarding records. Knowing the geographical and physical aspects of the area may aid us in determining migration patterns, lifestyle, and occupation.

Knowing the names of nearby towns and counties can be valuable as well. Mention of a certain town or city in our relative's correspondence, for example, suddenly makes more sense. It may also offer new possibilities for search sites—we may have to look for records in a neighboring town.

Maps may lead us to clues about what port one's immigrant ancestors were likely to have departed from, and may even give us hints as to possible occupations (fishermen, miners).

Many times these maps list names of property owners, neighboring businesses, and dimensions of the building, which allow us to look around the neighborhood for possible leads. And because many of these maps are available on film, once the desired information is found it can be printed out using the microform reader (for $.10 per page).

The 1874 Atlas of Cuyahoga County is a way to locate streets, although there is no index to the streets. It does list townships and villages located outside Cleveland proper. It's very easy to read and shows each ward for Cleveland proper. The pages are protected with plastic covers.

The Cleveland Street and Avenue Guide (a printout by the service desk) lists street names prior to 1906 and then the current street names. Actually, this was taken from the 1906 City Directory, so you could get the same information from the directory itself.

Census Enumeration Books for the 1910 and 1920 census surveys are kept in the locked cabinet near the service desk. These are helpful because the defined area searched is smaller than the ward, so it takes you closer to the exact spot on the census form, which you will then need to research. This eliminates frames of film through which you will need to search.

Sanborn Insurance Maps can be very helpful. I don't have an insurance claim, you say. Why should I use such a map? Because these maps were used for insurance purposes, they contain accurate and concise details about homes and businesses in Cleveland as early as 1858. You can search these by special topics such as by a school or church name. The index is contained in large oversized binders on the index table, which is just a table across from the service desk. There is an ex-

MURPHY   *Famous Families*

When you think of Cleveland families that go way back, the names Hanna, Case, Severance, Rockefeller, and Kelley come to mind. But what about Murphy, as in Murphy's Oil Soap? Many Clevelanders are unaware that the originators of this powerful cleaning agent made a clean sweep of things in Cleveland—or at least started to.

Like many other family histories, theirs is the tale of how a downtrodden immigrant family met success only after many failed attempts, and with the help of some luck—Irish luck in this case.

Jeremiah T. Murphy (to avoid confusion we will refer to this Jeremiah as Jeremiah I) was born in Cleveland, Ohio, 10 May 1857, the eldest of seven children of Michael Murphy and Bridget Bonfield Murphy.

Jeremiah I married Mary Ellen Whelan in 1880, and this union also produced seven children.

A family business can have many benefits. It also can interfere with and possibly disrupt family life. Sometimes we see the results, in little but significant ways, generations later, such as the break with tradition that occurred in the naming patterns for the Murphy family.

Jeremiah I founded the Ohio Oil Company. The company originally produced petroleum products for "valves, cylinders, dynamos, and machines." Jeremiah's father, Michael, his brother, Frank, brother-in-law Charles Whelan, and James his nephew (by marriage) all worked in the business. When financial difficulties arose, Jeremiah I borrowed a total of $4,250 from Michael, Charles, and James. However, a lawsuit by the three family members forced Jeremiah to pay back the loan, and although the company stayed in business it led to further strained relations within the family. It is for this reason that Jeremiah I did not name his firstborn son Michael but instead named him Murlan Jeremiah (Jermiah II)—with the name Murlan created by combining MU from Murphy with LAN from Whelan—Jeremiah's wife's maiden name.

Sometime in the 1920s, a German man visited the plant and showed the Murphys a soft soap—explaining that it was a unique product and he knew the formula for it. The formula used potassium instead of sodium (the standard at the time) and had better solubility. The selling point was that it worked best on grease and oil. And that's how Murphy's Oil Soap started in Cleveland.

Jeremiah I had already been in the car, paint, and real estate businesses with little or no success. He named his new company Phoenix, hoping it would be a success—rising like a phoenix from the ashes of the previous failed ventures. In 1968 the name became Murphy-Phoenix in order to keep the family name connected with the company. About this same time, they were battling to keep pace with the big soap companies such as Lever Brothers, Proctor & Gamble, and Colgate.

Advertising proved a powerful tool in the ensuing "soap wars," and the Murphy family had some positive results from an ad campaign many of us remember. It was Jeremiah III who chose to run the ad with the ladies cleaning a church—showing the beautiful wood banisters and other features in a charming old church in New York. With this "spot advertising," the only kind they could afford, the Murphy Oil Company was able to continue to compete in the market. The fact that the product contained no phosphates was appealing to the newly aroused concerns about the environment.

Jeremiah III was invited to witness the "shooting" of the commercial. The special effect of smoke, which was supposed to permeate the set and give the church an ethereal look, was an important aspect of the ad. The special effects person went a little too far and smoked up the entire church. Production had to be postponed, literally, until the "smoke cleared."

Eventually even the ad campaign could not keep the company from financial loss. In 1991, Murphy's Oil Soap was sold to Colgate Palmolive.

The local publicity surrounding the sale brought an interesting phone call. A child, or grandchild, of a former Murphy's Oil Soap employee had an old photograph of a company party. Without that phone call, the Murphys would not have the picture you see here.

Although the family knew that their old house in Cleveland Heights still had the Murphy coat of arms above the fireplace, they really didn't know much else about their roots. As the current generation became interested in their family history (actually spurred on by the interest of one of their spouses) they realized how little they knew. So Jeremiah III (grandson of the founder) and his three children, Jeremiah IV (Jerry), Ray, and Rita decided to hire someone to do genealogical research. They contacted the Church of Latter-day Saints and received a list of certified genealogists in the Greater Cleveland area. After speaking with one of the women on the list, they felt comfortable with her responses to their questions and hired her.

They had more information on the paternal side of the family but of course gave the researcher whatever information and records they had for both sides of the family. The researcher obtained many vital records and put together a five-generation family tree. Although

Figure 4-2: Photo of Murphy Oil Soap company party in 1917 (note flags on table for Armistice Day) saved by a former employee. Circled L to R; Jeremiah T. Murphy; Murlan Jeremiah Murphy (Jermiah II).
Courtesy of the Murphy family

they were generally pleased with the results, the Murphys would like to have found out more. Jerry was disappointed that "we weren't able to find out anything about the Murphys in Ireland." But he realizes that may have to do with the fact that so many records were destroyed and that the potato famine affected so many people at the time his family emigrated. He and other family members realize they made a contract with certain specifications. And perhaps if they had been willing to spend more time and money on the project, the researcher could have gone back further in time.

Rita recalls the initial excitement as the researcher first began obtaining records documenting their family's history. "Early on, the stuff comes quickly; but the farther back you go, the slower the progress. You get disappointed and think that's all there is. And then you don't push it further."

And those are good words for all of us to contemplate. It does take more work to obtain information as we go further back in time. But it can be done successfully whether you hire a professional researcher or do the work yourself.

It's not as if the research did not yield any new information—because it did. In the summer of 2000, Jerry and his wife Susie took a trip to Ireland. There they met for the first time Rita Scanlon, Jerry's mother's first cousin. The only information Jerry had was that the cousin lived in the town of Killaroo. So Jerry and Susie went to the town late one day and decided to go into the local tavern. They mentioned who they were looking for and learned that the tavern owner's mother was Rita Scanlon. By 10 p.m. that night they were sitting in Rita's house talking about the family. The next day they were taken to the house where Jerry's maternal grandfather grew up in the 1900s. Later a caretaker took them around to see the old stone house built in the 1800s where his maternal great-great-grandfather lived.

Another result of the family history research was that Rita found out some historical medical information of interest to her. Rita was recently diagnosed with a celiac spur—as she describes it: "basically the inability to digest gluten." One of the records produced by their paid researcher was a death certificate for Rita's great-aunt that states that she had a similar condition.

Is the family done with their interest and research into their history? Not really.

The Murphys would like to get in touch with other direct descendants of their ancestors and be able to trace the family back further in Ireland. And they believe that definitely is possible.

cellent tutorial on how to read Sanborn maps at: www.oplin.lib.oh.us (choose "genealogy," then "maps," then "Ohio maps").

The Hopkins Plat Books cover the period from 1912 to the1950s. While not as accurate as Sanborn maps, these may fill in when there are no Sanborn maps, and particularly for certain downtown areas during the 1920s and '30s. Hopkins has an index available in binders on the index tables across from the service desk. There is one index for Cuyahoga County and another for the City of Cleveland.

Another category of maps is Wall Maps/Landowner Maps. The 1858 Cleveland map shows the name of the landowner and the number of acres owned. Some of these, such as that for Cuyahoga County in 1874, are available in book form (these show wards); others are available on microfiche, such as those for Cleveland in 1852 and 1858. The original wall maps were often shellacked and displayed on the wall and did not hold up well. Those therefore tend to be accessible only via microfiche. Atlases are available on both microfilm and paper copies.

Historical County Atlases show how the county boundaries changed from about 1840 to 1900. Some of these are available in hard copy (books) as well as on microfiche; for some Ohio counties they are only available on microfiche. This will help you find where records are kept.

Gazetteers

Gazetteers are geographical dictionaries for other countries, some of them very old. Use the gazetteer to look up the name of a city or town where borders may have changed and the town therefore became part of another state or country (this enables you to find the correct jurisdiction for records). The gazetteer also provides latitude and longitude coordinates. Locate the military map for the relevant country (staff will gladly assist) and, using those coordinates, find the city and determine what country it is in now and what towns are next to it. Military maps are used because they are the most detailed.

The Columbia Gazetteer of the World by Cohen is a three-volume set of books kept in the "quick reference section"—the open shelves behind the reference desk.

Gazetteer of the World, published by Columbia Lippincott, is an earlier edition of the Columbia Gazetteer that might be helpful if you can't find a town or city name in the other editions.

To locate a Town Using a Gazetteer:

Using the Columbia Gazetteer, search alphabetically in the book by city or town (not country). The gazetteer lists recent population (1991), the county or prefecture the city or town is located in, the country, and whether it is in the northeast, northwest, southeast, or southwest portion of that country.

It may state that the town is near a certain river or mountain range. It also mentions the primary industry of the area and sometimes gives a short history of the town. Longitude and latitude coordinates are listed—write these down.

Next, go to the maps, which are kept in map cases that have extra-wide drawers and take up the majority of the space in this room. The cases are arranged by country, and most countries will have several maps from which to choose. These detailed maps of the country (many of these are military maps made during or just after World War II) allow you to use the longitude and latitude coordinates to find the particular city you are researching. The tabs on the bottom left of the maps indicate if they are reference maps, thematic maps, counties, or cities. The maps are generally from the 20th century, with the bulk of them from the 1950s.

For genealogical purposes this map research not only provides an indication of the current country in which the city is located, but also pinpoints nearby countries and cities. As I mentioned earlier, this information can be invaluable in understanding migration patterns, language groups, and possible leads for future searches. For example, on the 1920 census my paternal grandfather gave his nationality as Russian. His birthplace is currently in Hungary, but it is in the extreme northeast portion of the country and very close to what was then (1880s) Russia.

Quick Reference Section

In the "quick reference" section are large three-ring binders with:

Historical maps on file—commercial maps showing country boundaries, well-known battles, and population distribution by language and/or ethnic group.

Country outline maps—simple black-and-white maps showing the outline of the country (these can be reproduced for educational purposes only). You might use these in your family record to show the whereabouts of your family within a country or countries.

State outline maps—another set of simple, black-and-white, 8" x 11" outline maps showing the counties. Knowing county names is essential for record retrieval.

Figure 4-3: Patron retrieves map from drawer in the map case of the Map Room at Cleveland Public Library.
Courtesy of Michelle Jones

There are also African history maps—showing outlines of countries in Africa—that can be reproduced for educational purposes.

Historical U.S. Atlases indicate the major migration routes used during the 17th and 18th centuries. You might consult such atlases when trying to pinpoint the next location for a family on the move. If you have only a few clues it makes sense to begin with the assumption that the family followed the established routes as they moved west, or south, for example.

The following two map books can help you understand and trace the movement of people throughout the country:

- The Settling of North America (edited by Helen H. Tanner) covers the Ice Age to modern times.
- Atlas of American Migration (by Stephen Flanders) encompasses the pre-Columbian to suburban eras.

The Ohio Memory Project has digitized some pages of the 1874 Cuyahoga County Atlas. It can be accessed online at www.ohiomemory.org. As graphical images, maps adapt well to the Web format.

This library has so much to offer, both online and in person. I hope this chapter encourages you to visit often and helps make your visit profitable. If you have not been to this facility, you are missing out on a great experience. The depth of information available at the Cleveland Public Library is extraordinary.

5 The Cuyahoga County Archives

Cuyahoga County Archives (CCA)
Rhodes House
2905 Franklin Ave.
Cleveland, OH 44113
216-443-7250
Fax: 216-443-3636

Website:
www.cuyahoga.oh.us/cs/archives
E-mail: archive@cuyahoga.oh.us
Hours: Mon, Wed, Thu 8:30 a.m.–3 p.m.;
Fri 3–4 p.m. by appointment only. Please
call 1–2 days in advance for appointment. Closed Tuesdays to visitors but
staff is working and available for phone
calls. Property searches by appointment
only; call 216-443-7250 or ask at reception desk.
Parking: Free in an adjacent lot
Sign in: Required when you enter and
leave
Copies: $.25 each and are made by staff
or patron if using microfilm reader

At an archive, visitors are permitted to use the material, but nothing leaves the building. The Cuyahoga County Archives is the storage facility for a number of records important in family history research. The staff is only responsible for maintaining records; they did not create the records. And sadly, everything is not always complete.

Due to the physical limitations of this facility (they make use of space in a Victorian Italianate mansion built in 1874, so shelving and access to it are sparse), finding records usually requires the assistance of the staff. There is often more than one way to find records here, so don't be surprised if staff suggests another path to the same goal.

Visitors from all over the country and all over the world use the CCA. If you cannot visit in person, personnel respond to phone, fax, e-mail, and mail requests for documents. However, it takes at least two weeks to research most requests. If the need for the information is urgent (for instance, someone applying for Medicare who needs to prove their date of birth; or sometimes funeral home officials need to verify information quickly), be sure to mention this and they will try to accommodate you. While there is no research fee, there is a $1.00 minimum charge for copies once the information is found. Including a SASE is nice but not required.

It is helpful to remember that:

- The Archives may not have a certain record you are looking for.
- Certain records may never have existed—for example, the midwife present at a birth should have recorded certain information, but many midwives in earlier times didn't read or write English.
- You may need to wait for assistance because other patrons came in first, or because only one individual is permitted in the tax record room at a time.

Fortunately, the staff at CCA is friendly, knowledgeable, and extremely helpful. The following is a rundown of the types of records you can find at CCA.

Vital Records

Birth Records (1849–1908)

There are very few records for the early years (1849–1873). These early records were not created at the time of the birth but rather were based on an affidavit.

The Archives has two sets of birth records: one from the City of Cleveland and one from probate court.

Cleveland Institutions Help from Afar

The U.S. roots of Josie Banks's husband's family are in Northeast Ohio. Josie lives in New Mexico. Through the Internet Josie found the e-mail address of the Cuyahoga County Archives. She wrote asking for information on the McManaman family—an Irish name with a variety of spellings. Marriage records located on microfiche at the County Archives listed their marriage on 23 December 1856. The surname was spelled both "McMamum" and "McMannum."

Staff at the Cuyahoga County Archives also searched the records of births from probate court records and found the records of Ellen McMamnon, the seventh child, born 1877. According to Josie's research, this is the first record that actually had the name spelled correctly, even though alternative spellings also were recorded. An added bonus: the County Archives staff also sent Josie copies of several listings from the Cleveland Leader's City Directory showing the family and where they lived.

Dr. Cetina also sent Josie the address for the archives department of the Catholic Diocese of Cleveland. Josie wrote to the archivist at the Diocese and received by return mail records confirming the marriage date, and birth and baptismal dates for six of the seven children born between 1857 and 1870. Surnames on these various documents are given as McManum, McManamy, and McManamon.

"Perhaps it was the lilting Irish brogue that led to these misspellings, but it just goes to show that a dauntless researcher can overcome all odds," writes Josie. And, she is grateful for the abilities of the dauntless staff at the County Archives as well.

City of Cleveland Births

These are on microfilm only. Ask staff to help you determine the appropriate reel of microfilm and use the reader machine to locate the individual. Press the green "print" button to make a copy.

Probate Court Births

Several of the years have been indexed, and these indexes can be found in three-ring binders in the East Parlor. Still others are handwritten in original volumes with indexes at the beginning of each volume.

Information Provided

Birth records list child's name and date of birth, parents' names and their country of birth, and residence at time of birth.

How to Locate

Ask staff to help you determine which books or indexes to search.

Marriage Records

The exact document available varies depending upon the date. Earlier records merely confirmed that the marriage took place; later ones consisted of an affidavit and a return confirmation that the marriage occurred; by the 1890s, records contained the full application and the return.

A separate series from 1829 to 1875 also shows the actual marriage application. If you need this, ask a staff member. The family information contained in these includes the names of the bride and groom and perhaps the names of the parents of the bride and groom. However, if one party was underage, the name of the person giving permission for the marriage might be listed, in which case you might obtain verification of the existence of another family member. Sometimes an affidavit changing the mother's maiden name to her married name was not filed until a child was born, thus confirming that the marriage had occurred.

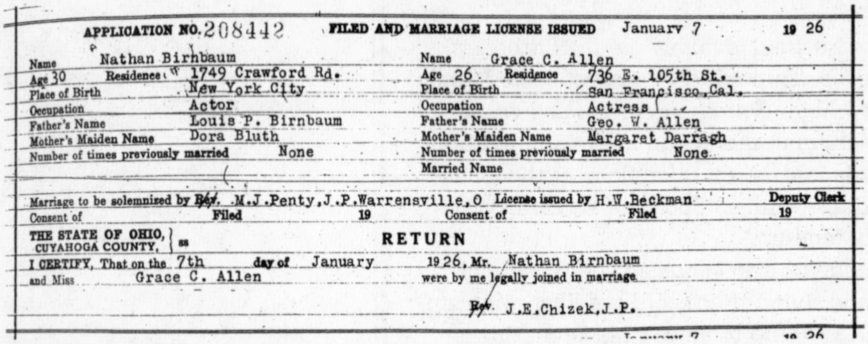
APPLICATION NO. 208442 FILED AND MARRIAGE LICENSE ISSUED January 7 1926

Name	Nathan Birnbaum	Name	Grace C. Allen
Age 30 Residence	1749 Crawford Rd.	Age 26 Residence	736 E. 105th St.
Place of Birth	New York City	Place of Birth	San Francisco, Cal.
Occupation	Actor	Occupation	Actress
Father's Name	Louis P. Birnbaum	Father's Name	Geo. W. Allen
Mother's Maiden Name	Dora Bluth	Mother's Maiden Name	Margaret Darragh
Number of times previously married	None	Number of times previously married	None
		Married Name	

Marriage to be solemnized by Rev. M.J.Penty, J.P. Warrensville, O License issued by H.W.Beckman Deputy Clerk

Consent of Filed 19 Consent of Filed 19

THE STATE OF OHIO, CUYAHOGA COUNTY, ss

RETURN

I CERTIFY, That on the 7th day of January 1926, Mr. Nathan Birnbaum and Miss Grace C. Allen were by me legally joined in marriage.

Rev. J.E.Chizek, J.P.

Figure 5-1: The marriage license for Nathan Birnbaum (better known as George Burns) and Grace C. Allen is filed at the Cuyahoga County Archives. It appears they decided to get married while passing through Cleveland during the vaudeville era. *Courtesy of Cuyahoga County Archives*

Information Provided

The marriage license lists the full name of both bride and groom; age in years; residence (usually the exact address); occupation; father's name; mother's maiden name; number of times previously married; date of marriage; and who performed the marriage and where.

How to Locate

The Archives has two sets of marriage records:

- 1829 to 1875: separate series—request from staff
- 1810 to about 1989 (index only for later records)

Look at the microfiche located on the table in the West Parlor. These records are arranged alphabetically by name of both bride and groom (check top of fiche for alphabetical ranges included on that piece of fiche). The microfiche lists a volume and page number, which leads to the marriage record on microfilm.

If the marriage occurred between 1810 and 1941, a copy of the license, the license application, or the original marriage application is available here on microfilm. Using the volume and page number from the microfiche, staff will assist you in locating the film from the gray file cabinet in the West Parlor.

Use the nearby microfilm reader to look at the film. Page numbers are in the upper right-hand corner. If you want to make a copy, center the document between the guidelines on the screen and press the green "print" button on the machine.

The Marriage Index covers the years 1810 to 1989, but the Archives does not have those marriage licenses issued later than 1941, or any that go past volume 200; the rest are at the county courthouse. Write down the volume number and page number from the index here to take to the county courthouse.

What this index list will help you determine, particularly with common surnames or incomplete information, is whether the marriage license you are searching matches the time of the marriage.

- Volumes 1 to 589 cover 1810 to 1960.
- Volumes 590 to 947 cover 1960 to 1982.
- Volumes 948 to 1024 cover 1982 to 1999.

Serendipity

On a recent Monday in June, Ceal went to the County Archives and got a copy of her great-grandparents' marriage certificate. It contained the parties' names (with the bride's misspelled), the date (23 September 1873), and the signature of T. P. Thorpe. Although she was hoping for more, Ceal was pleased to at least have the date of their marriage.

A few days later Ceal visited the grave of her other great-grandmother in section 11 at Calvary Cemetery. At a fork in the road, there was an island with a single monument in it. This tiny spot of land was designated Section 17. Ceal wondered why someone would have his or her very own section. Getting out of her car, Ceal walked over and saw the grave of the Right Reverend Thomas Patrick Thorpe (1838–1907), erected by the people of Immaculate Conception Church. She then knew what church her ancestors were married at. Interesting, isn't it, to get such a great answer from one great-grandmother about the marriage of the other great-grandmother?

Divorce Records

Divorce case files are found in records from various courts:

- 1811 to 1858—Ohio Supreme Court records
- 1876 to 1882—Court of Common Pleas files
- 1876 to 1922—Court of Common Pleas Special Docket
- Pre-1912 to about 1935—"Appearance Dockets" (no index)

Information Provided

Often the reason for the divorce is disclosed. The date and place of the marriage are given, as well as the age of both parties. Most important from a genealogical standpoint is the listing of minor children and their ages.

Information from the "appearance dockets" is usually a one-page description of the proceedings, and may state if alimony or child support was granted and whether the plaintiff was granted his or her request.

How to Locate

Because there are various courts involved and some overlapping time frames, ask staff for help locating the records from the first three of the above courts.

Appearance dockets are individually bound volumes indexed by time periods and then alphabetically within each volume. There will be a number after the person's name. Give staff the number, and they will retrieve that case file.

Death Records

There are a few different sets of death records. Some are categorized as City of Cleveland death records for 1840–1900 and for 1901–1908.

Others are probate court records for 1867–1890 and 1891–1908.

Information Provided

The death records list the person's name, date and place of death, cause of death, place of burial, country of birth, and sometimes names of parents. Staff will retrieve any of these records at your request.

Other Records of the Deceased

Necrology Files

These are copies of death notices that appeared in Cleveland newspapers. The necrology files cover two time periods: 1850–1950 and 1951–1975. The good news is that you do not need to know the exact date of death—just if it was before or after 1950. However, with common surnames, you may need other details to distinguish your William Smith who died in 1892 from several other William Smiths who died anytime from 1850 to 1949. Usually the information provided in the death notice—survivors, age of the decedent, and burial location—clarifies the issue or narrows down the possibilities.

Information Provided

Information will include the name of the individual; death date and perhaps burial date; sometimes an attached copy of the actual newspaper notice, listing survivors; residence of decedent; funeral home; and cemetery where buried.

How to Locate

The necrology files are on microfilm, located on a circular stand in the hallway between the two parlors. Staff will advise you which microfilm reader to use for these files and how to get a copy if you so desire.

Cemetery Records

The cemetery plat book, once available on delicate onionskin paper to all who visited here, is now on microfilm. This book was created by the WPA in about 1933 and is valuable when trying to locate one of the county's more than 100 cemeteries. The beginning of the film has a table of contents that names all the cemeteries alphabetically, gives the address, and shows the location of each cemetery on a map. There is also a key for veteran burials (for example, the number "1" indicates service in the Revolutionary War).

Information Provided

The first page for each cemetery has a few sentences about when and how it was incorporated, states the size in acres, and gives the number of burials. Well-drawn, detailed maps of the sections of the cemeteries, including grave numbers, follow. Although many area cemeteries have maps available to the public, here you can access all you need at one time. Plus, many researchers may visit cemeteries when the office is not open, or the office may be out of the map for the particular section needed. If you happen to be researching a veteran buried prior to 1933, his name should be listed here.

How to Locate

In the West Parlor is a small filing cabinet. In the bottom drawer are a few rolls of film, but they are not well marked so ask staff to assist you.

Incomplete Necrology Files

The necrology files are *not complete*. All necrology files for Greater Cleveland, whether located at CPL, Fairview Library, Western Reserve Historical Society, or here, are copies of the same information. However, not all death notices are contained in these files. For whatever reason, certain time periods seem to be better represented than others.

Atlases and Maps

The seasoned researcher realizes how much information maps can provide. In some cases they may contain a legal description from the tax duplicates, which indicate taxes due for both real and personal (livestock and equipment) property. Maps often show the landowner's name, and sometimes a small square or rectangle on the map indicates a house or other structure on the property. These maps are often used when doing a thorough search of a house or other building, particularly when renovating old property. It can be helpful to know the names of those living next to your ancestors as well. Because people often moved in groups, if you cannot locate your ancestor at some point in time, you can often find the individual, or a sister or brother, by tracing the movement of neighbors.

Cuyahoga County atlases for the years 1852, 1874, 1892, and 1903 (this one shows some of the suburban areas) and City of Cleveland 1881 and 1898 atlases can be found by asking staff.

Plat maps from 1860 to 1950 are not inclusive of all areas. (A project is under way to microfilm some of these.) These were created by the county auditor's office and indicate plots of land, the name of the owner, and the date title transferred. You will need to know where (east or west of downtown, and other specifics) the land was situated. These plat maps are available only for limited years and are not complete for all areas and times.

Information Provided

Plat maps indicate ownership of land and transfer dates. Sometimes names of neighboring landowners offer clues to married siblings, or denote group migration patterns that can lead to other clues. Noting nearby businesses or churches may provide further research possibilities.

How to Locate

Look in the index of the three-ring binder in the East Parlor for the address you need. This will reference a volume number. Ask staff to retrieve the map, which will be either the hard-copy map or microfilm indicated by the number. These maps will show the layout of streets according to year.

City Directories

These books, dating from the mid-1880s to 1939, provide a fairly comprehensive record of businesses, organizations, and people in Cleveland.

By following the dates for which an individual is listed in the city directory, you may be able to pinpoint when the individual lived somewhere and when they moved away or when they died. At first this can only be a working hypothesis, but it does provide a place from which to begin the search.

Most city directories at the Archives are in book form; those years missing are filled in with microfiche.

Information Provided

The beginning of the directory usually lists the names of public officials and such city institutions as the chamber of commerce, area businesses, libraries, temperance and philanthropic societies, and local religious organizations.

The bulk of the directory follows. Information for individuals will be listed alphabetically by last name, followed by occupation, work address, and home address. In the more recent volumes the wife's name is listed in parentheses after her husband's, or sometimes as "wid of Chas." (i.e., widow of Charles). The directory lists businesses as well as individuals, and business information often includes

❗ Ward Maps

Cleveland was divided into wards, and maps indicate the ward boundaries. When doing census research in urban areas like Cleveland, the ward usually translates into the enumeration district, thereby indicating which census film to access.

❗ Rural Routes

The 1905 city directory (microfiche number 17) includes rural routes in Lorain and Medina counties.

dates of incorporation and names one or two owners or officers (agents, president, vice president, etc.).

How to Locate

On the bookshelves in the East Parlor are city directories from 1837 to 1939 (not inclusive).

A three-ring binder in the East Parlor has microfiche copies of directories for 1879, 1880, 1904, 1905, and 1908. There is a microfiche reader machine on the nearby table. Copies can be made from microfiche. You may be able to copy from books, depending on the condition of the book and whether it will be compromised in the process. Ask staff.

Biographical Clipping File

The biographical clippings found here at CCA are the originals upon which the Cleveland Public Library's microfilm is based.

The clipping file is an alphabetical list of people whose names were in Cleveland newspapers from about the 1920s (some actually before) to the 1970s. Inclusion in this file, compiled prior to the advent of computers, was based on the librarian's decision that the person or the event connected with the person was worth noting. A volunteer is currently working on creating a database for this information. The file is indexed according to last name. Request this file from staff

Information Provided

Information varies, depending upon the news item. It may be about an honor someone received, a crime committed, or some other newsworthy item.

How to Locate

Find the binder titled "Biographical Clipping File" on the bookshelves in the East Parlor. Names are listed alphabetically. If you find a name you are interested in, ask a staff member, who will get the file for you. It will be a hard copy of the original newspaper article and come in a bound volume.

Coroner's Files

If a relative's probate record, death notice, or other information indicates the person died of unnatural causes, checking the coroner's file may provide important details. Coroner's files from 1833 to 1900 (not inclusive) are indexed by name of decedent.

Information Provided

These files contain witness testimony, medical information, and court records.

How to Locate

The index is on the shelf in the West Parlor. It will list a case number after the person's name. The actual case can be viewed on film, or the original can be viewed. (Because they were handwritten, often the film copy is difficult to decipher, so viewing the original can be helpful.)

For Files after 1900

Contact the Cuyahoga County Coroner's Office (listed in the appendix) for files after 1900. The file may consist of a lab report, coroner's verdict, and autopsy. Current charges are $5 each for lab report and coroner's verdict and $10 for the autopsy; however, not all cases included an autopsy. I suggest calling first to deter-

Noteworthy Files

Some interesting cases detailed in the coroner's files include Eliot Ness's investigation of the Torso Murders; the East Ohio Gas Explosion; and the Cleveland Clinic fire. Although these are outside the 1833–1900 time frame, the files ended up here and they remain here.

Haunted House Stories

Often people come to the CCA researching a house, but they aren't really specific as to why they are looking or what they are looking for. Usually it turns out they've had a paranormal experience and think perhaps the house is haunted. Residents of a home on Madison Avenue saw words appearing on the windows. They came to check out city directories to see who used to live at the house. Another lady came in and asked Cetina if she could use a ouija board.

Cetina has had her own ouija board experiences. While in college Cetina, like many other students, engaged in asking questions on a ouija board. These usually were questions about who liked whom, will I get good grades, etc. However, one night she and another person asked the question, "What important thing is going to happen?" and, according to Cetina, it spelled out "George Wallace." A few days later there was an assassination attempt on Wallace, resulting in his being paralyzed.

Staff at CCA have had paranormal experiences in the building as well. There have been instances of a chandelier swaying right after staff members talked about the possibility of ghosts in the building. One time Cetina went near the chandelier and said, "We acknowledge your presence but please stop," and it did.

About five years ago, Cetina went to pull down a book in the back room. She was holding a sheet of paper with a research request that had led her to this particular book. Suddenly the paper fell from her hands and disappeared. "It felt like the paper was taken, pulled, from me," recalls Cetina. She bent down and searched but never found the paper, which meant she could not retrieve the information requested, either. Cetina hoped that when the person requesting the research did not receive anything, they would contact her. But she never heard from them, and could not make contact herself since all pertinent information was lost on that sheet of paper. Perhaps the individual moved, found the information elsewhere, or even died. Or, well . . . what do you think?

mine which records are available. Send a SASE with detailed information on the individual (full name, date of death).

Estates and Wills

These records also have great potential genealogically. Probate records often provide names of persons and relationships; they establish that a person was at a specific place during a specific time. The inventory sometimes offers a look at possible occupations, hobbies, lifestyle, and at a person's station in life. This type of information-gathering is referred to as "putting the meat on the bones": getting more than just names and dates, and having a feel for who the person was—what she did with her time, what his life was like.

- For the years 1852 to 1941, files are indexed according to last name.
- For the years 1852 to 1918, files are located at CCA.
- For the years 1919 to the present, files are kept at probate court.

> **❗ Death Outside Cuyahoga County**
>
> Even if your ancestor resided in Cuyahoga County, if the death (from unnatural causes) occurred outside the county, the records will be in the coroner's files of that county.

Information Provided

Included in these files may be a copy of the will, which usually lists the date of death, names of heirs, and what they inherited. Other details often gleaned from estate records are ages and addresses of heirs and relationship to the decedent, and names of witnesses.

How to Locate

The white three-ring notebook in the East Parlor has microfiche sheets filed according to the name of the deceased. Use the microfiche reader to locate the individual and write down the case and/or file number. If the file number is 92,800 or under (or death was prior to about 1918), it will be found in the records for 1852 to 1918, which are kept here. Give the file number to staff and ask them to retrieve the paper copy for you. If you wish to have copies made, ask staff.

Naturalization Records

The laws regarding who could become a naturalized citizen of the United States and under what conditions changed several times including or excluding different groups (women, minor children, etc.). Three different courts in Cuyahoga County processed early naturalizations and kept the records, depending upon the time period (though in some cases these periods overlap).

Cuyahoga County Court of Common Pleas had jurisdiction over naturalizations from about 1818 to 1931. These records are stored at the County Archives.

Cuyahoga County Probate Court had jurisdiction over naturalizations from 1859 to 1901. These records are stored at the County Archives.

United States District Court had jurisdiction over naturalizations from 1855 to 1967. These records are not at the County Archives. Although once available locally, these records now are housed at the National Archives Great Lakes Region in Chicago, Illinois. They can be accessed numerically by petition number. National Archives staff will search for petition numbers if supplied with specific identifying information, including name, country of origin, place of naturalization, port and date of entry, and passenger ship. (You may not need all of these details, but the more, the better.)

The United States District Court Northern District has records from 1968 to the present. They can be contacted at:

U.S. District Court Northern District
201 Superior Ave.
Cle veland, OH 44114
216-522-4355

The United States Immigration and Naturalization Service maintains duplicates of all naturalizations after 26 September 1906. They can be contacted at:

U.S. Immigration and Naturalization Service
421 I St. NW
Washington, DC 20536
202-514-4316

Information Provided

The courts did not keep the actual certificate of naturalization—it was given to the individual. But the court has a reference to the fact that it was granted. Many visitors seek naturalization papers of their ancestors, hoping to obtain a gold mine of genealogical data. Dr. Judith Cetina says that in all her years as manager of the Archives, she has never seen parents' names on naturalization papers in Cuyahoga

You Found That Where?

One individual had his naturalization papers filed with his will, and included were two letters from a sister in Ireland—unknown to the family historian until the estate file was accessed many years later.

◆

Homeland Security

Recent reorganization has the Bureau of Citizenship and Immigration as part of the department of Homeland Security. This department has information previously part of the United States Immigration and Naturalization Service.

◆

Cleveland—a Long Way from Tipperary

Jim from Canton was researching his mother's maternal family line. Mary, his mother, had little recollection of her grandfather, who died when she was only three years old. By searching census records and city directories, Jim learned that William and his wife Eliza emigrated from Ireland about 1845, and that William was a bootmaker and shoemaker. William and Eliza had seven children, five of whom lived to adulthood. Jim contacted the Catholic Cemeteries Association and located the graves of William and Eliza. A visit to St. John's Cemetery brought new information—William's father and mother were buried there as well. But, good genealogist that he is, Jim wanted still more information.

At the Cuyahoga County Archives Jim located William's will, which showed that in addition to his five surviving sons, William also named a daughter, Anna, living in Wisconsin. Jim then checked the 1900 Wisconsin census under Anna's married name and found her husband Michael and their five children listed. Jim then corresponded with the University of Wisconsin, which provided copies of obituaries and cemetery information for most of the family. Information about Anna disclosed she had died in Cleveland in 1926.

Jim knew Anna died in Ohio, so he wrote to the Ohio Historical Society for her death certificate. It gave her father's name but stated that her mother's name was unknown. Anna's son was listed as the informant. But best of all, this document identified the civil parish in Ireland where Anna was born. From this, Jim was able to identify County Tipperary as Anna's county of birth. Now the search in Ireland could begin.

Jim contacted the Tipperary Heritage Unit, which was very helpful in obtaining baptismal records, one of which listed Anna's mother's name.

Jim is forever grateful for the research accomplished at the Cuyahoga County Archives that located the will with Anna's name. Furthermore, he is thankful to Anna's son for providing the information about the parish and the town on Anna's death certificate.

County. So consider why you are looking for these in the first place. Many beginning researchers think their immigrant ancestor surely was naturalized (many were not) and that once they find these papers, they will get lots of new data. It's not that simple—most things in genealogy aren't.

Still, if naturalization papers exist, they are worth having. The most important information found is probably the town where the individual was born. This one detail provides the researcher with an important link abroad from which to possibly obtain more records, notably birth, baptism, and marriage records. Other information on naturalization papers, depending of course upon which papers are found, includes: port and date of arrival, country of birth, and names, ages, and birthplace of children. The information about the children sometimes provides a timeline from which we can follow the family's migration within the United States.

Different court records sometimes provide different details:

- **Probate court records** usually indicate country of origin, arrival date, and the date the papers were signed.
- **Records from United States district court** include country of origin, present address, date of naturalization, age when naturalized, age when the naturalization was recorded, and number of years in the state, county, and city.
- **Records from court of common pleas** include a petition—which gives birth date and current address only, and a Declaration of Intent (DOI), which has very little information, just name and date of the DOI.

After about the turn of the 20th century, these records contain more detailed information, such as country of origin, passenger ship, port of entry, date of naturalization, age at naturalization, age when it was recorded, occupation, and number of years in the state, county, and city.

Not surprisingly, documents filed after 1923 offer even more details, such as where a spouse was born, and possibly names and ages of children.

How to Locate

You will need to know when (or about when) your ancestor came to the United States and if he or she became a citizen. Census records can provide this information. (That requires research elsewhere, as the Archives does not have census records—see Chapter 9: Making Sense of the Census.) If the individual did become a citizen, then locating naturalization records is possible, but not guaranteed.

Probate Court Records

There are two black binders and six white binders titled Index to Probate Court Naturalizations, 1859–1901 in the East Parlor. Find the alphabetical listing for your person and write down the volume number and page number next to the name. Ask staff to pull the record—it will be a paper copy showing country of origin, arrival date, and the date the naturalization papers (or declaration of intent) were signed.

Common Pleas Court Records

There are two ways to locate these records, but it is confusing. Staff make it look simple, so ask for their assistance.

The index itself lists the individual's last, first, and middle name; country of origin; date of arrival; date of declaration; date of naturalization; and if there is a "record problem."

If you are fairly certain your ancestor was naturalized, but all efforts to locate these papers have been fruitless, you could try the following method. If the individual served in World War I, look him up in a book such as the Official Roster of Ohio Soldiers and Marines in the War, *1917–1918* (located at these Archives, see below; other states have similar books) and find out when and where they "mustered out" (were discharged). Then check for naturalization records in that county. Many alien residents who served in World War I were granted citizenship after their service. Obviously this is a long shot, but others have done it successfully.

Tax Duplicates

Do we really care or need to know if our ancestors paid taxes? Not only can this be interesting from the standpoint of mere curiosity, but the diligent family historian values the important data that may be contained in such records. For instance, by looking through several years of tax records one may be able to:

From the Manager's Office

Dr. Judith Cetina, who has been manager of the Archives for eighteen years, is extremely knowledgeable about county history and the records in her keeping. Through the years she's read some interesting records. One record from about 1870 describes a suicide pact made by a man and woman married but not to each other. Another is a divorce case in which the husband claimed cruelty because his wife was chasing him around the barnyard with a hatchet. In another case a man accused his wife of abusing her elderly mother.

Such documents provide insight into family dynamics as well as a record of the everyday lives of people of the time. In one will, a father stipulated he was not going to leave his daughter anything except in a trust because he did not trust his son-in-law.

Sometimes the very lack of information also says something. If a woman took her life, we may wonder why. Some records say "see Coroner's File" and we get another view—perhaps she was pregnant and attempted an abortion.

Looking at early records we may learn about the number of farm animals owned, and often there is an inventory of the home including pots and pans, trunks, etc. Again, the information gives us a broader perspective on life in an earlier era.

1. Track an individual—By searching personal property tax records year by year, you may be able to determine when a person or family left the area, especially if it was between censuses. This helps answer the all-important "where" question.

2. See a pattern—By plotting when and where the person was in different communities, you may discover a migration pattern.

3. Get accurate information—You found a name in the census, but it is so "garbled" you are not sure it is "your person." These records may help confirm or refute your hunches. Therefore, taking the time to go through these records year by year may help you conclude when an individual arrived, or left, the area.

Information Provided

Tax records show name, amount of taxes due, and for what they were assessed. We may even learn the number of horses and cows owned, as these were considered personal property. Early tax duplicates help discern if someone was passing through Ohio between censuses. Perhaps the individual was not a property owner; still, listed in these records were professionals such as doctor or lawyers, who were assessed a licensing tax.

Books containing tax duplicates are cataloged by year and township, then by name. The first half of each township or city entry in each book lists land or other real property owners and the amount of tax the person owed and/or paid. The second half contains personal property records for those who lived in the township. This includes tenant farmers and others who lived on the land but did not own it. Doctors, lawyers, and others who were taxed a licensing tax are also sometimes included. Take into account the fact that someone can own land but pay no personal property tax on it, perhaps indicating they did not live there.

Land records can be traced by deed, although not all deeds are recorded—it was

MORGAN

Figure 5-2: Garrett A. Morgan.
Courtesy of The Western Reserve Historical Society

Garrett Morgan was born 4 March 1877 (some records state 1879) in Paris, Kentucky. His father, Sydney, was a former slave and the son of a Confederate colonel. His mother, Eliza Reed was also a former slave. Morgan left Kentucky for Cincinnati at the age of 14 and came to Cleveland three years later in 1895. His 1896 marriage to Madge Nelson ended in divorce two years later. In 1908 Morgan married Mary Hasek. Their union produced three children: John Pierpont Morgan, Garrett A. Morgan, Jr., and Cosmo Henry Morgan.

Shortly after arriving in Cleveland Morgan found work as a sewing machine adjuster and by 1907 was in business for himself. In his shop on West 6th Street he repaired and sold sewing machines. A few years later his tailor shop had 32 employees and was producing dresses, suits, and coats. While testing solutions to reduce the tension on sewing machine needles, Morgan discovered a hair-straightening formula that led to his manufacturing of "Morgan's Hair Refiner."

Morgan's knowledge of machinery and his curious mind led him to become one of the most important inventors of his time. By 1912 Morgan had invented a safety helmet, and a special "breathing device" that was patented in 1914. The "breathing device" was used in 1916 following the Cleveland Waterworks explosion. Unfortunately the officials at the time judged Morgan by the color of his skin rather than the efficacy of his invention. So he wasn't called to the scene of the disaster until very late; and even then, white workers didn't trust his device, and it was left to Morgan and his brother to go down into the tunnel and save the one or two workers they could get to.

The breathing device was later patented as a "gas mask," and it saved many lives during World War I.

In 1923 Morgan patented the first three-color traffic-signal and it continues to be one of his most well-known inventions.

Although they didn't know him for very long, his grandchildren have fond memories of Garrett Morgan. Cosmo's stepdaughter Zoe Tyler was only five or six years old when Grampa Morgan died. She remembers Morgan as a hunter who shot deer and rabbit, and remembers eating Sunday dinner sitting around the large table in his house. "At the dinner table he would officiate–telling us hunting and fishing stories. And often we'd be eating the game he just shot," recalls Tyler.

Tyler remembers what an excellent seamstress and baker Grandma Mary (Morgan's second wife) was. Her wonderful lattice cookies were one of her specialties. She was from Czechoslovakia, and her family of shoemakers and craftsmen did not approve of the interracial marriage. They would see the grandchildren, but at their home in Little Italy, not at the Morgan house.

The Morgan house in Cleveland had a garage behind it big enough for six cars. This was his workshop. Tyler remembers the old Cadillac he drove. "He'd throw coins in the back seat and tell the kids to look for money–that was a great treat for us," continues Tyler. But when his eyesight failed, Morgan resorted to traveling by bus.

Of visits to Morgan's house Tyler reminisces: "He'd sing songs with our names in them. And there were pictures of him and Teddy Roosevelt and his Raiders. And there was Grampa with long braids. He pretended that he was an Indian–it was more acceptable" [than being African-American].

Tyler remembers genealogy as an interest in her family until Cosmo, her stepdad, died in 1985. In fact the last thing Cosmo was involved with was a program called "Portrait of an American." He was learning about his father's background and trying to trace it back as far as he could.

Morgan was also involved in area newspapers. In fact he is credited with starting the Cleveland *Call and Post*. He continued his activities within the Greater Cleveland African-American community even when he became ill with glaucoma. Even though he had a live-in nurse caring for him Morgan did not want outsiders to know the seriousness of his illness.

In 1967 Mayor Ralph Locher dedicated a plaque in Morgan's honor. The plaque was placed in Cleveland Public Auditorium.

Other descendants of Morgan have memories and stories to contribute to the family history as well. And not unlike that of many other families, this family history is far from complete. Sandra Morgan (whose father was Garrett A. Morgan II, one of Morgan's three children) laments how little she knows about her grandfather's parents. Sandra, who lives with her children in Cleveland, says that for Grandma Mary, there is "all kinds of information going back to 1834," but sadly very little on Grandpa Garrett. She knows "the Morgan name came from great-grandfather Sidney, who worked on the railroad and just kind of blew into town. Sidney was originally from West Virginia, and supposedly his father was the Morgan of Morgan's Raiders" [first battle of Civil War to take place in the North]. As Sandra says, "there is no substantiation for this, so though it is a good story, it remains just that–a story."

Although Sandra is clearly interested in her family background and history, this wasn't always true. When she and her sister went to Claysville, Kentucky, in the 1970s the trip consisted mostly of looking at old tombstones, talking with the mayor, and searching through old records–sadly, fire had destroyed a lot of detailed information. Sandra credits her interest in genealogy as stemming from a committee she worked with at Western Reserve Historical Society. While typing information for the committee at the library a friend of hers looked up his family name and quickly came up with pertinent genealogical information. So Sandra, who was less than two years old when her grandfather died, is trying to get to know him better.

"I'd like to know how he saw himself and what he did–what were his motivations. We have some ideas as to why he invented these things, but what was going on in Cleveland at the time and what gave him the courage to buy a bunch of chemicals and mix them up? How did he see himself?" wonders Sandra.

Figure 5-3: Morgan's National Safety Hood. *Courtesy of The Western Reserve Historical Society*

originally done only as protection for the new owner. Deeds did not have to be recorded until the 20th century. So it is possible for a property owner to not have a deed. (Deeds are kept at the recorder's office, not at the county archives.)

The researcher may also be able to ascertain when someone died because the owner's name is suddenly changed to that of someone else—usually a surviving spouse or child.

How to Locate

You need the year and the township or municipality, and then the owner's name. For the 19th century and some parts of the 20th in Cleveland, it is important to know if the property was located east or west of downtown.

Voter Registrations

An easy first step in determining whether naturalization documents exist is to check the card file of registered voters located in the West Parlor. This lists all naturalized Americans who chose to record their naturalization with the board of elections. Listed on each card are the individual's name, address, birth date and birthplace, date and port of entry, and the date of naturalization and name of witnesses. Be sure to look in the remarks column, which should say in which court they were naturalized.

If you believe your ancestor did vote and cannot find him or her in the card file described above, ask staff for the bound volumes of registered voters. It is possible the original index was faulty (human error) and you may be able to find the appropriate voter registration forms.

Information Provided

The book will list a volume number and page number, then say if the naturalization was from one of the courts whose records are here (common pleas 1818–1931, or probate 1859–1901). Get film with the help of staff and find your person according to the volume and page number.

How to Locate

Request the books of voter registrations. Each volume is arranged by year and then more or less alphabetically. These books are countywide and include all three courts

Other Helpful Books and Records

Official Roster of Ohio Soldiers, Sailors, and Marines in the War, 1917–1918

There are twenty-three volumes, including an addendum. Information given includes name; where enlisted or drafted from; city and state of residence; race; age at entrance; birthplace; service dates; rank and company when discharged. Also listed are major engagements participated in, whether wounded, and in which battle(s). This source is on the bookshelves in the East Parlor.

Cuyahoga County Soldiers and Sailors and Marines Killed and Wounded 1914–1918

This four-volume set is on the bookshelves in the East Parlor.

Errata

Always check the table of contents and first or last book in a series to see if there is an addendum or listing of "errata"—this was how mistakes were corrected. Your relative might have been omitted in the original listing and added later, so be sure to check.

Civil War Bounty Books, 1862

These books contain the names of individuals who enlisted in the Civil War in Cuyahoga County and received a bounty (government payment, about $25; sometimes an individual paid someone to stand in for him). This may help verify military service and lead to other military records.

These books are shelved in the storage areas of the Archives. Request retrieval by a staff member.

Record of Commission on Burial of Ex-Union Soldiers

This is a 23-volume set of oversized, musty old books. In about 1880 the county commissioners realized that many veterans of the Civil War were impoverished and unable to pay for their or their spouses' burials. A law was passed providing for these services; therefore separate records were kept verifying that the service was provided and documenting it. The set is arranged according to death dates beginning with 1895 and ending in 1953.

Information includes where the Civil War veteran or his mother, wife, or widow died, cause of death, where buried, and other details such as unit and rank in service, occupation, and cost of funeral.

These books are shelved in the storage areas of the Archives. Request a staff member retrieve them for you.

Annals of Cleveland, 1933–1936 and Annals of Cleveland Foreign Language—(Slovak, Carpatho-Russian, Roumanian, Czech, Lithuanian Jewish)

Use the index to search for individuals or events mentioned in the newspapers of the time. Helps to pinpoint the whereabouts of an individual at a certain time and provide more biographical information as well. This series of books is on the bookshelves in the East Parlor.

Miscellaneous

There are numerous other records in the Archives that may be of interest, depending upon many variables. You can browse the shelves in the East Parlor to determine if some of these records might be of interest to you. Or discuss your research with a staff member, who may be able to provide suggestions.

Justice of the Peace Records

There are some interesting entries in the justice of the peace records at the county archives.

On 16 December 1878, there was a complaint against Mine Washingbauer for "using obscene and licentious language in the presence and hearing of a female." According to the affidavit, "Mine Washingbauer, being an adult of the age of fourteen years and upwards, unlawfully did in the presence and hearing of a female, one Mrs. Keifer, make use of the following obscene and licentious language: 'God dam liar' and 'God dam shit ass' contrary to the form of the statute in such case made and provided and against the peace and dignity of the State of Ohio."

The accused consented to have the case tried by Justice of the Peace John P. Green, entered a guilty plea, and was found guilty and ordered to pay a fine of $1 plus court costs.

A similar case offers a foreign-language lesson:

On 26 May 1878, J. M. Novak filed a complaint that Joseph Froch "spoke and uttered in the presence of a female in the Bohemian language the following obscene and licentious language: Ti Soine, Ti pravo, Ti shuroo, Ti cupno, which . . . when translated into English means "you sow, you cow, you whore, you bitch. . . .," Mr. Froch did not consent to have his case tried by the justice of the peace and therefore was ordered to procure a bond in the sum of $100 and appear before probate court on the first day of the next term.

And lest you think that women were above using such language, there is this case:

Ann Mullen Quinn of W. 25th and Bismark Street lodged a complaint against Mrs. Delaney, first name unknown, who "unlawfully and in the presence and hearing of an adult . . . made use of and uttered certain obscene and licentious language . . . 'God dam bastards I will pull the guts out of you.'" However, in this instance, the case was "dismissed for want of prosecution at costs of complaining witness." It seems Ann Quinn did not show up in court and therefore had to pay costs in the amount of $4.30.

Another case was a landlord complaint filed 4 Oct 1892, in which Frank Gawn, A. T. Gawn, and Margaret Morris claimed that E. Risenweber unlawfully and forcibly detained from their possession certain property. Mr. Risenweber was found guilty and gave restitution of the premises as well as paying the plaintiff's court costs of $6.80.

Other cases are for goods sold and delivered but not paid for. At times it is noted: "Plaintiff in court, defendant came not, nor for one hour thereafter." In those instances the plaintiff was ordered to "recover of the defendant" the amount originally in dispute.

In the coroner's files are copies of witness statements such as the following, regarding a fatal industrial accident.

On 26 December 1900, Fredrick Dranse, being duly sworn, testified as follows:

"I live at the corner of Tod and Newman. I knew Godleib Laderer. I saw him on the afternoon of the 21 of December. He was in John Walter's saloon. This was 2:30 p.m. He stayed there about three quarters of an hour. The foreman of the carpenters came over to the saloon. He said to Godleib, 'Come over and help on the elevator.' He went over with him. I never saw Godleib again alive."

Other cases include investigation of a suicide; the purchase of cocaine prior to a domestic dispute; and a fire in which one of the parties in a dispute died following the quarrel.

6 The Western Reserve Historical Society

The library of the Western Reserve Historical Society (WRHS) is a private archival library. No materials leave the premises—nothing circulates. Upon entering the library you must check in at the library registration desk and put briefcases, cameras, and bags in a locker (no charge). Of course research materials such as notebooks, paper, and pencil and even laptop computers can be accommodated in the library.

First-time visitors are asked to read a list of regulations on library use. New patrons should also speak to staff at the registration desk. They will provide you with fact sheets, offer a free ancestor chart, and interview you on your goals for the day.

To preserve the materials handled, you must use pencils when fragile materials are viewed, and sit in designated areas when handling manuscripts. There is a sign-in sheet for using the microfilm readers. Information sheets explaining these and other procedures are available in the case across from the registration desk.

To the casual observer the library appears modest in size. Most of the books that family historians use are on the open stacks. However, others may need to be requested by filling out a call slip. You use one kind of call slip for books and periodicals, and another for manuscripts (items in manuscript form are identified by the letters "ms"). Call slips are submitted at the library registration desk. Library staff retrieve books beginning at 9:15 a.m. and continue paging every half hour.

The library has an active volunteer group, the Genealogical Committee of WRHS, which volunteers both in the library and behind the scenes, taking on projects such as indexing large groups of records, teaching "how to" classes, and sponsoring seminars. Some classes are geared specifically toward the beginning researcher and include topics such as exploring family history, how to use the library, and how to fill out a five-generation chart. Other classes cover how to use maps and atlases for genealogy, use of the computer, and researching your immigrant ancestors, to name just a few. Classes are usually on a Saturday. A modest fee is charged (usually $15 or $20) and preregistration is necessary to ensure your space.

Seminars feature guest speakers from around the country: recent topics have been "DNA Links to Genealogy" and "The Library of Congress."

The Western Reserve Historical Society
10825 East Blvd.
Cleveland, OH 44106
Phone: 216-721-5722

Website: www.wrhs.org
Hours: Tue–Sat, 9 a.m.–5 p.m. (Wed until 9 p.m.); Sun noon–5 p.m.; closed Mon
Admissions: $7.50 for adults, $6.50 for seniors, and $5 for students; memberships can be purchased for $40 per individual.
Photocopies: Made at the front desk (fill out a request sheet) are $.35 each. The microfilm section has three coin-operated reader machines available for making copies. Cost is $.50 per page.
Parking: The adjacent attended parking lot charges commercial fees. Street parking at meters on Magnolia Drive. Special sustaining members get free parking as part of their membership.

Figure 6-1: Patron talks with staff member at the registration desk. *Courtesy of The Western Reserve Historical Society*

Collections

The Western Reserve Historical Society was one of the first organizations in America to collect genealogical data. Its library is the largest American history research repository in Northern Ohio, holding over six million items including books, newspapers, photographs, and manuscripts.

Regional Collections

The Historical Society's regional collections focus on Cleveland and the Western Reserve, including topics related to architecture, education, farming, immigration, law, social welfare, politics, and transportation. Individual abolitionists, clergy, journalists, lawyers, and business and political leaders are represented in journals, newspapers, manuscripts, and photographs. Special populations within the community are recognized and served by specialty divisions including: the African-American Archives, Philanthropic Archives, Irish Archives, Gay and Lesbian Archives, Jewish Archives, and Ohio Labor History and Urban Archives.

Genealogical Holdings

Family Histories—over 18,000 genealogies and publications from genealogical associations

Family Bible collection

Federal records—all census schedules on film from 1790 to 1930

Local records—vital records for several Ohio counties, Cleveland necrology file, and Ohio surname index to county histories, as well as an extremely strong collection for all locales east of the Mississippi (New England, Midwest, and mid-Atlantic states)

Military Records – Revolutionary War pension applications and bounty land files (index available); War of 1813 pension application file index; index to Ohio Civil War records; Daughters of the American Revolution lineage books; World War I Cuyahoga County draft registrations; World War II and Korean War picture files from the *Plain Dealer*; see WRHS website, "genealogy collections" for more.

Special Collections

Special Collections include the Wallace Hugh Cathcart Collection of Shaker Literature and Manuscripts, the Charles Baldwin Collection of Maps and Atlases, the William Pendleton Palmer Civil War Collection, and also manuscripts for each of the signers of the Declaration of Independence.

Using the Library

Online Catalog

The online catalog, known as IPAC (Internet Public Access Catalog), is a work in progress. Currently major manuscript collections and major newspaper titles are completely represented. Records for microfilm of U.S. census schedules and soundex are represented. Yet to be added are manuscript vertical file items, and holdings for other newspapers. The general book collection and family histories are being added at the rate of 3,500 titles per month. The library holdings at the James A. Garfield National Historic Site in Mentor, Ohio, can be searched online. Also in progress is inclusion of the records for the museum holdings (added at the rate of 4,000 holdings per month) and cataloging the automobiles and aircraft of

❗ Do Your Homework

Before visiting this or any other facility, it is prudent to check their website. You will get up-to-the-minute information on changes in hours or programs, and be alerted to new acquisition. You can also begin searching online in advance and have ready the titles and call numbers for books you plan to request. This can only help you make the best use of your time while in this library, or any other facility you visit.

❗ Using Registers

If the print catalog or online catalog refers to a manuscript collection and then states "register available in library," be sure to use this time-saving device. The registers are filed alphabetically by collection name in a filing cabinet in the corner by the computers. The register offers a folder-by-folder description of the manuscript containers, thereby saving time so the researcher knows which folders within the entire collection to look in.

Two Women Make Use of the WRHS

An elderly woman was given a surprise gift by her family—a trip to Europe. Unfortunately, she'd lost her birth certificate and could not get a passport without some proof of birth.

She came to WRHS, looked herself up in the 1920 census, photocopied the information, and was able to get a U.S. passport.

Marilyn K. was interested in tracing her husband's great-grandmother, known as "Greaty." When she became a widow, Greaty moved into a house in the side yard of her daughter and son-in-law in Howland Township near Warren, Ohio. Marilyn saw pictures of Greaty in the family photo album and then went to WRHS to check the 1920 census schedule. Sending to the Ohio Historical Society for Greaty's death record, Marilyn got the exact date of death as well as the name of the cemetery where she was buried. A visit to the cemetery, and a talk with the caretaker yielded not only the grave of Greaty but also the graves of two of her sons. Until this discovery, no one in the family knew where they were buried.

Figure 1-1: Mrs. Sanders, her first husband, and their children. *Courtesy of Cheryl J. Marone*

the Crawford Auto-Aviation Museum. Ask reference staff and look at the "Help Guides" at workstations for assistance.

Print Catalog

These are located by the library registration desk:

Main card catalog – cites the bulk of material available; indexed by subject, title, and author. Cards in this file are removed as its contents are added to the on-line catalog.

Main card catalog II – contains newer titles cataloged since 1997.

Manuscript card catalog – cites original records. Entries are arranged alphabetically by collection name and cross-referenced by subject.

Family history card catalog – citations to over 18,000 family histories arranged alphabetically by surname

Local records card catalog – citations to transcribed local records arranged alphabetically by state, county, and town (look under "C" for citations to records about Chicago, Illinois).

Deaths and Marriage Index – an index of all deaths and marriages published in the *Jewish Review and Observer* and the *Jewish Independent* from 1898 and continuing through the 1960's. A database of these abstracts eventually will be on the WRHS website. The first phase, 26,000 death records, will be completed soon.

Checklists

Microfilm checklist – provides exact cabinet and drawer number in the microfilm room for microfilm and microfiche collections.

```
              SURNAME EXCHANGE FILE
ANCESTOR'S INFORMATION  ** PRINT **
_____   _____
          LAST NAME                FIRST NAME
BIRTH _____   _____
            DATE                     PLACE
MARRIAGE _____   _____
              DATE                   PLACE
DEATH _____   _____
            DATE                     PLACE
SPOUSE'S NAME (Maiden Name Women) _____
_ _ _ _ _ _ _ _ _ _ _ _ _ _ _ _ _ _ _ _ _ _ _ _ _
YOUR NAME _____
ADDRESS _____   CITY _____
STATE _____ ZIP _____   PHONE (optional) ( ) _____
                                             2001
```

Figure 6-2: Surname exchange cards can be filed at WRHS so researchers with names in common can find one another.
Courtesy of The Western Reserve Historical Society

City directory checklist – lists city directories that are available in the library collection.

Map checklist and catalog – lists to available historic maps arranged alphabetically by country, state, county and city.

Atlas checklist and catalog – refers to historic atlases also arranged alphabetically by country, state, county, and city.

Picture group checklist – citations for more than 400 photograph collections (alphabetically by name of institution, business, or person). See library staff regarding research in the photographic archives.

Periodicals checklist – lists available magazines and journals

Automotive and aviation periodical checklist – lists available periodicals for this subject matter and specific issues of those periodicals that are available.

Surname files – individuals are invited to contribute to this file by listing their name, the name of the ancestor they are researching, and a way to contact the researcher, in hopes of finding and connecting with others who are researching the same surname.

Frequently Used Materials

A number of frequently used materials make their home at the registration desk. These include:

- Genealogical "how to" books
- Dictionary of Cleveland Biography and Encyclopedia of Cleveland History
- Civil War index—(also available online) refers to records from the National Archives and Records Administration (NARA) and require a written request for a specific record
- Guide to the Shaker Manuscripts in Library of WRHS 1974
- WRHS Portrait File Collection Inventory
- Guide to WRHS Cleveland Picture file Collection—over 8,000 photographs on eight rolls of film
- Guide to WRHS Newspapers on microfilm
- Guide to CD-ROM list—lists CDs available at WRHS
- Census catalogs for 1900 and 1930—gives the reel number and tells how to order individual reels (at times this is consulted if researchers feel there were mistakes on the roll of census film)
- Guide to the microfilm edition of the Cleveland, Cuyahoga County, and Western Reserve maps—lists those maps available on microfilm
- "Handybook for Genealogists"—a list by state and county of repositories for local records, such as probate courts
- Guide to local government records at WRHS—lists all eight Ohio locations for the Network of American Historical Resource Centers; continues alphabetically by county, listing available records such as Civil War bounties, cemetery records, auditors' records, and board of education records.

The bulletin board near the registration desk lists some of the frequently used holdings including: censuses and census indexes; military records; passenger lists; newspapers; local records within Ohio (necrology, marriage, tax duplicates, naturalizations for Cuyahoga County, Columbus phone books) and outside Ohio (city directory for Chicago, Accelerated Index System International [AISI], passenger lists); and other items such as genealogies on microfiche, Freedmen's Savings Records, the International Genealogical Index (IGI), and the Church of Jesus Christ of Latter-day Saints (LDS) Card Catalog.

Church Trail in Bath

Researching the surname "Brown" is enough to make genealogy a challenge.

Mathew Walling, son of Revolutionary War soldier James Walling, was born in Austerlitz, New York, on 14 September 1787 and died in Wood County, Ohio, on 29 January 1858. His second wife was Annis Brown, born 22 March 1808 somewhere in New York State. She died 27 January 1855 in Wood County.

Although their marriage was performed in Medina County in 1832, deeds in Summit County showed that Mathew resided in both Bath and Richfield (then in Medina now in Summit County).

The researcher, Suzanne, frustrated with the common name "Brown," checked the card file at WRHS under "Bath" and found a reference to church records. This led her to the manuscript collection of Jonathan Hale. Included in the Jonathan Hale Papers (Manuscript 3630) are records of Bath Congregational Church. Pages 13 to17 cover a church trial in which William Jones charged Mathew Walling with "slander and gossip." During the two-week trial, Mathew was said to have told several men that Jones had unlawful intercourse with Nancy Smith and that "in telling the story [Mathew] was chearfull [sic] and sometimes laughed." Church members agreed Mathew was guilty of reporting a story on William Jones "in an unchristian like manner" and Mathew was required to make a public acknowledgment before the congregation.

The records had very little information about Annis Brown except to state that she was admitted to the church on 16 September 1828 and her brother Morris Brown was admitted on 17 May 1834, the same day as Jonathan Hale. The church record also shows that Mathew and Annis were dismissed from membership by letter on 6 January 1839.

Of interest is the comment by Evaline Bosworth Cook that Mr. Morris Brown was one of her teachers in Bath, after Nancy Smith—the same Nancy Smith whose liaison with Jones is mentioned above.

Suzanne did not get the information she was looking for about Annis and Morris's parents. She did, however, find some colorful background information with perhaps a few new clues to keep in mind as she continued her search.

In addition, there is an explanation of how to use the soundex system to code a surname and a listing of those forms available either free of charge or for purchase at the registration desk for $.20 each plus tax.

Maps/Atlases

Some maps are in bound volumes, others are on microfilm. For those on microfilm check the map catalog across from the registration desk. It describes 860 flat printed road and land survey maps arranged by geographic area, then by size and content date. These maps date back as early as 1786. They depict transportation routes such as the interurban railway system and neighborhoods with names such as "Goldwood" (located between Rocky River and Fairview Park), and "Eastview" (situated between Shaker Heights and Warrensville). An 1886 map of Cleveland defines ward limits and voting precincts, and another map shows the distribution of Polish families in greater Cleveland in about 1930, showing that 37 percent owned their own homes.

To access the maps or atlases, use either the computer or the checklists for maps and atlases. Several atlases are located on the atlas rack in the open stacks along the east wall.

Atlases of interest for area researchers:

- 1874 Cleveland/Cuyahoga County Atlas
- Sanborn Insurance Maps of Cleveland for 1878, 1881, 1896, 1903, 1912, and 1931–1951
- 1881 City Atlas of Cleveland by Hopkins
- Hopkins Plat Books of Cleveland for 1912, 1921–1922, 1932–1933
- Hopkins Plat Books of Cuyahoga County 1914; 1920–1927; 1941–1957
- Hopkins Map of Cuyahoga County for 1858

There are also numerous maps and atlases that cover over eighty Ohio counties including the counties of Geauga, Lake, Lorain, Medina, Portage, and Summit.

The maps and atlases for other U.S. states focus on those states bordering Ohio but include many others as well. The collection also includes atlases from several different countries and regions of the world, and atlases of both world wars.

Examples of How to Research at WRHS

Cemetery/Funeral Home Search

The library at WRHS houses such a broad spectrum of genealogical material that even longtime users still find new sources. So let's experiment a little.

Using the online catalog's search feature on the computer, if you type in "Ohio cemetery," the results show 412 records, including, "Cemetery inscriptions—Preble (county, Ohio)." If you change the search term to "Cleveland cemeteries," a list of 45 records appears; some, but not all, are the same as the results of the first search. One record does not even have Cleveland in the title or the subject, but because it was compiled by the Cleveland Daughters of the American Revolution, it comes up in this search.

Several funeral home records turn up with a search of "funeral homes" and offer some new advice for those researching burial sites and death certificates. For example, if you look on the left side of the citation for the manuscript entitled "McGorray Brothers Funeral Home Records, 1876–1934," "register" is listed under "finding aid." The register tells specifically what records are included in the manuscript. This entry mentions that the funeral home was founded in 1873 and closed in 1934, and that the collection includes funeral record books, death certificates, and burial permits; then there is the statement "of particular interest to Irish Catholic family history."

How nice that someone has added this bit of genealogically significant information!

Likewise, the description of the manuscript collection for "Beilstein Young Company, 1907–1930" mentions the availability of a manuscript register. The citation tells us these undertakers were at 3311 Prospect Avenue in 1907 and in 1913 moved to 1795 Crawford Avenue. Genealogical information found in these records includes: birthplace of parent and cause of death.

The entry for the "Pease Family Funeral Home" mentions that a significant

City Directories Direct the Way

Louise B. Tucker was interested in finding the birthplace and parents of William Manuel Tucker, her husband's paternal grandfather.

W. M. Tucker came to Cleveland at the end of the Civil War and died here in 1915. Louise went to WRHS and, using the Cleveland City Directory, found W. M. Tucker first in 1871. Knowing Tucker had married the daughter of George S. Whitfield, she looked for that family as well and found them in the same 1871 directory. The Whitfields were free blacks who appeared in the Cleveland City Directory as early as 1851. Louise heard family stories about the Whitfields coming to Cleveland from Buffalo New York. So, back to WRHS and the Buffalo City Directories, where she found this same family from 1844 through 1848. In that directory George S. Whitfield is listed as "free black, place of birth Boston, Mass, occupation sailor, wife Lucinda." She had achieved her original goal but continued on.

Using city directories, Louise followed William Tucker as his address and occupation changed until finally he was Patrolman Tucker living at Lawnview Avenue in 1915 when he died. However, one address prior to that offered great clues. The listing for Tucker at 56 Euclid Avenue was quite in-

Figure 6-3: W.M. Tucker, June 3, 1881

teresting. This was also the address of the Herrick family—a wealthy white family living on Millionaires' Row. According to oral family history, William M. Tucker was a young contraband slave who went to a Union army camp looking for food, work, and housing during the Civil War. Colonel John French Herrick, the camp commander, was looking for someone to care for his horse and clean the stables. Young William Tucker got the job, followed Colonel Herrick to Cleveland after the war, and served as coachman to the Herrick brothers—John and Gamaliel.

When Tucker arrived in Cleveland he could neither read nor write. He soon went to classes and there met and married his teacher, Mary Elizabeth Whitfield. According to Louise, it was his wife who encouraged William to get a better job. At that time the police department's board of commissioners appointed police officers. The mayor was an active member of that board, and from 1879 to 1882 R. R. Herrick was mayor of Cleveland. William Tucker, who had been employed by the Herrick family for a long time, asked Mayor Herrick to appoint him a police officer. And so it was that William T. Tucker became the first African-American patrolman in Cleveland. Fifteen officers were appointed patrolmen that year. There were a total of 55 police officers in Cleveland, but no African-American ones—until William Manuel Tucker.

number of individuals of Scandinavian, Italian, and German heritage were served by this funeral home from 1883 to 1975, when they operated in Dover (now Westlake), Ohio. Another possible gold mine for the right researcher!

Also, "J. B. Deutsch Funeral Home Records, 1909–1960" note that burial books are available and contain mostly Jewish but some non-Jewish death records arranged chronologically.

One might at first wonder why a search under "funeral home" brings up a manuscript collection of the Slovene National Benefit Society. Upon closer examination we learn that included are funeral records from 1904 to 1975.

Slave Research

See the "African-American Research/Where to Find Information" worksheet in the appendix for further ideas on researching slave ancestors.

Finding Aids

The library staff has put together several selected bibliographies to aid in research on African-American, German, Irish, Italian, Jewish, Native American, and Scottish family history. These finding aids are in the rack facing the registration desk.

Census Search

- Census Holdings at WRHS:
- Federal population schedules, 1790–1930
- Printed indexes for most states, 1790–1870
- Complete 1880 and 1900 soundex (note that most of the 1890 census was destroyed in a fire)
- 1890 special census of Union veterans and their widows
- 1910 soundex or miracode for the following states: AL, IL, KY, MI, MS, NC, NY, OH, PA, RI, TN, VT, and WV
- Enumeration district description for 1900, 1910, 1920, and 1930
- Accelerated Index System International (AISI) index on microfiche
- Federal non-population schedules for Ohio, 1850–1880. This includes mortality (list of deaths within one year before the census), agricultural, and manufacturing schedules
- New York State 1855 schedules
- Slave Schedules, 1850–1860
- AncestryPlus—an online subscription service

Let's do a computer catalog search just using the word "census."

We find the information that the index/soundex to the 1920 population schedules on microform is in cabinet 38. It contains soundexed index cards for the entire 1920 census. A family card was typed by name of head of household and if someone in the household had a different last name that person had a separate card that referred back to the household card. Information consists of surname, given name, state and county of residence, city, age, place of birth, and U.S. citizenship. Each card also lists the enumeration district, volume and sheet number, and the line on which the person can be found on the population schedule. Each card gives names of people other than those in the immediate household who are enumerated with the family. These could include grandparents, boarders, cousins, and servants who resided there but may or may not be related. For Ohio in 1920 there are 476 soundex reels.

Another result from the online "census" search is a book, *The Town of Alexandria, Jefferson County, New York Cemetery Inscriptions*, published in 1994. Why would this book appear under a search for "census"? Because included in this book is the 1850 federal census for this town.

Another record under the "census" lookup is "Heads of Families in the First Census of U.S. Taken in 1790." This is a transcription from the original roster of heads of families in 1790 taken from census records. Apparently the returns for Delaware, Georgia, New York, New Jersey, Tennessee, and Virginia were destroyed in a fire in 1814. So here is another way to possibly locate an individual residing in one of these states in 1790. Also, because the 1790 federal census schedules for Virginia are missing, we learn from this record (still just from information at the computer) that lists of the state enumerations made in the years 1782 to 1785, while not complete, were substituted.

On all of these online catalog searches I used the "general keyword" category. You can also search by author, title, and subject. With the information from the computer, fill out a call slip (located near the computers and on top of filing cabinets) if you want to look at the item. Walk to the stacks and see if you can locate the item following the shelving indicators on the rows of open stacks. Remember, "ms" means it is a manuscript and you need to fill out a manuscript request.

Slave Ancestors

Sandra G. Craighead used records of the Freedmen's Savings & Trust Company Bank (on microfilm) to successfully locate and identify many family members. These records have the potential for revealing information that can be found nowhere else.

Included in these bank records are the Registers of Signature of Depositions for the branch located in Nashville, Tennessee, which Craighead accessed at WRHS. Interestingly, they were the first item donated to WRHS by the African-American Genealogical Society of Cleveland in 1993; Craighead is its current president.

The earliest deposit accounts asked for the depositor's birthplace, age, and occupation; names of the freedman's former master and mistress; name of the plantation they came from and where it was located; names of the depositor's parents and siblings, and if they were alive or deceased; and the names of their spouses and children, as well as their own physical description. Many depositors volunteered information not asked for on the form, such as "my mother Aggy was sold away before the war, haven't seen her since," and "my ole master was my daddy."

The accounts of six family members document Sandra's family from the Nashville–Davidson County area, other Tennessee counties, and Huntsville, Alabama. One of the depositors was Sandra's ancestor Milly Malone, who opened her account on 9 July 1873. Milly stated she was born and raised in Huntsville, Alabama, was about 30 years old, of medium brown complexion, and a self-employed housekeeper by occupation; her husband was named Dock Malone, her children were Isaiah and Laura, her deceased father was named "Fields," and her mother's name was Sally Robinson. Milly listed her siblings, all living, as Isaac, Martha, and Emily.

According to oral family history, Milly and her family came to Nashville from Alabama six weeks after General Hood's Raid ended in defeat when his Confederate Army was destroyed in the Nashville–Franklin area in Tennessee—a decisive battle in the Civil War. That was in 1864. Thus, this one federally created record documents three generations of Craighead's family: her great grandmother, Laura; great-great-grandmother Milly; and great-great-great-grandmother Sally.

By reviewing all of the Nashville accounts on one roll of microfilm, Craighead found the accounts of George Simmons and Catherine Craighead Allen. These helped confirm the family story that after slavery some Craighead members changed their surname to "Simmons." This was learned through the chance meeting of Craighead's Aunt Thelma with a stranger when Thelma was only 13 years old.

In an interview by Craighead in 1983, her Aunt Thelma revealed that the encounter with Aunt Janie Simmons took place in 1921 at a restaurant in Nashville. Thelma so resembled her father that a stranger came up to her and stated, "You must be my niece—isn't Carlton Craighead your daddy?—He's my nephew." Thelma mentioned the incident to her father later that day; he confirmed that he had not seen his father's half-sister, Aunt Janie Simmons, for years, and that they had the same father, James, but different mothers. Aunt Thelma remembered being told that Janie had brothers named Fremont and Oscar Simmons.

Craighead looked in the Freedman's Bureau records and found George Simmons's deposit account dated 25 March 1872, which along with oral history, census data, and vital records confirmed the Craighead-Simmons connection. George gave his address as 178 North Vine Street; he was 15 years old, was born and raised in Nashville, his parents were James and Mary Simmons, and his sibling were Jim, Oscar, Fremont, and Lewisa Jane Simmons. Craighead's great-great-grandfather, Jes Craighead Simmons, was listed along with other siblings—Jane, Watson, Joe, Susan, and Betsey—on another sibling's deposit account. Catherine Craighead Allen, their sister, noted on her account opened 27 August 1872 that she was born 29 years ago in Nashville, lived on North Vine Street, was of brown complexion, her husband and son were both named Hampton Allen, her father, Watson, was deceased, and her mother was Eva Craighead. Brother Joe Craighead's wife, Mary Jane, opened an account on 21 October 1872, indicating that their address was 178 North Vine Street and that their only child, Bibb, was adopted.

Famous Families
CLEAVELAND

The birth of Mary Artino's (nee Bacon) first child, Joseph, was heralded in the newsletter of the Early Settlers Association. Not that the Association wouldn't welcome any newborn in Greater Cleveland, but to them, this child was special. He was the sixth great-grandson, seventh generation, to Moses Cleaveland. What an honor! And yet the Bacon family had not always been aware of being direct descendants to the founder of the city.

In 1934 Emma Hawley, a librarian at the Western Reserve Historical Society, was tracing her family history. She discovered her relationship to the Bacon family and their direct relationship to Moses Cleaveland. That's when Mary's father (related to Hawley through their common Bacon ancestors) learned he was a fifth-generation descendant—making Mary a fifth great-grandchild, sixth-generation descendant. The members of this family continue to be the only known direct descendants to Moses Cleaveland.

From then on Mary's dad and later his children were routinely invited to the annual July 22 celebration of Cleveland's founding.

"As I was growing up," says Mary, "first my brother and then I were invited to go downtown for this ceremony. It was explained to me that I was related to Moses Cleaveland. At the time I didn't really know what it meant. I just heard bits and pieces of information. We just thought it was cake and ice cream and a big party."

As Mary's brother got older, soon she was called upon to represent the family. Sometimes on July 22 she would lay a wreath in front of the statue of Moses Cleaveland and be accompanied by members of the Cleveland Grays. Radio personality Larry Morrow used to dress up as Moses Cleaveland and talk about the city's historical significance.

Figure 6-4: Mary Margaret Bacon with Frederick C. Crawford and Judge Earl R. Hoover celebrate the 175th anniversary of the city of Cleveland.
Courtesy of Mary Bacon Artino

As she grew up, Mary learned more. Her brother Frederick went to college in Boston and began investigating the family lineage. He found the site of Moses Cleaveland's home. Although the home no longer stood, Frederick walked around the area and found some old handmade square nails and a leather baby shoe complete with buttons. The family has also visited Cleaveland's grave in Canterbury Court, and the Early Settlers Association still tries to keep in touch with the caretaker there.

Mary's brother Frederick made a family tree going back five generations. It is in her mother's house in Cleveland Heights. Mary has a scrapbook of newspaper articles featuring her family participating in ceremonies honoring the city's founder. But the articles and media attention have waned over the years. Mary's children are disappointed and saddened at the city's lack of interest in the historical significance of their family. Mary recalls Frederick bringing back research about Moses Cleaveland and wanting to do something significant with that information.

"Other than the historical society caring, no one else paid attention."

Mary's youngest son, Michael, was working on a school project on the history of Ohio. He was disappointed at how little was written about Moses Cleaveland.

That seems to be the theme. During times such as the city's bicentennial, we remember Moses Cleaveland and how and why the city was founded. But if you asked most residents of Greater Cleveland about the statue on public square, who it is and why it's there—most would have no idea. And to Mary Artino and her family, that is something that could easily be corrected

Pensions Search

Back to the computer for another search—this time let's type in "federal pensions." We are given information that *the Journal of Genealogy* from June 1979 has a list of federal military pensions in the U.S. compiled by William Glasson and entitled "English and Colonial Origins and Revolutionary Pensions, 1776–1789" with an index to claims made by persons with last names starting with A through C.

Page numbers referenced are to a book published by Gales and Seaton in 1834. (Wow!—yet another list to check for Revolutionary War veterans.)

CD-ROMs

How else can modern technology help in genealogy research? There is a 10-page notebook at the registration desk that lists all the CD-ROMs available for use at the library. These include everything from pre-1908 patents in Alabama to pioneers in Maine and New Hampshire. In between are numerous state censuses and census indexes a comprehensive 1880 census index (you don't need to know the state where the person was living for this one); marriage records and indexes (various states); the International Genealogical Index (over 200 million names recorded in genealogical files of the Mormon church); several military records from the

Attention to Detail and Persistence Pay Off

Drew's ancestor Anna Kral came to America in 1890 and died in 1907 at the age of 26. Unable to find any record naming her hometown, Drew began tracing her siblings. By writing to the Lorain County Common Pleas Court he got copies of naturalization records for Anna's sister Mary in Lorain, which gave Runou, Russia, as Mary's hometown and Rovno, Czechoslovakia, as her husband's hometown. Checking maps at the Cleveland Public Library, Drew found there were several towns named Rovno or something similar in Slovakia or regions near it. So the town of origin was not clear. He looked up Kral's married sister in the Lorain city directory by writing to the Lorain library and found relatives who provided more details. The Lorain relatives thought Mary Kral was from Czechoslovakia, not Russia. Drew asked them if they had any old records or papers referring to the town of origin and a few weeks later had obtained addresses of relatives in Europe. One of the addresses was to someone in "Rovne near Svidnik."

At WRHS Drew located Anna's civil marriage record. At the bottom of the marriage record it listed the clergy who performed the ceremony. Drew then checked the city directory for the year Anna was married to find the church where the priest officiated. Then he wrote to the church, which confirmed the town of origin as Rovne near Svidnik, located in what is now Slovakia.

New York Revolutionary War Records; an index of those who died in Korea and Vietnam; and PERSI, the Periodical Source Index.

This library has a well-deserved reputation as a prime resource for family history and genealogy materials as well as American history, and has much to offer that is not immediately visible. The depth and breadth of the collection are impressive and you are well advised to ask questions of staff and volunteers. Let your fingers "walk" through the catalogs and search on the computer using multiple terms. The fact that family Bibles from the 1700s are preserved here and available to look through (carefully, very carefully) is awesome.

7 Family History Centers

Family History Centers (or FHCs) are branch offices of the Family History Library that is part of the Church of Jesus Christ of Latter-day Saints (LDS) located in Salt Lake City, Utah. LDS members seek to identify their ancestors so that certain religious rites (known as ordinances) can be performed on their behalf. Thus, the LDS church has a long-standing interest in family history research and maintains vast amounts of genealogical material in a huge library in Salt Lake City. To make the materials from Salt Lake City available worldwide, the church set up Family History Centers all over the world. While much of what is at the Family History Center Library in Salt Lake can be sent to the individual FHCs, there are exceptions: books do not circulate unless they are on microfilm or microfiche, and some records, even though on microfilm, can only be used at the FHL as stipulated by the original "owner" of the material. The catalog entry will note when material is restricted. Other Family History Centers in Northeast Ohio are located in the cities of Ashtabula, Canton, Girard, Lisbon, Medina, Tallmadge, and Wooster. Family History Centers do not respond to mail inquiries.

On your first visit to a FHC, be sure to sign in and request or accept the offer of an orientation. One of the volunteers will give you a tour of the facility, show you where various materials are located, and even provide you with a "starter kit" containing an ancestor chart, family group sheets, research log, and information about the Mormon church.

Records in Common

You can access the same records from any Family History Center in the United States—or actually in the world. All Family History Centers have certain materials, such as sets of computer disks that can only be used at the center, including Scottish church records, Easton-Black books on early LDS church members, reorganized Church of LDS records (early members), AISI, PERSI, and the International Genealogical Index (IGI).

However, individual FHCs also maintain books, computer disks, microfiche, and other materials specific to the area where they are located. The specific in-house records kept by any FHC will be based upon (1) the frequency with which some records are requested (for example, Kirtland has many records for Campo Basso, Italy, because many patrons research that area) and (2) the region in which the FHC is located. Any items available at a specific FHC can be made available to patrons at any other FHC, given enough time for the transfer of the material. A phone call to the center you will be visiting is always worthwhile. And because FHCs use primarily volunteer staff, be sure to call in case hours have changed.

Family History Centers
Cleveland West
25000 Westwood Rd.
Cleveland, OH 44145
Phone: 440-777-1518
Hours: Tue–Sat 10 a.m.–2 p.m.;
Tues, Wed, Thu 6–9 p.m.

Cleveland East
Kirtland Heritage Center
(consists of the Heritage Center,
which has early LDS history, and
the Family History Center)
8854 Chillicothe Rd.
Kirtland OH 44094
Phone: 440-256-8808
Hours: Tue–Sat 10 a.m.–2 p.m.;
Thu & Fri, 7–9 p.m.

Control of Records

Some records are not as accessible to the public as others. For example, Catholic records, though controlled by the diocese, are also under the care and control of individual pastors. This applies not just to requests from non-Catholic organizations; Catholic church members as well have remarked on the inconsistencies in what is and is not permitted. And in some nations where there has been dramatic political change, records may have been destroyed, closely guarded, or simply not accessible.

FHCs will have very few church records from other religious groups. Most groups restrict access to these, citing privacy issues, for obvious reasons. FHCs also generally do not film newspapers, because they are not specific enough to genealogy.

Microfilms on Indefinite Loan at the Kirtland and Westlake FHCs:

- Maps of Western and Central Europe
- Historical and genealogical atlas of Germany
- Historical maps of Germany and Europe
- Maps of Poland, Lithuania, and Russia, 1944

But We're Not Mormons

If your family was in Northeast Ohio in the mid-1800s, or if you know they left Palmyra, New York, or Harmony, Pennsylvania, in the 1830s heading for Kirtland, you really want to check the early records here. Church affiliation can change from one generation to the next and may depend as much on convenience and the social climate at the time as on belief. And remember the effect that a charismatic clergyman can have on the public.

———◆———

Kirtland-Specific Records

- Early church (LDS) records, including original transfers of land from 1830 to 1848; early membership records from Novu, Illinois (Novu was the next stop for Joseph Smith and his party as they moved west); and early membership records of the Kirtland church, including vital records
- Atlases for: Summit County, 1891; Portage County, 1874; Allegheny, Pa, 1876; and Lake County, 1891 and 1915
- Family Group Sheet collections—family files (submitted by researchers) that become part of the posterity files
- 1881 British Census and National Index—a CD that includes England, Scotland, Wales, Channel Island, the Isle of Mann, and the Royal Navy
- 1880 U.S. Census and National Index—highly useful if your relatives were in the U.S. at this time. The index permits searching by name—you don't need to know where they were living, as long as it was in the U.S.
- Various rosters for Ohio soldiers in the Civil War and World War I
- Military Death Index—Korea and Vietnam participants. This is only available on a computer disk and cannot be accessed from the familysearch.org website
- Naturalization records
- Passenger lists
- Subscription to AncestryPlus
- Tax records for Geauga County
- Census—the 1880 Ohio soundex is the only census index kept in-house. Others must be ordered
- European gazetteers
- Out-of-state information kept in-house includes: Cook County, Illinois, death indexes, 1871–1933; Illinois death index, 1916–1938; New York City death index, all boroughs, 1888–1965; Wisconsin birth indexes prior to 1907; Ethnic groups represented heavily are Hungarian, Italian, and Slovenian

Westlake—Specific Records

- Databases on CD: Australian Vital Records; British 1881 Census; British Isles Vital Records Index, 2nd ed; Scandinavian Vital Records Index; Western Europe Vital Records Index; Canadian Census 1881; Cajun/Acadian Family Trees; Freedman's Bank Records; Middle America–Mexico Vital Record Index; Mormon Immigration Index; North American Vital Records; U.S. Census 1880; Family History Library Catalog for Windows and Pedigree Resource Files, vol. 1& 2 (CDs 1–50)
- Access to the Internet, primarily to FamilySearch.org and Ancestry.com
- Use of the "Family Search" computer disk provides access to Scottish Church Records. This is an index of approximately ten million names extracted from old Church of Scotland (Presbyterian) parish registers from the late 1500s to 1854. Individual, marriage, and parent searches of the data are possible.
- Reference books including family histories, local histories, indexes, periodicals, Genealogical Helpers 1965–1980, and other books, many covering England, Scotland, Ireland, Canada, Germany, Italy, Czechoslovakia, and Slovakia
- Lakewood city directories, 1950–1662

Connecting the "Dots"

Carole remembers visiting her great-grandfather on his deathbed when she was only five years old. When she got interested in genealogy, she wanted to find out more about him and her great-grandmother, Lucinda. Carole traveled to Warren to research another family line. At the Trumbull County Archives, in the basement of the courthouse in Warren, Ohio, Carole was going through a file box of dingy, poorly typed cards that showed deaths prior to 1905. There on the back of her great-grandfather's card was "Dot." Just that day Carole had been reading newspaper obituaries at the Warren City Library and came across something she'd never heard before. Her great-grandmother's nickname was "Dotty." Next, Carole went to the FHC and was able to print out records on more than 10 generations of ancestors, including Dot's great-grandfather, who was Isaac Goodwin, a patriot in the Revolutionary War, as well as others who lived in England in the 1500s.

- Berea city directory, 1963
- Women of Ohio (three vols.)
- Cleveland city directories, 1837–1860
- Gazetteers: Muellens, Meyers Ortz, Scotland, Canada, Czech, Hungary, Poland Spis
- Books on Immigration, including lists of passengers on the *Mayflower*; various indexes to passenger lists, including those by P. W. Filby and Morton Allan; and books that have pictures of ships, such as *Ships of Our Ancestors*.
- Atlases: Germany, Great Britain
- Microfilm frequently requested and therefore kept in-house reflects the special interest of patrons and includes: Cuyahoga County—marriages, deeds index 1860–1868 and 1810–1854, and death index 1868–1908. Other microfilms kept in-house contain vital records from Alabama, Illinois, Pennsylvania, and Tennessee, as well as from Canada, England, Germany, and Hungary

Census

All FHCs have the 1880 census on an "every name" basis, so you do not need to know the name of the head of household or even the exact location where the person lived to use soundex codes to search for someone.

Anything else is on microfilm and can be ordered from Salt Lake City at the nominal cost of $3.50. A phone call notifies you that the film has arrived, and you need to go to the FHC within three weeks to view it. Certain films get requested so often that the FHC keeps them in-house. Items on microfiche once ordered stay at the individual FHC.

How to Use Some of the Resources

The International Genealogical Index (IGI)

This index contains information on deceased persons that was obtained from church registers, censuses, wills, and other resources, including information on over 600 million deceased people from all over the world. Not all churches allow the Mormons to copy their records. Remember that depending upon the country, church registration often took the place of civil registration and does not necessarily imply church membership.

The majority of IGI listings are from the 1500s to about 1875. The index does not contain death records, although death dates can often be inferred from the information it does contain.

Codes for Recorded Events in the IGI:

A—Adult christening
B—Birth
C—Christening
D—Death or burial
F—Birth/christening of first child (when no marriage date found)
M—Marriage
N—Census
S—Miscellaneous
W—Will/probate

The IGI lists each life-cycle event individually. For example, you must look up births and marriages separately, finding the surname you want and searching that particular database. The index does list the original source for the information, allowing the researcher to check that source—which is always recommended. Anytime records are copied, filmed, or compiled, there is the possibility of error. So do not leave out this step of checking sources.

While at the FHC you can copy information found there onto a computer disk and then print it out for $.10 per page.

Personal Ancestral File (PAF; also called Ancestral Quest)

This genealogical program is offered free by the Church of Latter-day Saints. Printed worksheets (family group sheets, research log, pedigree chart, etc.) are also available at all FHCs. You can download the software onto your home computer for free from the website www.legacy.com. As with all genealogical computer programs, it offers a way to organize your family history, provides family group sheets and pedigree charts, and facilitates printouts of various sections and reports.

Ancestral File

This database contains genealogies from around the world and allows individuals researching the same family to "find" one another. Unlike the International Genealogical Index, these records are arranged with all information for the family in one place. However, these files were not compiled by an organization, or by simply filming available documents. They were submitted by thousands of individuals who have worked on their family histories and contributed their findings hoping to help others, and possibly themselves as well, link up families. Remember to check for accuracy. Some researchers may unknowingly submit information that is not accurate, or make mistakes when typing it into the computer. In the early days of family history research (less than 10 years ago), checking out sources was not emphasized. Thankfully, the entries include the contact information of the submitter. Upon finding a family record in the Ancestral File the diligent researcher will contact the submitter to find out what sources were used for specific data.

Using the Family History Library Catalog—With Internet Access

Many people make the mistake of skipping this item, and in effect they probably miss 90 percent of what the FHC has to offer. By using this very important tool you are accessing the database of everything available at the Family History Library in Salt Lake City. You can use FHLC by going to www.familysearch.org, either on your home computer or the one at the FHC (or at most other libraries as well). You can search the catalog under seven categories: by place, surname, author, subject, call

Time Is On Your Side

Drew was unable to locate any records mentioning the hometown for his direct ancestor Vasily Macko. Written notes from Drew's late grandfather noted the family was from "Berkaso Posta, Sid, Srem, Jugoslavia." Having no luck with Vasily, Drew traced Vasily's siblings. Information about George Mako's naturalization records from federal court as well as his death record received from Cleveland City Hall indicated his hometown was now known as Berkasovo, Yugoslavia. This agreed with Grandpa's written note.

However, Berkasovo was in a Serbian region, and the family was Ruthenian (a subdivision of Ukrainian) and spoke Russian, not Serbian. Furthermore, Vasily's marriage records, finally located in the civil marriage book at the Western Reserve Historical Society, gave his hometown as "Vencelia." According to maps consulted at the Cleveland Public Library, there was no such town near Berkasovo.

So Drew wrote to the parish priest in Berkasovo, who responded that he could find no record of this family. Drew did not feel this was conclusive because he could not be certain the priest looked in the right place or even made a serious effort.

More research located the marriage record, in a Ruthenian town in northeast Slovakia known as "Venecia," which was absorbed by another town in 1843.

At the Westlake FHC, Drew searched church records for Venecia. He searched for Vasily Macko's birth, just as the priest had supposedly done, in Europe. No records were found. Then he decided to look for anyone with the given name Vasily in the town of Venecia in that time period. He found "Vasily Fetzkov," born about two years earlier than Drew's records for his Vasily indicated. The parents had the same given names as the Vasily he was researching but a different surname. Carefully looking at the record, Drew noticed a note at the far right margin: "alias Macko." He had finally found Vasily's birth record.

It seems the family moved to Berkasovo from Venecia in about 1875. A persistent fellow, Drew wrote to Berkasovo again, ten years after his first letter. This time he received a positive response from the new parish priest. The records for the Macko family were found, including the birth of George. It took many years, but he found the answers to his questions

New Policy

There will be no new submissions to the Ancestral File. The database has become so huge that it outgrew the software's management capabilities. It seems that many researchers kept updating their submissions, and these kept being layered over the previous submissions—instead of having the new information incorporated into the old. So a new system has been introduced, called "Pedigree Resource File." It will serve the same purpose—a way to make your family genealogy available and to access that of others on a worldwide basis.

Tip: Search Three Times

To make optimum use of the FHL catalog, when doing a place search always perform the search on three levels: by name of town, name of province or county, and name of country. Doing this each time for each surname may seem time-consuming—until you find an elusive relative. Then you will realize how worthwhile it is.

---

number, microfilm or microfiche number, or title. Information appearing on the screen will be a description of the record, but not the record itself.

This information is worldwide in scope and includes records of births and marriages, census returns, church registers, wills, and family histories. When you find the record you are seeking, a film number will be listed as well. Write this down or print it out from the printer. Then fill out a request form, and request that roll of film be sent to your local FHC. There is a nominal fee (currently $3.50), and usually it takes a few weeks until the film arrives at the center. You are notified by phone when the film arrives. You then return to the FHC to look at the film on a reader machine. Once you indeed find the specific information you want on the film, you can make a copy of this by pressing the "print" button. When you use the catalog, you eventually will be finding original records.

Navigating the Website

From the home page at www.familysearch.org you will see four choices at the top of the page: Home, Search, Share, and Library. Choose "Library." There will be four choices under that. Choose "Family History Library Catalog." From there you will be offered the seven types of search modes. Just keep going until you find the film you want to order.

Using the Library Catalog—Without Internet Access

At some FHCs all computers can access the Internet. At others, however, patrons need to make use of the specific computer disks labeled FHLC. A volunteer will show you the appropriate disk. Then choose the type of search you want to perform, for example "place country." When researching, be creative in choosing the subject on the catalog disk. For example, "births" will be part of vital records, or civil registration. Wills and deeds will probably be under probate court.

Viewing the Film

Ordering a roll of film does not guarantee you will find your ancestor listed on it. Records of births in Budapest from 1880 to 1900 may not include your grandmother, even though information you have states that is when and where she was born. The place or time may be incorrect; the spelling of the name may be so different you don't recognize it. You will then need to search another category: for example a listing of Jewish residents of Budapest in 1880 to 1890; or the census from that time period. There can be more than one road to take to get your information—sometimes there are several rolls of film associated with your search. This can be frustrating and time-consuming: you have to decide which to order first, or whether to order several all at once.

Periodical Source Index (PERSI)

This is a microfiche index of articles published in over 2,000 genealogical and family history journals and magazines. Included are all English-language periodicals as well as some French periodicals. You can search by locations or surname, although not every surname listed in an article is in the index. PERSI actually is divided into two time frames. One index covers 1847 to 1985; the other, known as the Annuals Index, covers from 1986 to the present. PERSI will give the researcher references as to where an item was originally published. From there you can:

- get a copy of the article made from the Allen County Public Library in Fort Wayne, Indiana (fee-based)
- inquire if it is available on interlibrary loan
- check with local libraries to see if it's available
- write to the publisher and ask if they will copy what you want

Specific for LDS Members

The term "Temple Ready" refers to submitting ancestors' names in order for the ancestors to receive temple ordinance. This is an important procedure, one that members prepare for over a long time, and they may work on these files at any FHC but they must go to specially designated FHCs to actually submit the files.

---

❶ Ellis Island Website

Although this has been a wonderful additional resource, many names do not appear on this site, or are very difficult to read.

Family Here, Family There

A volunteer at the local Family History Center was helping someone look for information regarding his grandfather. This man's father had searched for years but found nothing.

The information that was known was the following: Grandpa left his home in Italy in about 1912 from the Port of Naples; there he boarded a ship to America, leaving behind a wife and two sons whom he was to send for later. The family never heard from him again and wondered if something happened to him en route, or after arriving in America.

As Coreen, the volunteer, writes:

"Using the passenger lists, we found that he had come to America, arriving at the Port of New York along with a friend none of the present family members had ever heard of. His final destination was listed as Chicago, Illinois, not New York, as the family thought.

"Using census records for Illinois, the grandpa was located in 1920 living in Chicago with a wife and two children; one of the children had the same name as the son he left behind in Italy. The death certificate for the man verified he was indeed the same man they were researching."

The patron was grateful to have a family mystery cleared up, but sad at the turn of events. The two boys left behind in Italy came to America, but their mother never left Italy.

International Research

You will need to know where your ancestor was when the event you are researching occurred. From FHC you can then order church records, vital records, or census information if you know the country, and the county, town, or district of residence. But first a search on the catalog disk is necessary to verify whether the specific records are available (that is, whether they have been "filmed" by the LDS).

Immigration Research

If the individual you are searching for was not naturalized, or those records have not been located, it is necessary to find them on a passenger list. This is a three-part process at the FHC.

1. First determine the port of entry and then order the index for the appropriate port and time frame (look for clues from the 1900, 1910, and 1920 censuses, which asked when people came to the U.S. and from where).

2. When that film comes in (after about three weeks), look for the surname on the index and order that film containing the ship's manifest. Be careful to take down the information next to the surname (page and line number). The index lists only the page and line number, not the ship's name.

3. When the next roll of film arrives (approximately three weeks later), you need to look through the entire roll for the page and line number to find your person's name. Hopefully you will find your ancestor on the passenger list.

Passenger list indexes after 1905 are searched using the soundex system and also give the person's age and a code consisting of a series of numbers, so you will order the passenger list according to those numbers.

By ordering and then viewing the film of the entire passenger list, you can see all the people who came from the same town at the same time as your relative. This may offer new names and possible clues to others who emigrated with your family member, and who may have been part of the family.

Can't Find Your Ancestor?

If the information you are looking for is not found on computer disk or via the online version, try looking at the microfiche version of the same record. Sometimes items are overlooked or left out.

Accuracy of Records

The Mormon church provides names and addresses of the people who submit information so you can write to them if you want to clarify something. Also, the church has a system of forwarding returned mail to the next of kin, if known. But it does not verify the accuracy of the information. Always, always go back to the original source.

A Story Leaves Its Mark

Coreen, the FHC volunteer, also helped her son-in-law research his family. Modestina Rizo arrived in America in 1907 at the Port of New York from Naples, Italy. The passenger list gave her final destination, height, color of hair, and color of eyes, and under "distinguishing marks" listed "wart." It seems the young Modestina had what we call a zit on her cheek. Although she insists she never had any such thing as a wart, it is recorded on the passenger list information sheet as just that.

The family got quite a laugh over this information. Poor Grandma had a zit back in 1907, and now it's recorded for all to see forever!

Figure 7-1: This copy of the manifest shows the notation "wart of cheek."
Courtesy of Coreen Bush

8 Fairview Park Regional Branch Cuyahoga County Public Library

The Fairview Park Regional Library is part of the Cuyahoga County library system and is one of four designated regional branches. Each regional branch has a specialty, and Fairview's specialty is genealogy and history as well as geography and travel.

Before going to any library, review their website or call to get updated information about hours, services, fees, and parking. It's a good idea to introduce yourself to the librarian on duty and let her or him know your goal(s) for the day. Reference librarians can be most helpful when they know what you hope to accomplish during your visit and which records you have already searched.

Bring in as few documents as possible, but do include your ancestor chart and any other materials you may need. For example, copies of census research (discussed in detail in Chapter 9) are often helpful in case you find a clue, perhaps in a newspaper article or book, that reflects on census information you already have or need to verify.

Fairview has many reference items and many books in their collection that circulate (patrons can request these at any Cuyahoga County library). This is a wonderful benefit, especially if you just need one specific book, don't have a lot of time to spend at the library, or want to read through a book (or books) at your leisure. It is easy to request the book in person from any Cuyahoga County library, by telephone, or online. And the book, if it circulates, will be sent to any Cuyahoga County library you designate.

Fairview Park Regional Library of Cuyahoga County Public Library
21266 Lorain Rd.
Cleveland, OH 44126
Phone: 440-333-4700
Fax: 440-333-0697

Hours: Mon–Thu 9 a.m.–9 p.m.; Fri, Sat 9 a.m.–5:30 p.m.;
Sundays 1–5 p.m. (Sep–May)
Website:
http://www.Cuyahogalibrary.org
Parking: A parking lot is located in front of the building.

Genealogy Collection

The genealogy collection is on the second floor. On the set of cabinets by the front windows are brochures detailing categories of items in the collection as well as offering a map of the open shelves that pertain to genealogy. Check here for information about local genealogy society meetings and classes. The Greater Cleveland Genealogical Society sponsors classes on beginning and intermediate genealogy as well as classes geared to special topics such as immigration, or computers and genealogy. Usually such classes are held once a week for three consecutive weeks. A $15 fee covers the cost of materials.

In this same section are nine computers that offer Internet use and also provide access to a paid subscription to AncestryPlus. This service offers access to large amounts of information, such as death, marriage, and land records from all over the world. They are constantly adding to their database. This is also where you can use the CD-ROM databases for FamilySearch and PERSI (Periodical Source Index; see Chapter 7: Family History Centers).

Everyday Resources Help in Genealogy Too

In searching for his St. Louis ancestors, Ray Tindira decided to get a phone book for the area. He went to the Fairview Park Library and accessed a current telephone book for St. Louis. A quick look under "Tindira" showed a listing for George Tindira. Ray called him and, yep, it seems that George, who is just a few years younger than Ray, is his cousin. George's father (George Sr.) had just passed away. From his own research Ray knew the married name (Shaeffer) of the sister from whom George Sr. had been estranged. Again using the phone book, Ray located the two sons of this sister (now deceased), who also lived in St. Louis. Calling George Jr. on the phone (by now Ray and his St. Louis phone book were fast friends), Ray asked, "Do you know where ___ street is?" "Sure," George Jr. replied. "It's about two miles from here." And that's how Ray from Cleveland introduced a set of cousins to each other in St. Louis.

The book collection begins with European countries in alphabetical order, followed by a section on immigration, and then covers the U.S. alphabetically by region and state. Next come volumes on surnames, heraldry, and military records. A large part of the information available focuses on the U.S. east of the Mississippi. Being able to browse the shelves is an added benefit. Sometimes seeing a topic or title will jog your memory and lead to new ideas or a new avenue of research.

Many of these books consist largely of indexes and abstracts to resources such as probate records, land records, and cemetery records. The index makes finding the information much easier but requires a second step—that of going to the original data, perhaps housed here, or possibly not, and then retrieving the information.

Nearby are reader machines for viewing microfilmed necrology files, old newspapers, city directories, and the census. The county libraries all permit you to make copies from these machines by simply pushing the "print" button—no fee is charged (that's right, it's free!).

Also available at the genealogy desk located in this section are blank 1930 census forms, pedigree charts, and other frequently used genealogy forms—all free of charge. On the first floor are copy machines (charge, $.10—change machine available).

Newsletters

This is one of the few sites in the county (another is WRHS) that keeps newsletters from genealogy societies. Current holdings date back to the 1960s and include newsletters from around the country. However, because of space issues, the library's future newsletter holdings will pertain only to those groups east of the Mississippi. These newsletters contain everything from names of schoolteachers in the 1900s, to where funeral home records can be found, to tricks to taking pictures of gravestones. Currently there are about 100 active titles in the newsletter file.

BELLAMY *Famous Families*

Author John Stark Bellamy II never thought he'd be interested in genealogy. In fact it was fate, not fascination that led him to the genealogy department at Fairview Park Regional Library. John was already working as a librarian at Fairview Park Regional Library when in 1993 he was asked to assume the responsibilities of genealogy specialist due to the untimely death of Barbara Musselman, who had served in that capacity.

John credits his luck in finding some of his family history information to the fact that he had a few well-known family members. A modest family tree was included in Arthur Morgan's biography of Edward Bellamy, John's great-grandfather. As proof that John has "author DNA," Edward Bellamy was the author of *Looking Backward* and first cousin to Francis Bellamy, author of the Pledge of Allegiance to the United States flag. John's father, Peter Bellamy was a well-known Cleveland journalist whose career spanned 50 years and included serving as the drama critic at the *Plain Dealer* from 1962 to 1976 and critic at large from 1976 to 1986; his grandfather, Paul Bellamy, was editor-in-chief at the Plain Dealer from 1928 to 1954 and for 18 years served as director of the Associated Press.

Information in the Morgan book led John to other books at Fairview Park Regional Library, including James Savage's *Genealogical Dictionary of the First Settlers of New England* as well as Grace Louise Knox's *Connecticut Divorces*. These helped fill in details about some of the minor scandals in the Bellamy family line. It wasn't long before the previously uninterested-in-genealogy librarian was buying his first genealogy software program (PAF). Having taken the plunge, John kept right on going–searching for and acquiring

Figure 8-1: Paul Bellamy, editor in chief of the Plain Dealer 1928–1954. *Courtesy of John Stark Bellamy II*

copies of documents such as census data, passenger lists, and city directories. Staying true to his literary family's calling, John soon produced his first family history, the subject of which was his father's direct line of descent. The book was produced by John using desktop publishing and presented as Christmas gifts to siblings and cousins in December 1994.

John sings the praises of the great improvements available to modern-day family historians including, of course, Internet resources and the expansive records available through the Mormon Church and subscriptions to private collections, all of which are also available at many of our public libraries.

John has continued his family genealogy to the point where he has been able to burst a few bubbles. The story about his maternal line coming from Alsace-Lorraine instead of (in reality) Prussia seems to have been used to ward off the anti-German sentiment of the time. He has also learned that his fourth great-grandfather, Joseph Bellamy, not only was a slave-owner but tried as well to convince Aaron Burr to become a Baptist minister. Now that might have changed history, as well as family history. He has found both sets of his mother's grandparents, and located records of his wife's great-grandmother, great-grandfather, and great-aunts who entered the United States through Ellis Island in 1913 and 1914. John even purchased an oversized reproduction of their Ellis Island records, which hangs prominently in his house. (See the Ellis Island website for the way to purchase similar items for your ancestors.) John views all the innovations and shortcuts brought on by computer-age technology as a huge benefit for genealogists. "In short," he says, "thanks to the computer age, there's never been a better time for living persons to search for the dead."

Genealogy Specialist

The library's genealogy specialist is available to speak locally as well as to assist you in your research. Staff will respond to e-mail or written requests as time permits. Be specific in stating the type of record needed, date and place the event occurred, and the full name of the ancestor you are researching. Staff does not perform in-depth research, but can provide a list of local researchers. Send e-mail requests to cwiggins@cuyahoga.lib.oh.us. Written requests should be addressed to Fairview Park Regional Library, attn: Genealogy, 21266 Lorain Rd., Cleveland, OH 44126.

City Directories

Fairview Park Library has city directories from 1837 to 1858 on microfiche; directories from 1861 to 1935 on 32 rolls of microfilm; and directories from 1936 to 1960 in books. All of these can be accessed on the second floor.

Newspapers

This library has "full runs" (the entire set) of several Cleveland newspapers, including:

- The Plain Dealer from 1845 to the present
- The Cleveland Press from 1878 to 1982
- The Cleveland Leader from 1854 to 1912
- The Cleveland News from 1945 to 1960
- Cleveland News index, 1982 to 1999
- Cleveland News death notices, 1975 to the present

Computer Menu

At any of the Cuyahoga County Public Library computer terminals, or from home, you can learn more specifics about what is available at the Fairview Park Library by going to www.cuyahogalibrary.org, clicking on "Branches," and then "Regional Library," then "FairviewPark," then "About your Branch," and finally "Genealogy."

Two excellent resources then come up on your screen: One is the word GENEALOGY written across the screen. By placing your cursor on different letters in this word, the following choices are then available:

- **G** – getting your genealogical research started
- **E** – electronic resources and Internet websites
- **N** – new additions to our genealogical resources
- **E** – ethnic heritage, Ellis Island, immigration
- **A** – about our genealogy collection, including e-mail link
- **L** – local resources for Cleveland and Cuyahoga County
- **O** – Ohio genealogy resources
- **G** – genealogical organizations and societies
- **Y** – your own genealogical record

From the "L" in Genealogy, I found a listing of local archives, and was fascinated to learn that the Cleveland Grays have an archive. Available by appointment only, they have local military and militia records from 1846 to 1935, including patriotic sheet music!

The second choice is to click on "Alphabetical List of Genealogical Websites Selected by Our Genealogy Librarian" on the bottom of the genealogy home page. This will lead you to many other excellent links, such as Allen County Library (the largest genealogical collection in the U.S. outside of Salt Lake City), RootsWeb (home to many online genealogy classes and other user friendly information), and many Ohio-based websites.

Take a "Walk in the Park"

Don't let the size of this chapter make you think the Fairview Park Library is short on material. Quite the contrary, the large collection of books (many of which circulate) on states (particularly east of the Mississippi) and other countries will aid in much of your research. The ease with which you can access historical newspapers from the area and the many computer terminals that allow access to AncestryPlus as well as other subscription databases will convince you that getting to know Fairview Park Library can make your genealogy trip a "walk in the park."

9 Making Sense of the Census

The United States Constitution requires a federal census be taken every 10 years. The purpose of the census is to determine congressional representation. Therefore, by 1790 a census taker visited or attempted to visit every household in the nation. Each successive census added to the questions of the previous one (as well as eliminating some). And the personal interview evolved into a form sent in the mail—sometimes followed up by a personal interview for those forms not returned. Hence the information available on the 1800 census is much less detailed than that on the 1900 census.

As with most genealogical data, the researcher needs to know the "where"—as in where an ancestor was living. This will determine in which part of the census to look. And the more detailed the information as to where your ancestor was living, the easier it will be for you to search—especially in large cities. Census records are organized by state, county, city, and then enumeration district.

Enumeration Districts

Townships, towns, and cities are divided into enumeration districts (1880–present), designated areas in which census information is collected. Each enumeration district is assigned a number. Enumeration district boundaries and numbers change each census year. By knowing the address where your ancestor lived during the census, you can find the enumeration district. If you don't know the exact address, maps can help you define an area or areas of the town in which to search. This may involve looking for records in more than one enumeration district, but it can be done relatively easily. However, for those records that are soundexed (soundexing is described below), you do not need to know the enumeration district before searching the index—it will be listed on the soundex card.

Because of the possibility of obtaining significant information on several generations of the same family, family historians relish searching through these records. The laws governing the census require these records to be closed to the public for 72 years, to ensure privacy. The 1930 census became available in 2002.

Schedules

For genealogical purposes, you want to look at the population schedules (1790–1930); mortality schedules (1850–1880); and special schedule for surviving Civil War soldiers, sailors, marines, and widows (1890). Other schedules include agricultural (specified size of farm and what was raised), manufacturing (owner's name, number of employees, amount of equipment, and what was produced), and Native American (separate listing of Native Americans living on reservations or who were not taxed).

Finding An Orphaned Grandmother

Kenneth Hicks was searching for information on his grandmother Elizabeth Ward. He knew her maiden name was Benson and that her West Virginia family did not raise her.

At the WRHS, Kenneth looked at the 1880 census. Although he did not know where in West Virginia Elizabeth lived, he had a hunch it might be in the capital—Charleston. He had no information as to Elizabeth's parents or siblings. Because the 1880 census is soundexed, Kenneth looked for the name BENSON (luckily not a common name) and found only one Elizabeth Benson, residing in the poorhouse in Harrison County. This matched family stories that Elizabeth was an orphan. From more recent family history Kenneth knew that Elizabeth Benson married William Thomas Ward shortly after moving to Pittsburgh, Pennsylvania. Now, with the new information from the 1880 census, Kenneth had an approximate birth year for his maternal grandmother, knew where she'd spent her formative years, and knew that her parents were born in Virginia.

Figure 9-1: Ward Hotel. *Courtesy of Kenneth W. Hicks*

Elizabeth's husband, William Thomas Ward, became well known in Cleveland Republican political circles in the 1920s and 1930s. He owned several hotels, including the Ward Apartment Hotel at East 40th and Cedar Avenue—one of the few dignified places people of color could stay in Cleveland.

If you've never looked at census records, be prepared. First of all, due to the sheer numbers of records and the fact that the census is not in alphabetical order (census takers went from house to house), there needs to be an organized method for arranging the information so researchers can find the family they are seeking. Indexes are used for this purpose. And for much of the U.S. census, a special type of index was created—this is referred to as the soundex.

The Soundex: What It Is, How It Was Created

In the 1930s, the WPA abstracted census data from 1880, 1900, 1920, and parts of 1910 onto card files. All surnames in the country were given a code consisting of a letter and three numbers. Basically, this is a phonetic method using the first letter of the surname, eliminating all vowels and the second letter of double letters (like the "l" in Kelly), and including the rest of the consonants. Records are therefore grouped together, so that Smith, Smyth, and Smythe will all be in the same section of the index. This allows for the many spelling variations of surnames as well as possible errors in spelling by the census taker or others. It is not, however, a perfect system.

These cards were coded, put on microfilm, and filed by state. They consist of complete family listings and help locate families in the census. Therefore, the census is always seen on microfilm using a machine—a microfilm reader.

Those facilities having soundexed microfilm will have an explanation of how to put any surname into the soundex system. There is also a top-rate description of the soundex system at www.archives.gov/research_room/genealogy/census/soundex. It is not as complicated as it seems, and once you've done it two or three times, it really isn't a bother. But, this is not to say that all the Le, Lee, and Leigh records will be kept together on one roll of census film. Rather they will be together in the index. You must first read the index to see in which enumeration district all of them were located.

Once you know where in Cleveland or Chicago or Medina County, Ohio, your relative lived in a given census year (knowing the "ED"—enumeration district) and you've referenced the various name spellings, you will be directed to look at specific rolls of microfilm. Be sure to write down all the information you find in the index. It gives not only the enumeration district but also page number and the line number on the page. This will save you from scrolling through many unwanted pages of microfilm. At this point you might want to look at the census worksheets in the appendix. Look first at the worksheet for the specific census year you are researching to prepare yourself for what to look for and document.

Indexes

An index is a listing, usually by name, of what or who is included in the entire document (census, book, court file), and it can be arranged alphabetically, by year, or in some other manner. Many indexes, especially those for census and court records, are not "every name" indexes. For example, a probate or court index will list only names of decedents, but not all heirs, or parties in a court case. Consulting the index is only one step in the process of finding a person, or the document relating to the person.

Indexes (soundex or others) allow you to find the precise page on which your ancestors appear. So while you may not find your entire "Newman" family on the same roll of film, you may find the ones who live on the same street as well as neighbors who seem to follow your Newman family from one census to another.

Just because a family or an individual is not listed in an index (be it census, probate, or whatever), this does not mean for certain they are not in the actual record. Remember that people created the index, and people make mistakes.

Be sure to write down exactly all pertinent information found in the index, as well as the microfilm number and volume for each census roll on which you find data (and any other details on the outside of the box it was in). We've all gone back to look at the same film more than once, and this will save you valuable time, and frustration.

Census Indexes

The number of details included in the census, and the fact that it was compiled by hand, mean that there are hundreds and hundreds of pages of census records for each city and county in the country. An index makes the task of locating individuals in the census reasonably easy.

If a library or archive states that the census has an index, this means there are separate books or films to look through to help determine which roll of census microfilm to view. If it says "soundex," you will look up your surname according to the soundex system and then determine which roll of census microfilms to view.

Different states are indexed for different years. Not all censuses are completely indexed. The federal government has indexed a small number of the censuses—1880, 1900, 1910 (partial), 1920, and 1930 (partial). So organizations (such as the Ohio Genealogical Society, local historical and genealogical societies, and commercial companies) pay for, sponsor, or provide indexing. It is a costly, time-consuming project. All the Ohio federal population censuses are either completely indexed or soundexed, except 1930. But individual repositories decide which of these to purchase (see Appendix).

Reading the Census Form

Upon arriving at the correct line, page, and date and finding the name of your ancestor, you may be surprised. The information is not typed, nor necessarily written in beautiful script. Let your eyes adjust to the handwriting on the page. If you have difficulty deciphering all the letters, look for other names written in the same hand and compare them. Soon you'll get the hang of how this person writes capital J's or doesn't cross T's. Now is the time to write down everything. If the person lived in a large city in the 20th century the street number will be along the left side of the page—don't forget to include that as well.

In the case of the Ohio 1880 census, all of it is indexed (book format) and part of it is soundexed. The soundexed portion (just the index, not the census itself) only includes those families with dependent children aged 10 and under. This was for Social Security purposes. (Social Security did not exist in 1880, but at the time the index was created it did.) The federal government wanted to be able to verify age for people who would be 65 when Social Security went into effect.

For this reason it is often stated that the 1880 soundex is "not complete"—because it only included households with children age 10 or younger. However, with the advent of computerized database census records, most of the possible glitches or difficulties relating to individual census indexes has been overcome.

Some Special Situations

1850, 1860, 1870 Census Reports

The census schedules for 1850, 1860, and 1870 list children but not their relationship to the head of household. From the data one may be tempted to believe that all the children in the household are children of the adult "head of household," but this is just a supposition, which must be proved. Proof can be obtained by checking a later census, land records, or wills of the adults to see if the same names appear. Also, look for corroborating information from death records and obituaries.

Until that is done, one must remember that if the relationship has not been proven it is still only assumed.

1880 Census

The index to the 1880 Ohio census is the most accurate of all the ones for that year, thanks to the fine editing provided by the Ohio Genealogical Society. This was the first census to list the birthplace of parents.

1890 Census

A fire in 1921 destroyed most of the 1890 population schedules. Part of the special schedule listing surviving Civil War soldiers, sailors, marines, and widows still

Census Day

At the top of the form it will state what day was "census day." This is not the day the census taker actually visited the house, but rather all information given was considered accurate for that day. Be sure to write this down. Obviously the ages stated on the census form would all be relative to that specific day.

As People Move, So Do Their Records

Let's say naturalization papers indicated a family arrived in Baltimore, Maryland, in 1908; one child is listed as born in New York in 1909; the next child was born in Cleveland in 1911. You've been checking Ohio Census records and could not find the family in the 1910 census. There is a good possibility you will find them in the New York Census.

African-Americans and the Census

Free African-Americans were included in the 1850, 1860, and earlier federal censuses. Slaves, however, were considered property listed under the name of their owners, so you should actually search for the plantation owner's name. Very little personal information was provided for slaves: only age, gender, and race (black or mulatto), and sometimes an occupation.

Those slaves 100 years old or older did receive special treatment in that their names were noted, and perhaps some biographical information included as well. Certain locales included more information, but this is a hit-or-miss thing. For example, in 1860 for Hampshire County, Virginia, they included names of all slaves. Generally speaking, the way in which slaves were listed in the census denoted not families but age (oldest to youngest).

The 1870 census is the first U.S. census to by name African-Americans who were slaves.

---

exists (covering half of Kentucky and all the states that follow it alphabetically), and includes Confederate soldiers as well.

1910 and 1920 Censuses

Finding your ancestor in the 1910 and 1920 censuses may be difficult due to the large numbers of people living in cities by then, and because not all states were soundexed. However all states were indexed for 1920. (This is not a problem for the 1900 census because the WPA soundexed the 1900 census for all states.)

The 1910 census has Miracode (similar to soundex but references a "visitation number" instead of page and line number), but only for 22 states: Alabama, Alaska, California, Florida, Georgia, Illinois, Kansas, Kentucky, Louisiana, Michigan, Mississippi, Missouri, North Carolina, Ohio, Oklahoma, Pennsylvania, South Carolina, Tennessee, Texas, Virginia, and West Virginia.

If your ancestor lived in a large city that is not indexed, or the family is not found in the index, look at the microfiche "1910 Cross Index to City Streets" (available at the WRHS; it can be ordered from the National Archives and Records Administration—refer to microfilm m1283). This may help you find your ancestor if you know the street address.

The following cities have a town soundex for the 1910 population index: Birmingham, Mobile, and Montgomery, Alabama; Atlanta, Augusta, Macon, and Savannah, Georgia; New Orleans and Shreveport, Louisiana; and Chattanooga, Knoxville, Memphis, and Nashville, Tennessee (also Philadelphia County, Pennsylvania). People living in these cities are not included in the statewide index.

So what to do if you're researching in one of the other states? If you know the address where the individual was living (city directories and telephone books should help with this) then either:

1. Get the Enumeration District Description—it is available on microfilm and covers both the 1900 and 1910 censuses. To use this, consult a map of the area and determine the enumeration district number according to the microfilm's description of street boundaries for the address of your ancestor.

2. Get the Cross Index to Selected City Street and Enumeration Districts—1910 Census Miracode. This is available on microfiche and includes 40 cities (in Ohio: Akron, Canton, Cleveland, Dayton, and Youngstown). Use the guide to coordinate the address for your ancestor with an enumeration district.

1930 Census

The 1930 census was released in April 2002. It consists of approximately 2,668 reels of microfilm (146 just for Ohio). The records are arranged according to place of residence: state, then county, and then township or city. Paid subscription services, such as those available through Ancestry.com, Heritage Quest, and Genealogy.com, have included Ohio in their 1930 census index, but you will find some omissions ("page not available"). To date, there is no complete index for Ohio for 1930, but there are two rolls of film with descriptions of enumeration districts. Several organizations are working on indexing Ohio by county, but it is still a work in progress. Still, most medium- and large-sized libraries have subscriptions to AncestryPlus, which offers free access to this information.

Tips on Using Census Records

What Information Do You Need?

Consider what information you will get from the census. What do you need in order to get that information? As in most instances with genealogy, you usually need to know the "where" in order to get the "what"—ages, occupation, and so on.

Name Searches

Check both index and actual census records under a variety of surname spellings. A rose by any other name (Ross?Roze?) is not spelled the same.

Though the census is searched according to the last and then first name of "head of household," who was usually male, there are exceptions. At times the name of a widow or an eldest son is used for that category, or even a wife whose husband is still alive. It's a good idea to look at the information for same or similar surnames in the same locale. Even though the census is not arranged alphabetically, always look at the names of 20 people before and 20 people after "your person." People often lived near relatives, traveled in groups, and stayed in the same neighborhood. You may find a brother a few doors away, but under the household name of a married aunt. You will often find related households in this way.

Similarly, if an ancestor had an unusual name and you see another person with the same or a similar name in the same area (neighborhood, ED, town)—check this out. People are often named after a relative or prominent person, and this may be another clue.

Incorrect Information

Whether it's the census or a death notice, it's an official document, so the information it contains must be correct, right? Not really. Probably every family history researcher has found errors in one or more official records. That is why acquiring a variety of records from various sources is important. And, having one piece of information repeated in more than one document does not make it true. It is up to each individual to evaluate the information. Errors could be the result of poorly paid, uneducated workers not particular about the accuracy of what they put down. (If only these census takers knew how important this information would be to future generations! Ah, wishful thinking.) Perhaps the family was not home and the information was supplied by a neighbor; the handwriting can be difficult to read; people did not like or trust government workers; people purposely gave wrong information (many have found this in the case of divorce); or the worker did not verify the spelling.

You have to think not just like a researcher, but like a resident at the time that the record was created. What was the reason for this record to be produced? Who produced it, and could there have been a reason to lie?

Generation Gap

The average span of time between parents' birth and the birth of their children is 33 years. Three generations equals a century. If you have data that does not fit this pattern, you need to investigate more carefully.

Children Out of Wedlock

Children born out of wedlock (particularly prior to 1900) may be "hiding" in the census as a child in the household of the grandparents.

Online Census Records

There are various websites that offer access to census records online. As mentioned earlier, some of these require a paid subscription. However there are websites that offer free access, such as www.us-census.org, which has a link where you can check which state and county records have already been transcribed and put

Same Surname

When looking at printed indexes, take note of other families in the same area with the same surname as your family member. If the number of names is small, write them all down and consider researching these as well.

It's The Real Thing

After looking through census data, or anything else that is compiled or transcribed, be sure to check both the index and the actual document itself, and do both using all spelling variations of the surname. Look at several entries prior to and after your ancestors. There may be other family members you missed, or never knew about.

online by volunteers. There is also a census lookup board at www.us-census.org/webbs//lookups. When using any of these sites be sure to look at the entire page, and take the time to read any tutorials offered on how exactly to access the information.

Can't Find 'Em

You've looked for your ancestor's name in an index or soundex and not found it. Now you must read the census house by house for the town, township, or county where you think they were living. If you are still dissatisfied, read the surrounding counties. Still not successful? Look for married siblings of your ancestor, as well as aunts and uncles.

Where'd They Go?

You found your ancestor in one census, but not the next. What happened? Remember that proximity of listings on the census usually indicates close neighbors. And people often knew their neighbors so well that their children intermarried, and/or they moved together to the next town or state. So if you've been unable to locate your relatives in successive censuses, try looking for their neighbors.

Census Substitutes

We are always seeking to place an ancestor in a specific place at a specific time. We'd like to know when they arrived and when they left there because we know that at each location our ancestor may have left us more clues: most records are created and stored by location. So we always want to know where people are.

The census only happens every 10 years; what other information can we look in these 10-year intervals?

- **State census**—some states conducted a state census at different times; Ohio did not.
- **City directories**—you knew where your ancestor was once; follow through consecutive years of a city's directories. See if others are listed at the same address.
- **School records**—school districts kept records, often an actual "enumeration" of youth between the ages of 5 and 21.
- **Land records**—See Chapter 12.
- **Tax lists**—see "Tax Duplicates" in Chapter 5: Cuyahoga County Archives.
- **Quadrennial census for Ohio**—available for very few counties (not Cuyahoga); check with archives or auditor's office.
- **Churches and other religious organizations**—records were kept for births and marriages, membership, minutes of meetings, pew rentals, Sunday school classes, and teachers.
- **Voting lists**—helpful but only for citizens, and don't include women until after 1920.
- **Military records**—remember men did not always serve from where they lived except if it was a local militia.

Assumptions

Sometimes we can get the most use out of census records by making some creative assumptions or educated guesses. But always be sure to verify that the ensuing information is valid. For example, free African-Americans in the 1870 census likely lived close to their previous owner, whose surname was the same as theirs.

CARTER   *Famous Families*

Shawn Godwin has known since he was a young child that he was a direct descendant of Lorenzo and Rebecca Carter, Cleveland's first permanent European-American settlers. Shawn recalls how he became seriously interested in genealogy at about age 10, and he sees it as a direct extension of his early interest in history.

"The connection between history and genealogy seemed logical. When I was younger and heard the family stories, I was fascinated by my family's connection to the frontier, the French and Indian War, the War of 1812, log cabins, Indians, and wolves."

Although members of his family took great pride in their family history, no one in several generations had bothered to record it or do new research. "It was just part of our family, something to talk about occasionally," explains Godwin. So when he was in his early teens, he began to compile records and to interview relatives. "Like many people, I was very inspired by the television show *Roots*."

Godwin came to see genealogy as a way to approach social history. He is interested in "seeing how families were part of economic and social migrations; how larger historical events affected the personal lives of individuals."

Like many beginning family history researchers, Godwin at first wanted to know "who is the earliest ancestor I can find, and how fast can I find them? As I got older," he says, "I realized I should focus on the people who are living right now. Oral history work was sometimes harder than documentary research because living relatives did not always share my detailed interest in family history and might have thought I was prying into their personal lives. A lot of these people have died, and I kick myself wishing I had been more sophisticated in my questioning as a child and checked out more facts with them."

This is not to say that Godwin hasn't done library research. He knows the thrill of finding family members in the census, and of that information supporting or calling into question information he already had and then giving him other questions to ask.

Godwin's method now is to approach family history by prioritizing. He feels the historical information

about Lorenzo Carter "will always be there—it will get even easier to access as time goes on." Right now he wants to focus on other branches of the family where he still has living relatives, particularly an aunt who shares this interest and who would like to "see her family's story compiled." Godwin has also been working to organize the years'-worth of records he has collected and to write up his notes. He does not use commercial genealogy software for this. Instead, he puts his information on his computer in a word-processing program using an adaptation of forms he developed as a teenager with lots of room for footnotes. "If it is not written down, it is not history, and if you do not list your sources accurately, it is not good history!"

While Godwin appreciates his connection to Carter, it is no more important to him than that to many other ancestors. "Carter's independence and self-reliance have been an inspiration to me, but I also feel a strong connection to many of my other ancestors, whether furniture makers or botanists," says Godwin. "For me the most important part of genealogy is the perspective it can supply—a strong connection to history and a sense of place. When I think of Carter I can see the deep hemlock forests he might have seen. When I look at Cleveland now, where I still live (only a few blocks from the land where Carter's daughter lived), I sometimes wonder what he would think of this city he so desperately wanted to build. Genealogy is like literature . . . it is a way to reflect upon your own life, why you live where you do, why you are who you are."

Godwin recalls one great-grandmother who was extremely proud of being a Carter descendant. She was a very proper Victorian woman, with a conservative demeanor and attitude out of sync with the times. For example, when he told her he was going to college she advised him to be sure to get into the "right" fraternity. Little did she know that he had chosen Oberlin, where not only was there no "right" fraternity; there were no fraternities at all! For this woman, Lorenzo Carter was the totality of family history to the exclusion of others with stories just as interesting.

And that's why Godwin cautions us not to place undue emphasis on lineage. There was, and perhaps still is, a certain Yankee elitism and class bias that went along with this family pride. In Godwin's family there was some tension between his grandmother and her mother-in-law based on the fact that one was descended from the earliest immigrants to New England and the other from common nursery workers (albeit also very early immigrants to North America—from Canada and backwoods Vermont, as well as mid-19th century immigrants from England and Germany).

Godwin says, "Every ancestor has an interesting story to tell once you move away from personal boosterism or trying to 'prove something' with your genealogy and focus instead on the individual's connection to larger historical forces. By trying to contextualize your family's history it is possible to reveal its rich diversity, to come to a personal understanding of the mechanics of history itself, and how history is constructed of a complex interweaving of people, their environment, and events."

For example, Lorenzo and Rebecca Carter, according to this descendant, were very much like many others of their time—post–Revolutionary War settlers from Vermont who came to the Western Reserve as the agricultural economy of New England was in collapse. Piecing together the small bits of information about the Carters gives us some insight into the bigger picture. Fragments of stories about the Carters' relationships with Native Americans and African-Americans offer a view not only of the Carters, but also of their times.

Godwin has heard many stories attributed to the Carters, but he wants documentation and source material before he accepts them as true. "Many stories told about early settlers offer more insight into the minds of the people who recorded them (usually local history boosters from the late 19th or early 20th centuries) than they do about the people they purport to be about."

One of Godwin's favorite stories (possibly apocryphal) is about a slave catcher who followed the trail of a slave from Kentucky to Cleveland. The slave had had a very difficult journey across Ohio and was exhausted. He was caught near Cleveland and was about

Figure 9-2: Lorenzo Carter, first permanent resident of Cleveland. *Courtesy of The Western Reserve Historical Society*

to be returned to Kentucky. The slave catcher talked him into voluntarily returning to Kentucky, where his master reputedly had been "kind" (although not kind enough for the slave not to want to escape in the first place). Hearing of this, Carter and a few of his "frontier types" waylaid the slave catcher and brought the slave back to Cleveland (apparently now liberating the man against his will).

However, when the group got back to Cleveland, they would not let the man live on the east side of the river where they lived; instead, they transported him west of the Cuyahoga to live alone in a crude cabin in the woods.

Whether a completely true story or not, this is an example of the need not to judge our ancestors by our current standards but rather to try and see them in the context of their times. The fact that Carter was intolerant of slavery and yet not willing to live with people of African descent does not indicate he was a bad person; he was actually progressive for his time. Anecdotes like this one help make the complexity of history tangible.

Genealogy is filled with such complexities, and that is why we need a good understanding of the historical context in which our families lived. By getting right in the middle of some of these muddy issues we see how ideas and events actually evolved and become aware of their relationship to larger movements such as abolition, women's rights, or peace.

As Godwin drives around the Western Reserve, his family's long connection to the area and the land is a major part of his spirituality. "It adds richness to my sense of place, my connection to the land, but it also contributes to an occasional feeling of melancholy as I watch things change—not always for the better; here was a beautiful farm or a wonderful old house completely erased from the land, there was a woods where my family had seen gentians growing, now gone with no sign that they were ever there.

So the researcher might want to look for that same surname for a slaveowner in the county in which the African-American family is found in 1870.

This chapter has explained not only why we look for census records, but how to find them—and some of the obstacles you may have to overcome in order to access and understand the records. This explains why census work is not advised until you have obtained other documents and information and have become familiar with genealogical terminology and researching methods.

The "New" D.A.R.

The Daughters of the American Revolution have had a reputation for snobbism or exclusivity. An article in *Town and Country* (October 1981, pages 208–278,"The D.A.R.'s Fresh Young Look") goes into some detail about a group that once was thought of as frumpy white-gloved WASPs that is now having its own "quiet revolution." Women's liberation, along with an emphasis on younger, more diverse membership, has changed both the attitude and "look" of the D.A.R. There are, of course, other lineage societies, such as the Society of Colonial Dames of America, the Mayflower Society, St. Nicholas Society of the City of New York (male descendants of people living in New York City or New York State before 1785), Society of California Pioneers (male descendants of California residents prior to 1850), and those of local interest such as the Early Settlers Association and First Families of Ohio. Most of these have strict requirements for potential members, including that they "prove" their lineage beyond a shadow of a doubt and that the local chapter accept them.

Certainly membership entails a sense of kinship and of service to the nation as well. The D.A.R has a strong history of rescuing and restoring numerous historic buildings and sites and providing aid to schools for Native Americans and poor Appalachians. More recently they have become involved in charitable work for animal protection, local conservation efforts, and anti-pollution concerns.

Being part of a group that boasts members (past or present) such as Rosalynn Carter, Mamie Eisenhower, Bess Truman, Ginger Rogers, Virginia Mayo, Grandma Moses, Clara Barton, Mary Baker Eddy, Susan B. Anthony, and Harriet Nelson may in the past have led members to feel they had reason to hold their heads, and perhaps their noses, just a little higher.

But the "new" D.A.R, and other lineage societies try to emphasize unity and sisterhood/brotherhood along with a commitment to patriotic duty and paying homage to family history. So, as with other things, we ought to view these groups in their historical context and then be sure to update that with current information.

10 Vital Records

Vital records are fundamental to family history research. Many of these records consist of information provided at the time of the event; called "primary" data, it often was supplied by the individual himself and therefore is considered especially reliable (though this is not always the case). Although some of what is included in this chapter can be found elsewhere in this book, this chapter, organized by "event" and then jurisdiction, puts it easily at your fingertips all in one place.

The information gleaned from vital records can often send us several steps backward (for genealogists, backward in time is forward in research). Consider the birth certificate; not only do we get the child's name and date of birth, but also parents' names and ages, and mother's maiden name. Then there are those details such as number of previous births, or place of birth, that can send a budding genealogist's heart aflutter. Information found in vital records can lead to solving a family mystery, or making us aware of a new one—so if this wasn't Mom's first child, then who was and what happened to that child?

Births

State of Ohio

Not until 1907 did Ohio require the registration of births. While many counties may have kept their own records, state records have been kept only from 1908 on. Keep in mind that many births occurred at home and may not have been recorded.

Ohio Department of Health/Bureau of Vital Statistics (1908–present)
Revenue Room
246 N. High St.
P.O. Box 15098
Columbus, OH 43215-0098
Phone: 614-466-2531 (recording)

Website: http://www.odh.state.oh.us/vitstats/certified
E-mail: vitalstat@gw.odh.state.oh.us
Cost: Certified copies are now $15 each (fee increase in effect since 1 July 2003); uncertified copies no longer available either at the state, county, or city level. Your request should include a check to Treasurer, State of Ohio, and child's name, names of birth mother (maiden) and father, date and place of birth, and a SASE or first-class postage payment. If you do not know the year of birth, research is $3 per name for searches in 10-year spans. It is a good idea to check first at the city or county level as fees may be less and the wait time much less.

Cuyahoga County

**Cuyahoga County Archives
(1849–1908; probate court originals)**
2905 Franklin Blvd.
Cleveland, OH 44113
Phone: 216-443-7250

Website: www.cuyahoga.oh.us/cs/archives
There are several sets of birth records here.

Probate court records from 1867 to 1908 as well as City of Cleveland records from 1849 to 1908 are available; however, those from 1849 to 1872 are based on affidavits filed after the fact (in 1873 a city ordinance was passed requiring documentation of birth). For genealogical purposes, records made after the event instead of at the time of the event are considered secondary sources and have a greater chance of being less accurate.

Cleveland

Cuyahoga County Courthouse (1868–1908)
1 Lakeside Ave., Room 31
Cleveland, OH 44113
Phone: 216-443-8935

Probate court (Room 31) had the original docket books, which were handwritten. These have been sent to the County Archives. However, in the 1930s the WPA indexed these books and probate court has the card file index. Information is usually just the child's name, date and place of birth, and the parents' names. Over the years it was noted in ink when the record was made. These records may be difficult to decipher.

Cleveland City Hall (1909–present)
601 Lakeside Ave.
Vital Statistics, Room 122
Cleveland, OH 44114

Phone: 216-664-3400; 216-664-2317 (message explains how to order records using credit card; mailing surcharges may apply)

Mail requests containing name of child, parents' names, mother's maiden name, and hospital of birth, if known. As of 1 July 2003, only certified copies are available, and the charge is $17. If you are not sure of the date of birth you may call 216-420-8865 to schedule a time when you can search for the birth certificate (8–10 a.m., Mon–Fri) at City Hall; only one individual can search at a time, and there is a waiting list for these appointments.

Suburban records:
These Cleveland suburbs maintain separate birth records, for which one must contact the respective city hall: Bedford, Berea, Cleveland Heights, East Cleveland, Euclid, Garfield Heights, Lakewood, Maple Heights, Parma, Rocky River, Shaker Heights, South Euclid, and University Heights.

Area hospitals

Birth records from the following hospitals, located in suburban areas, are also at Cleveland City Hall: Euclid-Glenville Hospital (pre-1952); Huron Road Hospital (pre-1936); and Southwest Community Hospital (September 1975–present).

Deaths

State of Ohio

Ohio Historical Society (20 Dec 1908–31 Dec 1944)
Archives/Library (death certificates)
1982 Velma Ave.
Columbus, OH 43211-2497

Phone: 614-297-2300
Websites: www.ohiohistory.org or http://dbs.ohiohistory.org/dindex
Costs: If you can find the certificate number on either of the above websites, the cost for copies of the certificate is $1 for the first four pages (include SASE), $.25 per page thereafter, plus additional postage. If you need library staff to get the certificate number, the research fee is $20 per name, for which they will search two of eight time periods between 1908 and 1944 (i.e., 1908 to 1912). Prepay with check or money order to Ohio Historical Society.

The websites above both lead to the index for deaths from 20 December 1908 to 31 December 1944. You can perform the search yourself, acquire the details of the record (certificate number and volume number), and avoid the research fees listed above.

You can also print out the request form from the website, fill in the blanks, include the copying fee, and mail it to the preceding address or mail the request to another repository mentioned below.

Not as many people know about and use the following two repositories that have the same information, so they get fewer requests and therefore, in my opinion, response time is faster. Of course you can visit any of these facilities in person—call or check websites for hours of operation.

Youngstown Historical Center of Industry and Labor (20 Dec 1908–31 Dec 1944)
151 W. Wood St.
P.O. Box 533
Youngstown, OH 44501-0533

Phone: 330-743-5934
Fax: 330-743-2999
Fees exactly the same as for Ohio Historical Society, above.

Akron-Summit County Public Library (1908–1932 and 1938–1944)
1040 E. Tallmadge Rd. (temporary location during renovation of Main Library)
Akron, OH 44310
Phone: 330-643-3000

Akron-Summit County Public Library, Main Branch
55 S. Main St.
Akron, OH 44326-0001
Phone: 330-643-9041
Website: www.ascpl.lib.oh.us

Accidental Death

Ancestor died in an accident?

Look in the county coroner's records for the place where the accident occurred.

For Cuyahoga County you can look at the Western Reserve Historical Society library and the Fairview Park Library for "Index to Cuyahoga County, Ohio Coroner Files, 1883–1900" compiled by the Cuyahoga West Chapter of the Ohio Genealogical Society in 1983. Included in this index will be: case number, name, age, and date and cause of death. Then go to the Cuyahoga County Archives to get the record itself.

❗ Tip: Finding Death Notices
Once you find the death certificate, try to find an obituary or death notice in the local paper.

Consider ethnicity (foreign-language papers), location of home or business (suburban papers), and religion (e.g., the Jewish Independent) when deciding exactly which papers to search.

Don't Know Much About Dates

Don't know the date or exact place of death, but pretty sure it was in Cuyahoga County after 1849? See Chapter 4 on the Cleveland Public Library for how to search online for death notices and obituaries. Remember: if the individual died out of state, she may be buried in Ohio, but the death record will be on file in the state where she died.

◆

Caveat: Early Scanners Not As Precise

The online death index at the Ohio Historical Society was scanned before the era of "good" scanners, hence there were some misreadings. For example, Drew had his relative's name and date of death from a newspaper obituary. He wanted the death certificate in order to obtain the names of the deceased's parents. In a search of the OHS death index online, no such person was found.

◆

**Ohio Department of Health/
Bureau of Vital Statistics (1945–present)**
Revenue room
246 N. High St., 1st Floor
P.O. Box 15098
Columbus, OH 43215-0088
Phone: 614-466-2531
Website: www.odh.state.oh.us/vitstats/certified
Cost: $15 for each certified copy—uncertified copies are no longer issued.
Send name of decedent, date and county of death, and check made out to "Treasurer, State of Ohio." If you do not know the exact year or date of death, there is a research fee of $3 for every 10-year time span researched.

Cuyahoga County

Cuyahoga County Archives (1840–1908)
2905 Franklin Blvd.
Cleveland, OH 44113
....
Phone: 216-443-7250
See Chapter 5 for researching records at the county archives.

Cleveland City Hall (1840–1880 [incomplete]; 1909–present)
Vital Statistics, Room 122
601 Lakeside Ave.
Cleveland, OH 44114
....
Phone: 216-664-3400
216-664-2317 for credit card orders
Mail-in requests for certified copies (at cost of $17 each) are honored if you provide the person's name and date of death. You can also go in person, or use the phone number indicated above for requests using a credit card (mailing surcharge may apply).
For deaths that occurred in Bedford, Garfield Heights, Lakewood, Maple Heights, Parma, Rocky River, South Euclid, University Heights, or East Cleveland after 1935, or Euclid after 1952, the records are not at Cleveland City Hall but rather at the city hall for the respective suburb.

Probate Court (1868–1908)
1 Lakeside Ave., Room 31
Cleveland, OH 44114
....
Phone: 216-443-8935
Cost: Copies are generally $.10 per page; certified copies are $1 per page—cash only. Checks accepted only from attorneys.

Divorce

State of Ohio

Ohio Department of Health/Bureau of Vital Statistics (September 1949–present)
Revenue Room
Ohio Department of Health
P.O. Box 15098
Columbus, OH 43215-0098
....
Phone: 614-466-2531
Divorce records are issued by the city or county in which the divorce occurred. If you

do not know the date of the divorce or the county in Ohio but do know it was after 7 September 1949, this office will do the research ($3 fee per 10-year period). This will provide you with the date and county of the divorce; for a copy of the divorce papers, you must contact the county where it occurred.

Cuyahoga County

Common Pleas Court, Clerk's Office
(Records and case number 1912–present; records only 1875–1911, get case number from County Archives)
1 Lakeside Ave.
Clerk's office, Room 37
Cleveland, OH 44113
....
Phone: 216-443-7939

By phone, provide the names of the divorced couple, and staff will get the case number and filing date. Then write and request a copy of the divorce papers (there is a fee), or go in person to the preceding address, provide the case number, and get an uncertified copy of the records for $.25 per page; certified copies are $1, cash only.

Cuyahoga County Archives
(Common Pleas Court: 1876–1882; Supreme Court 1811–1858; Common Pleas "appearance dockets" 1876–1922)
2905 Franklin Blvd.
Cleveland, OH 44113
....
Phone: 216-443-7250

You must get the case number for records from 1875 to 1911 from this facility before you can access the records for divorce files kept at the Common Pleas Court on Lakeside Avenue. Other divorce records are kept at the County Archives, depending on the date of the divorce and which court had jurisdiction at the time. You can request records by mail, e-mail (archive@www.cuyahoga.oh.us), by phone, or in person. Be sure to provide your home address; minimum fee is $1 for 1–4 copies and $.25 each thereafter.

Marriage

State of Ohio

**Ohio Department of Health/
Bureau of Vital Statistics**
(Records from 7 September 1949—present)
P.O. Box 15098
Columbus, OH 43215-0098
....
Phone: 614-466-2531

Marriage records are issued by the city or county in which the marriage occurred. If you do not know the date of the marriage or the county in Ohio but do know it was after

7 September 1949, this office will do the research ($3 fee per 10-year period). This will provide you with the date and county of the marriage; for a copy of the marriage record, you must contact the county where it occurred.

Cuyahoga County

Cuyahoga County Archives (1810–1941; 1810–1973 indexed)
2905 Franklin Blvd.
Cleveland, OH 44113
....
Phone: 216-443-7250

Probate Court (1811–present)
Cuyahoga County Courthouse
1 Lakeside Ave., Room 31
Cleveland, OH 44113
....
Phone: 216-443-8935

Western Reserve Historical Society (1810–1960)
10825 East Blvd.
Cleveland, OH 44106
....
Phone: 216-721-5722

Fairview Park Library (1810–1989)
21266 Lorain Ave.
Cleveland, OH 44126
....
Phone: 440-333-4700

Sometimes jurisdictions for records overlapped, as in this case. So both probate court and another court may have been responsible for (and kept) some marriage records within a given time frame, giving you two different places to look for these records in some instances.

Vital Records for Other Counties in Northeast Ohio

Now that you've seen how Cuyahoga County agencies handle vital records and land documents, let's see what other counties in Northeast Ohio have to offer.

Listed for every source are the years covered by the records they hold. I am including websites because they are good to check for last-minute changes and updates. However, be aware that websites and their URLs (addresses) change often.

I also provide the year each county was established; it's important to know this in order to understand not only why records are not available for an earlier time but also to get a historical perspective on your ancestors and what was happening in their lives. The first county established in Ohio was Washington County, in 1788.

Ashland County (est. 1846)
www.ashlandcounty.org

Birth and death (1808–1908)
Ashland County Courthouse
142 W. Second St.
Ashland, OH 44805
....
Phone: 419-289-0000
Copies: Certified $1; uncertified $.10
Hours: Mon–Fri 8 a.m.–4 p.m.

Birth and death (1909–present)
Ashland County Office
Vital Statistics, Third Floor
110 Cottage St.
Ashland, OH 44805
....
Phone: 419-282-4231
Copies: $15, certified only
Hours: Mon–Fri, 8 a.m.–4 p.m.

Marriage (1846–present)
Ashland County Courthouse, Probate Court
142 W. Second St.—Main floor
Ashland, OH 44805
....
Phone: 419-289-0000
Copies: Certified $2; uncertified $.25
Hours: Mon–Fri 8 a.m.–4 p.m.

Divorce (1846–present)
Ashland County Courthouse
142 W. Second St.
Ashland, OH 44805
....
Phone: 419-289-0000
Copies: Certified $2; uncertified $.25
Hours: Mon–Fri 8 a.m.–4 p.m.

Deeds (1847–present)
Ashland County Office
Recorder's Office
110 Cottage St.
Ashland, OH 44805
....
Phone: 419-282-4238
Copies: $2
Hours: Mon–Fri 8 a.m.–4 p.m.

Ashtabula County (est. 1808)
www.co.ashtabula.oh.us

Birth and death (1867–1908)
Ashtabula County Probate Court
25 W. Jefferson St.—First floor
Ashtabula, OH 44047
....
Phone: 440-576-3451
Copies: Certified $1; uncertified $.25
Hours: Mon–Fri 8–4:30

Homework

By checking either of these websites— http://198.30.212.15/ or www.cuyahoga.oh.us/probate/Probatehome.htm—you can obtain the volume number and page where a marriage license is recorded. Records are from 1810 to 1998.

Volume numbers 1–200 (approximate marriage date of 1940) are at the Cuyahoga County Archives as well as at probate court. Records in volumes 201 and upward are available at probate court (443-8923), in room 146. The exact marriage document available depends upon the time frame. The earlier records merely confirmed that the marriage took place; later records consist of an affidavit and a return confirmation that the marriage occurred; by the 1890s records contain the full application and the return. Uncertified copies are $.10 each.

The separate series from 1829 to 1875 also shows the actual marriage application but does not have much genealogical data other than the name of the parents of the bride and groom. However, if one party was under age, you might see listed the name of the person giving permission for the marriage, which may verify the existence of and/or relationship to another family member.

◆

❗
Double Marriage Records
There may be two marriage records—one civil and one religious. You will want to check both. Also check newspapers for marriage announcements—but consider this a secondary source.

Faith in the Process

From the time she was a young child, Betsie knew she was adopted. In 1985, while a student at Cleveland State University, Betsie read the book The Adoption Triangle (see bibliography) by Sorosky, Pannor, and Baron. She finished the book the night she started reading it. Years before, she had looked up the name of the agency that handled her adoption but did not call them. She thought they would misjudge her motives—that they might think her adoptive parents weren't doing the right things.

Yet the idea of finding her birth mother was always with her. Betsie wanted to connect with this person, to know something about her, to know whether Betsie looked like her, and know how her birth mother had felt about her, what the circumstances surrounding her birth were, and why she'd been placed for adoption.

As a nurse, Betsie also knew the importance of knowing her birth family's medical history.

Betsie finally called the local agency that handled the adoption. She was given "non-identifying" information and told that if her birth mother should call the agency, that information would be put in her file. Betsie soon learned that Ohio birth records for 1964 were open, so she wrote to the Division of Vital Statistics in Columbus for her birth certificate. There, on that piece of paper, was the name she had been given at birth. "My name had been Victoria Faith Boyer, a far cry from Betsie Lynn Norris! I had not known any of the names before this. I found the name inspiring and optimistic, which helped my determination to search."

Betsie's birth mother had listed her parents' address in Wallingford, Pennsylvania, as her permanent address. And she had listed the address of what had been the Florence Crittenton home on Euclid Avenue as her mailing address at the time of the birth. The woman listed on the birth certificate (Betsie's mother) had listed her mother's (Betsie's grandmother's) address.

Armed with a 25-year-old address, Betsie took a trip to the small Pennsylvania town. She looked through land records and found her birth mother's parents' names, but also found that they had moved from the area about 25 years earlier.

She wrote to the local high school to confirm the graduation of her birth mother. Later, Betsie went into the high school, looked through her mother's yearbook, made a copy of her picture, and also photocopied the class list. Later, from Cleveland, Betsie looked up and got names of classmates still living in the town. After making several phone calls, Betsie spoke with someone who had been involved in a recent class reunion, saying only that she was "a family member planning a reunion and that the person I was looking for was a lost relative" (not untrue!). Betsie got the married name and address of her birth mother—then living in another state. The class reunion information sheet she obtained also gave her birth mother's place of employment.

Knowing that her birth mother was currently married and had three teenagers at home, Betsie decided it would be best to call at work—rather than possibly cause a disruption at the house. It took Betsie one entire day to make that phone call. She had been preparing for this in her mind for years. She tried to prepare for disappointment and anger. Still, she felt sure "that the fantasy is always worse than the reality." After writing out a script of what she wanted to say, Betsie picked up the phone and called. Her birth mother responded, "I've been praying for this call for 26 years." Three weeks later Betsie met her birth mother.

Betsie is currently the executive director of the Adoption Network of Cleveland (291 E.222nd St., Euclid, OH 44123, 216-261-1511). She and agency staff and volunteers are available to help others within the adoption triangle search for their family members.

Figure 10-1: Birth certificate of Victoria Boyer. *Courtesy of Betsie Norris*

Birth and death (20 December 1908–present, excluding Ashtabula and Conneaut)
Ashtabula County Health Department
12 W. Jefferson St.
Jefferson, OH 44047
....
Phone: 440-576-6010
Hours: Mon–Fri 8 a.m.–4:30 p.m.
Copies: $15; certified only

Birth and death (20 December 1908–present, city of Ashtabula only)
Ashtabula City Health Department
4717 Main Ave.
Ashtabula, OH 44047
....
Phone: 440-992-7123
Copies: $15; certified only
Hours: Mon–Fri 8 a.m.–4:30 p.m., closed 12:30–1:30 p.m.

Birth and death (20 December 1908–present, Conneaut only)
Conneaut Board of Health
327 Mill St.
Conneaut, OH 44030
....
Phone: 440-593-3087
Copies: $15
Hours: Mon–Fri 8:30 a.m.–noon and 1–4:30 p.m.

Marriage (1812–present)
Ashtabula County Probate Court
25 W. Jefferson St.
Ashtabula, OH 44047
....
Phone: 440-576-3451
Copies: Certified $5; uncertified $1
Hours: Mon–Fri 8–4:30

Divorce (1811–present)
Ashtabula Common Pleas Court—Clerk's office
25 W. Jefferson St.—second floor
Ashtabula, OH 44047
....
Phone: 440-576-3637
Copies: Certified $1; uncertified $.25
Hours: Mon–Fri 8 a.m.–4:30 p.m.

Estate files (1811–present)
Ashtabula County Probate Court
25 W. Jefferson St., First floor
Ashtabula, OH 44047
....
Phone: 440-576-3451
Copies: Certified $5; uncertified $1
Hours: Mon–Fri 8 a.m.–4:30 p.m.

Deeds (1798—present)
Ashtabula Count Recorder's Office
25 W. Jefferson St.
Second Floor
Ashtabula, OH 44047
....
Phone: 440-576-3762
Copies: Certified $3; uncertified $2
Hours: Mon–Fri 8 a.m.–4:30 p.m.

Columbiana County (est. 1803)
www.ccclerk.org

Births and deaths (1908–present)
Columbiana County Health Department
321 South Beaver St.
Lisbon, OH 44432
....
Phone: 330-424-0272
Copies: certified only $16.
Hours: Mon–Fri 8 a.m.–3:30 p.m. (sometimes closes for lunch)

Birth and death (1908–present) if occurred in East Liverpool
City of East Liverpool Health Department
126 West Sixth St.
East Liverpool, OH 43920
....
Phone: 330-385-7900
Copies: $16 certified only
Hours: Mon–Fri 8 a.m.–3:30 p.m. (sometimes closes for lunch)

Birth and death (1908–present) if even occurred in Salem
785 East State St.
Salem, OH 44460
....
Phone: 330-332-1618
Copies: $16
Hours: Mon–Fri 8 a.m.–4 p.m.; closed noon–1 p.m.

Birth (1903–present) and death (1908–present)
City of East Palestine Health Department
82 Garfield Avenue
East Palestine, OH 44413
....
Phone: 330-426-4367 ext. 24
Copies: $15
Hours: Mon–Fri 8 a.m.–4 p.m.
(If writing to request records, mail to: P.O. Box 231, East Palestine, OH 44412)

Birth and Death (1867–1908)
Columbiana County Courthouse
Probate Court
105 S. Market St.
Lisbon, OH 44432
....
Phone: 330-424-9516
Hours: Mon–Fri 8 a.m.–4 p.m.
Go to probate to search index and get a file number; then proceed to this address for the actual record:
Juvenile Justice Court
260 W. Lincoln Way
Lisbon, OH 44432
Phone: 330-424-4071 (ask for "Records")
Copies: .25 plus postage; money order or certified check
Hours: Mon–Fri 8 a.m.–4 p.m.

Marriage (1803—present)
Columbiana County Courthouse
Probate Court
105 South Market St.
Lisbon, OH 44432
....
Phone: 330-424-9516
Copies: $.25
Hours: Mon–Fri 8 a.m.–4 p.m.

> **❗ Informal adoptions**
>
> If the adoption took place prior to the time when legal adoption was practiced in a certain area, consider checking charitable organizations. They likely were involved in informal adoptions or "placements" and may have records.

Private Service

By calling 800-255-2414 or going to the website www.vitalcheck.com, you will be connected with VitalChek network—a private company that contracts to expedite your receipt of these records and for this service charges an additional fee. By calling the toll-free number, or visiting the website, you will get specific instructions. The current fee is $15 plus $9.95 shipping and handling.

Estates and wills (1803–present; records for 1853–present are here; for 1803–1852, get case number here then proceed to Juvenile Justice Court (address follows)
Columbiana County Courthouse
Probate Court
105 South Market St.
Lisbon, OH 44432

Phone: 330-424-9516
Copies: $ .25 if you look them up. $1.00 if staff does.
Hours: Mon–Fri 8 a.m.–4 p.m.

Juvenile Justice Court
260 W. Lincoln Way
Lisbon, OH 44432

Phone: 330-424-4071 (ask for "Records")
Copies: $ .25 plus postage; no personal checks
Hours: Mon–Fri 8 a.m.–4 p.m.

Coshocton County (est. 1810)
www.co.coshocton.oh.us

Birth and death (1867–1909)
Probate Court
426 Main St.
Coshocton, OH 43812

Phone: 740-622-1837
Copies: $ .25
Hours: Mon–Fri 8 a.m.–4 p.m.

Birth and Death (1908–present)
Coshocton Board of Health
724 South 7th St.
Coshocton, OH 43812

Phone: 740-622-1426
Copies: certified only $ 15.
Hours: Mon–Fri 8 a.m.–4 p.m.

Marriages (1811–present)
Probate Court
426 Main St.
Coshocton, OH 43812

Phone: 740-622-1837
Copies: certified $ 2.00 uncertified $.25
Hours: Mon–Fri 8 a.m.–4 p.m.

Divorce (1810–present)
Clerk of Courts
318 Main St.
Coshocton, OH 43812

Phone: 740-622-1456
Copies: certified 1.25 uncertified $.25
Hours: Mon–Fri 8 a.m.–4 p.m.

Estates and wills (1811–present)
Probate Court
426 Main St.
Coshocton, OH 43812

Phone: 740-622-1837
Copies: certified $2.00; uncertified $.25
Hours: Mon–Fri 8 a.m.–4 p.m.

Deeds (1800–present)
County Recorder's Office
394 Main St.
P. O. Box 817

Coshocton, OH 43812
Phone: 740-622-2817
Copies: certified $3.00; uncertified $ 1.00

Geauga County (est. 1806)
www.co.geauga.oh.us/communities
Birth and death (1867–1908); transcriptions on Web:
www.rootsweb.com/~ohgeauga/geauga.html

Birth and death
(microfilm of originals 1867–1908)
Geauga County Public Library—Chardon Branch
110 E. Park St.
Chardon, OH 44024

Phone: 440-285-7601
Copies: $.10
Hours: Mon–Thurs 9 a.m.–9 p.m.; Fri–Sat 9–5;
Labor Day–Memorial Day same as above except Fridays 9 a.m.–6 p.m., Sundays 1–5 p.m.

Birth and death (1867–1908, original records)
Geauga County Main Courthouse—Probate Court
100 Short Court—3rd floor
Chardon, OH 44024

Phone: 440-285-2222
Copies: Certified only, $10
Hours: 8 a.m.–4:30 p.m.

Birth and death (1909–present)
Geauga County Health Department
Bureau of Vital Statistics
470 Center St.—Bldg. 8
Chardon, OH 44024

Phone: 440-285-2222 x 6407
Copies: Certified $15; printout for genealogy $.10
Hours: 8 a.m.–4:30 p.m.

Marriage (1806–1919)
Geauga County Public Library—Chardon Branch
110 E. Park St.
Chardon, OH 44024

Phone: 440-285-7601
Copies: $.10
Hours: Mon–Thurs 9 a.m.–9 p.m.; Fri–Sat 9–5
Labor Day–Memorial Day same as above except Fri 9 a.m.–6 p.m. Sun 1–5 p.m.

Marriage (1920–present)
Geauga County Courthouse, Probate Court
100 Short Court St. Suite 3A
Chardon, OH 44024

Phone: 440-285-2222, ext 2000
Copies: Certified $1; uncertified $.25
Hours: 8 a.m.–4:30 p.m.

**Divorce (Feb 1990–present, available online;
case number only for divorces prior to Feb 1990)**
Geauga County Main Courthouse
Domestic Relations
100 Short Court
Second floor—Room 2B
Chardon, OH 44024
....
Phone: 440-285-2222
Copies: Certified $1; uncertified $.25
Hours: 8 a.m.–4:30 p.m.
Then order file from archives (it will arrive next day) or go
to archives at:
470 Center Place Bldg. 8—lower level
Chardon OH 44024
....
Phone: 440-285-2222 , ext. 6277
Copies: $.25
Hours: Mon–Fri 9 a.m.–12 p.m.

Estates and wills (1806–1917, indexed)
Geauga County Archives
470 Center Place Bldg. 8—lower level
Chardon, OH 44024
....
Phone: 440-285-2222, ext 6277
Copies: $.25 uncertified only
Hours: 9 a.m.–12 p.m.

Estates and wills (1917–present)
Geauga County Courthouse—Probate Court
100 Short Court St. Suite 3A
Chardon, OH 44024
....
Phone: 440-285-2222
Copies: Certified $1; uncertified $.25
Hours: Mon–Fri 8 a.m.–4:30 p.m.

Deeds (1806–present)
Geauga County Archives
470 Center Place Bldg. 8
Lower level
Chardon, OH 44024
....
Phone: 440-285-2222, ext 6277
Copies: $.25
Hours: 9 a.m.–noon

Deeds (1806–present)
County Recorder's Office
Courthouse Annex Building
231 Main St.
Chardon, OH 44024
....
Phone: 440-285-2222, ext 3680
Copies: $2
Hours: 8 a.m.–4:30 p.m.
Email: recorder@co.geauga.oh.us

Lake County (est. 1840)
www.lakecountyohio.org

Birth and death (1867–1908)
(Card file is in "the caves," in the archives—must be re-
trieved for you)
Lake County Courthouse, West Annex
25 N. Park Place
Painesville, OH 44077
....
Phone: 440-350-2830

Parking: Park in front; enter at rear of building
Copies: Certified $1; uncertified $.25
Hours: Mon–Fri 8 a.m.–4:30 p.m.

Birth and death (1920–present)
Lake County Health Department
33 Mill St.
Painesville, OH 44077
....
Phone: 440-350-2543
Copies: Certified only, $15
Hours: Mon–Fri 8 a.m.–4:30 p.m.

Marriage (1840–present)
Lake County Courthouse, West Annex
25 N. Park Place
Painesville, OH 44077
....
Phone: 440-350-2830
Parking: Park in front; enter at rear of building
Copies: Certified short form $2; long form $3; uncertified
$.25
Hours: Mon–Fri 7:30 a.m.–5 p.m.

Divorce (1840–present)
Lake County Courthouse, West Annex
25 N. Park Place
Painesville, OH 44077
....
Parking: Park in front; enter at rear of building—office is
on lower level
Phone: 440-350-2657
Copies: Certified $1; uncertified $.25
Hours: Mon–Fri 8 a.m.–4:30 p.m.

Estates and wills (1840–present)
Lake County Courthouse, West Annex
25 N. Park Place
Painesville, OH 44077
....
Phone: 440-350-2830
Parking: park in front; enter at rear of building
(Go to marriage department—they handle estates and
wills also)
Copies: $.25
Hours: 7:30 a.m.–5 p.m.

Deeds (1840–present)
**Lake County Administration Building, Recorder's
Office**
105 Main St.
Painesville, OH 44077
....
Phone: 440-350-2510
Copies: $.25
Hours: Mon–Fri 8 a.m.–4 p.m.

Lorain County (est. 1822)
www.loraincounty.org/government

Birth and death (1867–1908)
Lorain County Probate Court
226 Middle Ave., 4th floor
Elyria, OH 44035
....
Phone: 440-329-5175
Copies: Certified $1; uncertified $.30
Hours: Mon–Fri, 8 a.m.–4 p.m.

Birth and death (1908—present, excluding cities of Lorain and Elyria)
Lorain County Health Department
9880 S. Murray Ridge Rd.
Elyria, OH 44035

Phone: 440-322-6367
Copies: Certified only $15
Hours: Mon–Fri 8 a.m.–4:15 p.m.

Birth and death (1908–present)
Elyria Health Department
Vital statistics
202 Chestnut St.
Elyria, OH 44035

Phone: 440-323-7595
Copies: Certified $16
Hours: Mon–Fri 8 a.m.–4:30 p.m. closed 12–1

Birth and death (births: mostly1908–present, some back to 1878; deaths: 20 December 1908–present)
Lorain City Health Department
Vital Statistics
1144 West Erie Ave
Lorain, OH 44052

Phone: 440-204-2300
Copies: Certified only $16
Hours: Mon–Fri 8:30 a.m.–4:30 p.m.

Marriage (1824–present)
Lorain County Probate Court
308 Second St., Fourth Floor
Elyria, OH 44035

Phone: 440-329-5175
Website: www.loraincounty.com/probate. Records online for last names A–V from 1824–present
Copies: Certified $1; uncertified $.30
Hours: Mon–Fri, 8 a.m.–4 p.m.

Divorce (1824–1960)
Common Pleas Court—Domestic Relations
Lorain County Courthouse
308 Second St., Fifth floor
Elyria, OH 44035

Phone: 440-329-5386
Copies: Certified $1; uncertified $.10
Hours: Mon–Fri 8 a.m.–4 p.m.
(Divorces from 1960 on were handled by family court; records may be located elsewhere, but your search begins in this office.)

Estates and wills (1824–present)
Lorain County Courthouse
Probate Court, Fourth floor
308 Second St.
Elyria, OH 44035

Phone: 440-329-5295
Copies: Certified $ 1; uncertified $ .30
Hours: Mon–Fri 8 a.m.–4 p.m.

Deeds (1803–present)
Lorain County Courthouse, first floor
226 Middle Ave.
Elyria, OH 44035

Phone: 440-329-5140
Copies: Certified $2; uncertified $.50
Hours: Mon–Fri 8 a.m.–4:30 p.m.

Mahoning County (est. 1846)
www.mahoningcountygov.com

Birth and death (1846/47–1908)
Mahoning County Court House
120 Market St.—basement
Youngstown, OH 44503

Phone: 330-740-2310
Copies: Certified $1; uncertified $.05
Hours: Mon–Fri 8 a.m.–4:30 p.m.

Countywide births, 1908–present; deaths 1892–present
Youngstown Health Department
Vital Statistics
345 Oakhill Ave.
Youngstown, OH 44502

Phone: 330-743-3333
Copies: Certified $10; uncertified $.25
Hours: Mon–Fri 8 a.m.–4 p.m.

Marriage (1846–present)
Mahoning County Court House
120 Market St.—basement
Youngstown, OH 44503

Phone: 330-740-2310
Copies: Certified $1; uncertified $.05
Hours: Mon–Fri 8 a.m.–4:30 p.m.

Divorce (1840–present)
Mahoning County Court House
120 Market St.
Clerk of Courts, 2nd floor
Youngstown, OH 44503

Phone: 330-740-2100
Copies: Certified $1.10; uncertified $.10
Hours: Mon–Fri 8 a.m.–4:30 p.m.

Estates and wills (1846–present)
Mahoning County Court House
120 Market St.
Probate Court, first floor
Youngstown, OH 44503

Phone: 330-740-2310
Copies: Certified $1; uncertified $.05
Hours: Mom–Fri 8 a.m.–4:30 p.m.

Deeds (1848–present)
Mahoning County Court House
120 Market St.
Recorder's Office, basement
Youngstown, OH 44503

Phone: 330-740-2345
Copies: $ 1 by staff; $.25 self-serve
Hours: Mon–Fri 8 a.m.–4:30 p.m.

Medina County (est. 1812)

www.co.medina.oh.us

Birth and death (1867–1907)
Medina County Courthouse

Probate Court—First floor
93 Public Square
Medina, OH 44256

Phone: 330-725-9703; Brunswick/Hinckley: 330-225-7100, ext 9703; Wadsworth: 330-336-6657, ext 9703
Copies: Certified $3; uncertified $.25
Hours: Mon–Fri 8 a.m.–4:30 p.m.

Birth and death (1908–present)
Medina County Health Department

4800 Ledgewood Drive
P.O. Box 1033
Medina, OH 44258

Phone: 330-723-9511
Copies: $15
Hours: Mon–Fri 8 a.m.–4:30 p.m.

Marriage (1818–present)
Medina County Courthouse

Probate Court—First floor
93 Public Square
Medina, OH 44256

Phone: 330-725-9703; Brunswick/Hinckley: 330-225-7100, ext 9703; Wadsworth: 330-336-6657, ext 9703
Copies: $3 certified; $.25 uncertified
Hours: Mon–Fri, 8 a.m.–4:30 p.m.

Divorce (1818–present)
Medina County Courthouse

Clerk's Office
93 Public Square
Medina, OH 44256

Phone: 330-725-9722; Brunswick/Hinckley: 330-225-7100, ext 9722; Wadsworth: 330-336-6657, ext 9722
Copies: Certified $1.25; uncertified: $.25
Hours: Mon–Fri 8 a.m.–4:30 p.m.

Estates and wills (1833–present)
Medina County Courthouse

Probate Court—First floor
93 Public Square
Medina, OH 44256

Phone: 330-725-9703; Brunswick/Hinckley: 330-225-7100, ext 9703; Wadsworth: 330-336-6657, ext 9703
Copies: Certified $1.25; uncertified $.25
Hours: Mon–Fri 8 a.m.–4:30 p.m.

Deeds (1818–present)
Recorder's Office
Medina County Administration Building

144 N. Broadway—3rd floor
Medina, OH 44256

Phone: 330-725-9782
Copies: $28 for first two pages; other charges apply after that
Hours: 8 a.m.–4:30 p.m.

Portage County (est. 1808)

www.portageworkforce.org/portagecounty

If you cannot come in person for any probate records, write to: P.O. Box 936, Ravenna, OH 44266-0936. Include a SASE, and a clerk will send a form, which you can mail back, and then your request will be processed.

Birth and death (1867–1907)
Portage County Courthouse

Probate Court—2nd Floor
203 W. Main St.
Phone: 330-298-3247 (records office)
Ravenna, OH 44266

Copies: Certified $ 1.25; uncertified $.25
Hours: Mon–Fri 8 a.m.–4 p.m.

Birth and death (1908–present, Ravenna only)
Ravenna Health Department

220 W. Spruce Ave.
Ravenna, OH 44266

Phone: 330-296-4478
Copies: Certified $15
Hours: Mon–Fri 7:30 a.m.–3:30 p.m.

Birth and death (1909–present, excluding Ravenna)
Kent Health Department

325 S. Depeyster
Kent, OH 44240

Phone: 330-678 8109
Copies: Certified $15
Hours: Mon–Fri 8 a.m.–4:30 p.m.

Marriage (1819–present)
Portage County Courthouse

Probate Court—Room 204
203 W. Main St.
Ravenna, OH 44266

Phone: 330-298-3247 (records office)
Copies: Certified $1.25; uncertified $.25
Hours: Mon–Fri 8 a.m.–4 p.m.

Divorce (1885–present)
Portage County Courthouse

Domestic Relations clerk—Room 201A
203 W. Main St.
Ravenna, OH 44266

Phone: 330-297-3475 (records office)
Copies: Certified $1; uncertified $.10
Hours: Mon–Fri 8 a.m.–4 p.m.

Estates and wills (1817–present)
Portage County Courthouse

Domestic Relations—Room 201A
203 W. Main St.
Ravenna, OH 44266

Phone: 330-298-3247 (records office)
Copies: Certified $1.25; uncertified $.25
Hours: Mon–Fri 8 a.m.–4 p.m.

Deeds (1790–present)
Recorder's Office
241 S. Chestnut St.—2nd Floor
Ravenna, OH 44266
Phone: 330-297-3553
Copies: Certified $3; uncertified $2
Hours: Mon–Fri 8 a.m.–4:15 p.m.

Stark County (est. 1808)
www.co.stark.oh.us

Birth and death (1867–1908)
Stark County District Library
715 Market St. N.
Canton, OH 44702
Phone: 330-452-0665
Copies: $.15 (self-serve); $1 (mail requests)
Hours: Mon–Thu 9 a.m.–8 p.m.; Fri, Sat 9 a.m.–5 p.m.

Birth and death (1908–present, Alliance only)
City of Alliance Health Department
207 E. College
Alliance, OH 44601
Phone: 330-821-7373
Cost: Certified $15
Hours: Mon–Fri 8:30 a.m.–noon; 1–4:30 p.m.

Birth and death (1908 to present, Canton only)
Canton Health Department
420 Market Ave. N.
Canton, OH 44702
Phone: 330-489-3231
Copies: $ 15
Hours: Mon–Fri 8 a.m.–4:30 p.m.

Birth and death (1908–present, Massillon only)
City of Massillon Health Department
Administrative Building
100 City Hall S E
Massillon, OH 44646
Phone: 330-830-1710
Copies: Certified only $15
Hours: Mon–Fri 8:30 a.m.–4:30 p.m.

Birth and death (1908–present, excluding Alliance, Canton, and Massillon)
Stark County Health Department
3951 Convenience Circle NW
Canton, OH 44718
Phone: 330-493-9904
Copies: $15
Hours: Mon–Fri 8:30 a.m.–4:30 p.m.

Marriage (1900–present; index from 1850, but no records until 1900)
County Office Bldg.—corner Market & Tuscarawas
110 Central Plaza N. 5th floor
(corner of Market & Tuscarawas)
Probate Court
Canton, OH 44718

Phone: 330-451-7762
Copies: Certified $2/page; uncertified, first five pages free, $.05/page after that
Hours: Mon–Fri 8:30 a.m.–4:15 p.m.

Marriage (1809–1900)
Stark County District Library
715 Market St. N.
Canton, OH 44702
Phone: 330-452-0665
Copies: $.15 (if you make them yourself; $1 for requests by mail)
Hours: Mon–Thu 9 a.m.–8 p.m.; Fri, Sat 9 a.m.–5 p.m.

Divorce (1968–1994)
Stark County Records Center
201 Third St. NE, Suite 5
Canton, OH 44702
Phone: 330-451-7372
Copies: Uncertified, free for first five pages; $.15/page after that
Hours: Mon–Fri 8:30 a.m.–4:30 p.m.

Divorce (1809–1968)
Stark County Office Building
110 Central Plaza N.
Sixth floor
Canton, OH 44702
Phone: 330-451-7365

Divorce (1994–present)
Stark County Clerk of Courts
Domestic Relations
110 Central Plaza S.
Canton, OH 44702
Clerk's Office, Suite 690
Phone: 330-451-7796
Copies: Certified $1; uncertified $.10
Hours: Mon–Fri 8:30 a.m.–4:30 p.m.

Estates and wills (1810–present)
Stark Count Probate Court
110 Central Plaza S., Room 501
Canton, OH 44702
Phone: 330-451-7753
Records Center: 330-451-7953
Copies: First 5 pages are free; succeeding pages are $.05/page
Hours: Mon–Fri 8:30–4:30 p.m.

Deeds (1809–present)
County Office Building
110 Court Plaza (corner of Market & Tuscarawas)
Suite 170
Canton, OH 44702
Phone: 330-451-7443
(Come to front office to let them know you are waiting.)
Copies: $2
Hours: 8:30 a.m.–4:30 p.m.

Summit County (est. 1840)

www.co.summit.oh.us

Birth and death (1869–1908)
Summit County Courthouse
209 S. High St.
First floor—Records room
Akron, OH 44308

Phone: 330-643-2352
Copies: Certified $3; uncertified $.05
Hours: Mon–Fri 8 a.m.–4 p.m.

Birth and death (1909–present, Akron only)
Akron Health Department
368 S. Main St.
Akron, OH 44308

Phone: 330-375-2976
Copies: Certified $10
Hours: Mon–Fri 8 a.m.–4:15 p.m.

Birth and death (1908–present, Barberton only)
City of Barberton Health Department
571 W. Tuscarawas St.
Barberton, OH 44203

Phone: 330-745-6067
Copies: Certified $11
Hours: Mon–Fri 8 a.m.–4:30 p.m.

Birth and death (1908–present, excluding Akron and Barberton)
Summit County Health Department
1100 Graham Circle
Cuyahoga Falls, OH 44223

Phone: 330-923-4891
Copies: Certified $16
Hours: Mon–Fri 8 a.m.–3:30 p.m.

Marriage (1840–present)
Summit County Courthouse
Probate Court
209 S. High St.
First floor—Records room
Akron, OH 44308

Phone: 330-643-2352
Copies: Certified. $2; uncertified $.05/page

Divorce (1840–present)
Summit County Safety Building
53 University Ave.
Clerk of Court's office—first floor
Akron, OH 44308

Phone: 330-643-2205
Copies: Certified $1; uncertified $.05/page
Hours: Mon–Fri 7:30 a.m.–4 p.m.

Estates and wills (1840–present)
Summit County Courthouse
Probate Court
209 S. High St.
First floor—records room
Akron, OH 44308

Phone: 330-643-2352
Copies: Uncertified $.05/page
Hours: Mon–Fri 8 a.m.–4 p.m.

Deeds (1795–present)
Summit County Auditor's Office
Ohio Building 4th floor
175 S. Main St.
Akron, OH 44308

Phone: 330-643-2713
Copies: Certified $3; uncertified $2
Hours: Mon–Fri 7:30 a.m.–4 p.m.

Trumbull County (est. 1800)

www.trumbullprobate.org

Birth and death (1867–1908)
Trumbull County Archives
118 High St. NW
Warren, OH 44481

Phone: 330-675-2374
Copies: Uncertified $.10
Hours: Mon–Fri 9 a.m.–3:30 p.m.

Birth and death (1908–present, excluding Northside Hospital, Youngstown, and Girard)
Trumbull County Health Department
418 Main St.
Warren, OH 44481

Phone: 330-841-2596
Copies: $15
Hours: Mon–Fri 8 a.m.–4 p.m.

Marriage (1800–present)
Trumbull County Archives
118 High St. NW
Warren, OH 44481

Phone: 330-675-2374
Copies: Uncertified $.10
Hours: Mon–Fri 9 a.m.–3:30 p.m.

Divorce (1854–present, some as early as 1803, but not complete until 1854)
Trumbull County Courthouse
Domestic Relations
150 High St.
Warren, OH 44481

Phone: 330-675- 2625
Copies: Certified $1; uncertified–$.10
Hours: Mon–Fri 8:30 a.m.–4:30 p.m.

Divorce (1953–present)
Trumbull County Courthouse
Family Court
220 S. Main St.
Warren, OH 44481

Phone: 330-675-2302

Divorce (1803–1854)
Trumbull County Archives
118 High St. NW
Warren, OH 44481
Phone: 330-675-2374
Copies: $.10
Hours: 9 a.m.–3:30 p.m.

Estates and wills (1803–1984)
Trumbull County Archives
118 High St. NW
Warren, OH 44481
Phone: 330-675-2374
Copies: $.10
Hours: 9 a.m.–3:30 p.m.

Estates and wills (1985–present)
Trumbull County Courthouse
Probate Court
150 High St. NW
Warren, OH 44481
Phone: 330-675-2521

Deeds (1795–1896)
Trumbull County Archives
118 High St. NW
Warren, OH 44481
Phone: 330-675-2374
Hours: Mon–Fri 9 a.m.–3:30 p.m.
Copies: $.10

Deeds (1896–present)
County Recorder's Office
160 High St. 44481
Warren, OH 44481
Phone: 330-675-2401
Copies: $2
Hours: Mon–Fri 8:30 a.m.–4:15 p.m.

Wayne County (est. 1808)
www.wooster-wayne.com/county

Birth and death (1867–1908)
Wayne County Courthouse
Probate Court
107 W. Liberty St.
Wooster, OH 44691
Phone: 330-287-5575
Copies: Uncertified $.25
Hours: Mon–Fri 8 a.m.–4:30 p.m.

Birth and death (1909–present)
Wayne County Health Department
203 S. Walnut St.
Wooster, OH 44691
Phone: 330-264-9590
Copies: $15.
Hours: Mon–Fri 8 a.m.–4:30 p.m.

Marriage (1813–present)
(Get volume and page number at:)
Wayne County Courthouse—Probate Court
107 W. Liberty St.
Wooster OH 44691
Phone: 330-287-5575

(Use volume and page number to view microfilm at:)
County Administration Building
Microfilm room (lower level)
428 W. Liberty St.
Wooster, OH 44691
Phone: 330-287-5418
Copies: No charge
Hours: Mon–Fri 8 a.m.–4:30 p.m.

Divorce (1820s–present)
Wayne County Courthouse, Clerk of Courts
107 W. Liberty St.
Wooster, OH 44691
Phone: 330-287-5596

For divorces before 1970, get case number at courthouse, then proceed to:
County Administration Building
428 W. Liberty St.
Wooster, OH 44691
Copies: $.05
Hours: Mon–Fri 8 a.m.–4 p.m.

Estates and wills (1820s–present)
(Get case number at:)
Wayne County Courthouse, Probate Court
107 W. Liberty St., Second floor
Wooster, OH 44691
Phone: 330-287-5575

(Then view microfilm at:)
County Administration Building
428 W. Liberty St.
Microfilm room
Wooster OH 44691
Copies: No charge
Hours: Mon–Fri 8 a.m.–4 p.m.

Deeds (1812–present)
Wayne County Recorder's Office
County Administration Building
428 W. Liberty St.
Wooster OH 44691
Phone: 330-287-5460
Copies: $2
Hours: Mon–Fri 8 a.m.–4:30 p.m.

11 The Courts

The "old" county courthouse is located on Lakeside Avenue. It is just down the street from city hall, and often the two are confused. This explains the many notices along the walls stating, "This is not city hall." Enough said. Street parking is not close enough to be convenient. Though costly, parking at the Huntington Garage allows easy access to the building (current cost is $1 for every 15 minutes with an $8 daily maximum). When entering from the underground parking facility (above-ground spaces are limited), use the elevator and press "1R"—the elevator doors will open in the rear, and the door to probate court is directly in front of you. You are on the ground floor/basement. Security measures in effect include a metal detector.

Cuyahoga County "Old" Courthouse
1 Lakeside Ave.
Cleveland, OH 44113
Phone: 216-443-8764 (probate court)
Hours: Mon–Fri 8:30 a.m.–4:30 p.m.

Getting Around the Courts

Many of us are unfamiliar with courts, and it can be confusing determining which courts have jurisdiction over what types of records. There are civil and criminal courts. Most family historians will be concerned with civil courts. And in Cuyahoga County, most of the historical records involve probate or are housed in the same building as probate court.

Probate court handles wills, estates, and matters of individuals adjudged incompetent, as well as marriage licenses and some birth and death records, as described below. Probate records can be most valuable, as they help pinpoint people to a specific place on an exact date. They also may contribute biographical details of a person or group of persons. In the case of common surnames, these records often help to differentiate between people with similar names.

Mail Requests

Departments within the court will respond to requests for copies via mail. Be sure to supply them with the most definitive information you have, and pay the required fee (listed here) in advance. In some instances, you might want to ask the size of the file before requesting "all records."

> **❗ All Requests are Filled, Sooner or Later**
>
> With the increased popularity of genealogy, the influx of these requests has mushroomed. Therefore it is possible that the record may have to be mailed to you a day or two after you request it. But all requests are filled.

Births and Deaths, 1868–July 1907 (Probate Court)

Cuyahoga County "Old" Courthouse
1 Lakeside Ave.
Room 31
Cleveland, OH 44113
Phone: 216-443-8764
Hours: Mon–Fri 8:30 a.m.–4:30 p.m.

This court maintains early birth records (prior to 1908 they are records, not certificates of birth) and death records held in county courts from about 1867. Although recording of births and deaths at this time was not required, it was strongly encouraged. Such information was sometimes reported to the census enumerator or justice of the peace. This might occur long after the event, perhaps when family members visited neighbors in the township in which this official was located. A few Ohio counties did keep some death and birth statistics in 1852/53, but this soon stopped and it is unclear where those records, if they still exist, are held.

The only birth and death records in this building are from 1868 to July 1907, and they are only for births in the city of Cleveland. These will have fewer details than later birth records.

Go to Room 31 and ask the staff. Be prepared for a record that may be very difficult to read. These are filed alphabetically by the child's name and will give parents' names, address, and date of birth. Copies are $.10 per page or $1 per page for certified copies.

Marriage Records, 1810–Present (Probate Court)

Cuyahoga County "Old" Courthouse
1 Lakeside Ave.
Room 146
Cleveland, OH 44113
Phone: 216-443-8921

You can go in person to Room 146 to get a marriage record. You will need the license number and volume number. To obtain them you can either:

1. Go to the website www.cuyahoga.oh.us/probate and put in the names of the bride and groom (or just one name), and you will be given the volume number and license number. Then proceed to Room 146 and request a copy of the record (supposedly the short record is no longer offered, just the longer, more detailed one, and copies are $.10 each).

2. Go to Room 146. One microfiche machine in this room permits individuals to look up the marriage record, thereby obtaining the volume and license number. Then request the record from staff. If the machine in this room is in use, you can also use the computer down the hall in Room 129 to get the same information. The early records, those listed in volumes 1 through 200 (which corresponds to about 1940), are also available at the Cuyahoga County Archives—and may be easier to read because they are the originals.

Divorce Records (Court of Common Pleas, Division of Domestic Relations)

Cuyahoga County "Old" Courthouse
1 Lakeside Ave.m Room 41
Cleveland, OH 44113
Phone: 216-443-8560 (clerk of courts)

A different court maintains these records, but don't let that confuse you. It is in the same building as probate court. The clerk of courts has divorce files from 1875 to the present, which can be accessed on the computer in Room 41. Records prior to 1975, going back to 1912, are on microfilm and are looked up manually at the Index Department (phone: 216-443-7966). Before you come in for research, call the Index Department to get the case number. Provide the names of the parties and the approximate date of the divorce, and the indexing operator will give you a case number. If you are unable to call beforehand for the case number, then you first have to go across the street to:

Cuyahoga County Justice Center
1200 Ontario St.
First Floor, Indexing
Cleveland, OH 44113
Phone: 216-443-7966

Return to Room 41 of the Old Courthouse with the case number, and staff will pull the records for you. Copies are $.25 per page. If the record has been microfilmed (records prior to 1995), you will go to Room 37 to look at it and to make copies.

Another group of records, from about 1912 to the early 1930s, are on "appearance dockets" (see Chapter 5).

Docket papers for current divorce or civil cases can be obtained at the Justice Center across the street at 1200 Ontario. Go to window 14 for a copy of the item.

Estates and Wills (Probate Court)

Cuyahoga County Courthouse
1 Lakeside Ave.
Room 131
Cleveland, OH 44113
Phone: 216-443-8792

Lost Heir?

Wondering if you or someone you know or love might be a "lost heir"? Check out the website:
http://7341.foundmoney.com

These records contain information on a person's heirs and next of kin. They also establish when someone was at a specific place. The researcher will find names of persons and their relationships to each other. Often a will contains an inventory of the household, which offers a look at possible occupation, hobbies, lifestyle, and station in life.

While these records usually have to do with legal arrangements made after someone has died, they can also be used in connection with illegitimate births, orphans, adoption, insanity, and apprenticeships.

Once it is determined that such a probate file exists, be sure to ask about the original file—the probate book may have copies of some but not all items from the original file. Also, if other names are mentioned in these records, look up those names in the index as well. Information may include the name of the executor of the will, or some heirs to the deceased's estate whom you never knew about before.

To obtain records of estates and wills, go to the clerk's office on the ground floor (Room 131, "Data Entry"). Here can be found:

• Index to estates and wills from 1868 to 1974 on microfiche
• Index to estate and wills from 1975 to the present on computer

The film provides a one-page description of the case, called a "statement of proceedings." This is a chronological accounting of the process of filing, probating, and recording the will. It may list the name and address of the appointed adminis-

Legal Lingo

Docket books, case files, journal books—people in this building speak a whole different language. So I asked for some clarification:

Journal book—a book of all the actual orders signed by a judge. Sometimes a person just wants a copy of a journal entry; for example to prove that they have been given custody of a minor.

Docket book—a running record of all the filings on a case.

Case file—all the original papers filed on a case. It includes the complaint and the outcome and is the most comprehensive record you can get.

Finding Courts

Here is yet another website that helps you track various courts in the U.S.: www.sconet.state.oh.us/web_Sites/Courts. Just choose "U.S.," then the state you want, and then the county.

---

trator, the appraisers, and the amount of the attorney fees. Handwritten across this will be another number. If you want the entire record (which is advisable), write down this number, go to the file room (the entrance is almost directly in front of you), and request the file.

This will be another reel of film that you need a different machine to view—this time one located by the window. Staff will show you how to load and operate the machine. Information contained in these records varies widely. The file may consist of a few or a number of pages and may include: names, addresses, relationship of heirs; address of decedent; address and phone number of applicant; name of attorney or notary public; and value of real or personal property. In the event an individual died intestate (without a will), there may be information regarding debts and value of real or personal property.

How to Locate

Use either the computer on the counter or the microfiche machine at the small wooden table to look up your ancestor. When viewing microfiche, be careful to view both columns of names for each section on the sheet. Write down the case number listed for the person you are researching. If there is more than one listing for your named individual, look in the drawer of the desk the machine rests on. There is a sheet that matches case numbers to year of death, which will help you determine which case number is appropriate for your individual.

Armed with the case number, proceed to the wide metal cabinet at the south end of the room (close to Room 125) and get the docket film filed according to case numbers. Use the reader machines located opposite the metal cabinet.

Copies

For copies of either of these records, note the file or case number and heading at the top of the page. Remove the film from the machine, take it to the Quality Assurance Department (you're standing almost in front of it), and request a copy. Copies are $.10 each and are paid for at the cashier's window next door in Room 135.

To Retrieve the Actual File

Packets from 1813 to 1918 are at the Cuyahoga County Archives (see Chapter 5).
Packets after 1918 are at probate court in Room 150.

Guardianship

Records prior to and including 1940 are also kept in Room 31. Those after 1940 are accessed by looking them up on the computer in Room 129. Once you get the file or case number, go to the file room to request the record.

Probate Court Inquests/Mental Illness Cases

For records of inquests and mental illness cases proceed to Room 107, where staff will assist you.

Civil Cases

Located in Room 37 are records of civil cases as well. Remembering the old adage "follow the money"—let's think like a private investigator. What else happened in our ancestors' lives that could bring them to court? Civil lawsuits, of course. Suing someone for not paying a bill, for doing shoddy work, or perhaps because they defaulted on a loan. Think Depression, think mortgages. Think Room 37.

Closed cases are located in the archives, also known as the file room. Of course it is in the basement—Room 37. This area is home to hundreds of reels of micro-

Decent Descent

About 45 years ago, attorney John Q. wrote a will for Mr. and Mrs. B. John knew the couple socially, and they had always insisted neither one had any living relatives. When Mrs. B died, the attorney encouraged Mr. B to make a new will. When the gentleman died of a stroke a few years later, no will was found. So John filed an application in probate court and stated that the deceased had no next of kin. An Akron lawyer who specializes in finding lost family saw this and discovered 28 relatives living in England who will share in a substantial inheritance.

The only reason these second and third cousins can inherit from this estate is that there was no will, or no will could be found. Making a legal determination of the rightful heirs was a long and tedious process, including much genealogical digging, lengthy correspondence, and the exchange of much legal documentation with England. It took more than two years to settle this estate. It seemed that each time the lawyers felt they had determined all the successors, more heirs were found, or one would die and leave heirs, and the matter would have to be continued.

After two years and about $20,000 in lawyers' fees (both in the United States and England), the estate was finally settled. Some individuals received one twenty-eighth, others two twenty-eighths of what was a rather substantial sum.

Unfortunately, as far as the Cleveland lawyer is concerned, instead of the estate going to people the deceased wanted it to go to (people who had been good to Mr B. all his life), it went to these previously "nonexistent" relatives.

While states have different laws, in Ohio under the law of "descent and distribution," first, second, and third cousins have rights of inheritance (if there is no will) over the state.

---

film from as early as 1865. You definitely want to visit this room and make friends with the staff. Believe me—they can be very helpful in deciphering these old records, especially on microfilm.

It helps if you have the case number for civil cases—available at the Indexing Department at the Justice Center across the street—but you don't have to.

Records of genealogical interest here include:

- Civil journal books, 1865–1965
- Civil case files, 1875–1993

There are also some judgment lien records and income tax books. Call the microfilm room (216-443-7939) for more information. Copies may be made from the microfilm readers. They cost $.25 per page, or $1 per page for certified copies.

If you are interested in current civil, criminal, or judgment lien cases, that information can be found in the Justice Center across the street at 1200 Ontario. The main phone number is 216-443-7950.

HALLE

Famous Families

"Basically it's what families love to hear," says Dennis Sherwin when asked why he cares about family history. "And," he continues, "even if you're not interested, your children are or will be." It seems Sherwin knows whereof he speaks. As the youngest son of Margaret and Francis Sherwin, and the grandson of Samuel Horatio Halle and Blanche Murphy Halle, Dennis is surrounded by family history at his office and home, and proud to share it with others.

Lately Dennis has been receiving e-mails from cousins in their 20s and 30s "saying they want to know more about the family," and he is pleased to oblige. However, Dennis isn't writing any of this down. Whether or not he's counting on others to do so is unclear, but as far as he's concerned, "it's not going to get written," at least not by him.

Dennis shared a memory of the time Randolph Churchill stayed with his family in Cleveland while in the states "giving a series of speeches across the U.S. to revive his political career." He continues, "while Randolph was visiting, Aunt Kay fell asleep on the couch. She had very, very long hair at the time, as was the fashion. Randolph cut her hair off while she was asleep (to the length of what we today consider long). From that time on they became best friends."

Ann Crile Esselstyn, Dennis's cousin, has memories of when Winston Churchill visited as well. "My mother told about playing backgammon with Winston during his visits.

"My clearest memory was in 1964 when my husband took a year of training in London. Thanks to Katy we had lunch with Randolph, his son Winston, and Winston's son Randolph on the day his house was open to the public—and people looked in the window at us as

Figure 11-1: Sam Halle and Sir Winston Churchill.
Courtesy of Ann Crile Esselstyn

we ate. It was definitely surreal . . . just being there and then being looked at as well."

Moses Halle and his brother Manuel came to Cleveland in 1846. Manuel arrived first and then sent money for Moses to make the trip.

Moses married Rebecca Weil and had two sons, Salmon P. Chase Halle and Samuel Horatio Halle. (After the death of Rebecca, Moses married Rosa Loentritt, and they had two children, Jessie and Minnie.)

Manuel married Rebecca Weil's sister Augusta Weil ("Gusty"), and their offspring were Ida, Nora, Della, William, and Eugene.

By 1865 brothers Moses and Manuel Halle had established the M and M Halle Co.—specializing in wholesale men's furnishings and notions. The business was successful, and both brothers were able to retire by the time they reached the age of 50.

Moses gave his sons Samuel Horatio and Salmon P. Chase $10,000, which they could use either to pay for a college education or to begin their own business. Following in their father's footsteps, and not unlike many other Jews of the time, the brothers decided to open a dry goods store. On 7 February 1891, Halle Bros., located then on Superior Avenue, opened for business. The success of that store and the suburban stores that followed continued for almost a century, ending in 1982, when the Halle Brothers store on Euclid Avenue closed. But the name Halle continues to evoke pride, sentiment, and nostalgia for many Greater Clevelanders. And the Halle family continues to be representative of a certain era and style as well.

When Salmon P. Halle married Carrie Bloch Moss, they were following the tradition and expected norms of the time, but when Samuel Horatio Halle married Blanche Murphy, they were not. In fact, the union of a German Jewish man and an Irish Catholic woman made headlines in Cleveland.

Samuel and Blanche had five children: Katherine (Kay), who never married and died in 1997 at the age of 93; Walter, who married Helen Chisholm (both deceased; their only surviving child is Kate Halle Briggs); Margaret, who married Francis Sherwin (both deceased) and had three sons: John, Brian, and Dennis–who shares his story here); Jane, who married Dr. George Crile Jr. (both deceased–their children are Joan, deceased, Ann Crile Esselstyn, Susan Crile, and George Crile III), and Ann Halle, their only surviving daughter, who married Robert Little; their children are Sam Little and Reeve Little (deceased).

As Dennis continues, he mentions the visual reminders of his family and extended family that he has in front of him in his office. "One is of my father, Francis McIntosh Sherwin, with his father John standing by an old car, probably a 1932 Ford; there's one of my dad in a polo shirt–he looks very much like the McIntosh he was. And there's my mother (Margaret Halle Sherwin) leaning against a pillar at about age 25; and here's a picture of Sam and Blanche and all the kids sitting on a marble seat in the front entrance to the house on Harcourt Drive; another picture of Aunt Kay with a gorgeous hat a la 1940s–probably designed by Mr. John. She's reading into a microphone. She was the first woman national broadcaster. She conducted interviews during intermission at the Cleveland Orchestra. I remember one was with Rachmaninoff–the world-renowned composer.

"There are many more pictures: one of grandfather Halle (Samuel) done by the cartoonist from the *Plain Dealer* and below that a picture of Winston Churchill with Grampa Halle."

Because he lived in Washington, D.C. for many years, Dennis probably knew his Aunt Kay better than any of his contemporary cousins. "She was not a snob," he declares with conviction. The reason she be-

Figure 11-2: Kay Halle broadcasting on WGAR. *Courtesy of Ann Crile Esselstyn*

came such fast friends with Randolph Churchill is that she "appreciated his guts, his brilliance, his energy. That's a definition of the Halle family–active people who appraise people on their ability and what they do with themselves."

Kay Halle was a beautiful woman, a journalist and author, well known in Washington circles and linked romantically with Joseph P. Kennedy, W. Averell Harriman, and George Gershwin, to name a few. Gershwin wrote "Summertime" on Kay's piano in her New York apartment.

Halle family members were accomplished in other arenas as well. Esselstyn recalls that Sam Halle got his pilot's license at the age of 65, and her mother, Jane Crile, also was a licensed pilot, as was Ann Halle Little. There was even a landing field at what is now Penitentiary Glen, the family farm in Geauga County.

Esselstyn talked about her parents' joint writing venture. "During World War II, George Crile Jr. (Barney) was in the Navy stationed in San Diego. Barney and Jane started skin diving and eventually invented a way to take a movie camera underwater using the re-breather bag from an anesthesia machine and silica gel. Jacques Cousteau was starting to take underwater movies at the same time. My parents showed their underwater movies around Cleveland and then the world. It was the first time people had seen underwater photography. They were true pioneers. They wrote a number of books about their underwater adventure–one of which was *Treasure Diving Holidays*. Jane also was a serious photographer and had several works in the May Show."

Knowing that "accomplishment was the goal of Halle–to do your best," Dennis describes his mother as "unhappy that all she did was produce three boys– and keep them out of jail." But Dennis of course can add much to that. Margaret Halle Sherwin "was someone who would say just what came to her mind. She loved to say things to shock kids. She knew exactly what they were thinking." His mother was also "an environmentalist before her time and a well-known birder. We raised Canada geese on our farm–South Farm in Lake County. I remember when we were burying her, suddenly a whole bunch of geese flew overhead in a V formation."

As for farms, Sherwin remembers the Halle farm and the annual company picnics held there. "At that time companies were like families, and we had a family day out at the Halle farm every year. It was no small event–there were often as many as 3,000 people at these events."

Figure 11-3: Pilot Sam Halle. *Courtesy of Ann Crile Esselstyn*

And, as Dennis remembers it, the atmosphere of the Halle Company was also one of family. "Grandma Murphy knew the names of each employee. We just called it 'the store' and we visited daily."

Equally interesting are the points at which families interconnect and become part of other families and forge new lifelong relationships.

Ann Crile Esselstyn explains, "While in medical school at Yale, my future father-in-law, Caldwell B. Esselstyn, coached my father, George Crile Jr., in freshman football. Esselstyn was a cadaver partner at Yale with a young man named Benjamin Spock. Spock later taught at what was then Western Reserve University in Cleveland and my husband, Caldwell B. Esselstyn Jr., was one of his students. We had many enjoyable evenings with the Spocks at their house and at our little rented house in Chagrin Falls."

Caldwell B. Esselstyn Jr., later took his internship and residency at the Cleveland Clinic and stayed on as a general surgeon specializing in the parathyroid and thyroid and breast. His passion over the years changed to arresting and reversing heart disease. In 1984 Dr. Esselstyn began working with 24 patients with severe heart disease with the purpose of reversing the illness. He is still following 18 of those patients.

There are more interconnections as well. After Jane Crile's death (Ann's mother), George Crile Jr. married Helga Sandburg, the youngest daughter of Carl Sandburg. Helga has lived here almost 40 years and has become one of Cleveland's preeminent writers and poets.

And that's what draws many of us to an interest in family history–the challenge to find those links, explain them, learn about them, and understand them.

12 Land and Property Records

Looking at land and property records becomes important when trying to match two or more records using a legal description without benefit of names. Also, by looking at property records you may be able to determine when someone died, because the original owner's name may have been changed—perhaps to that of a spouse or child.

Land records provide the name of the landowner, dates of transfer of the property, and correct spelling of names, and may offer another method of verifying whether a person was living in the area at a certain time. (Remember, though, that you can own land but not live on it.)

How to Find a Deed

Property records are traced by searching for the deed. The purpose of recording a deed was to protect the new landowner; in Cuyahoga County deeds did not have to be recorded until 1810.

You must have the permanent parcel number and the transfer date in order to get the deed. Such information may be found on records you have already collected. Otherwise, go to the auditor's office for this information. Bring with you the address of the property and any other details you know about it.

Auditor's Office Room 310
Cuyahoga County Administration Building
1219 Ontario
Cleveland, OH 44113
Phone: 443-7010 or 443-7091

For property owned from the early 1900s until the present, begin with a lookup on the computer. Staff will assist you, as there are several steps in this process. Eventually you will be looking at microfiche and getting all the dates on which the property was transferred. Be sure to write down every detail provided: dates and names; descriptions of the property; mention of its location as it relates to streets and landmarks. (This will be important if you end up consulting tax duplicates in your research.)

Each date associated with the transfer of the property allows you to get a copy of the deed, and in this manner you can trace a property's ownership back though time. These records date back to about the 1810s.

Your ability to get a deed depends upon the transfer date. Whatever the very first date of transfer is, as given to you by the auditor's office, that deed should be

> **! Ownership Before 1810**
> The auditor's office cannot search for parcel numbers or sublots (another record-keeping system) prior to 1810, but the Cuyahoga County Archives does have some earlier records.

A Little Help, Please

Sometimes the number you get from the auditor's office is a little unusual, and the recorder's office will do their best to help you find what are probably township records. If you are unable to find a deed in the recorder's office, return to the map room in the auditor's office and ask to speak to the genealogy expert.

Special Saturday Opening

Recently the Stark County recorder's office conducted a "genealogy day" on a Saturday from 10 a.m. to 2 p.m. Their offices are usually open only on weekdays, making it difficult for those who work to access materials. The county recorder, along with staff members, offered to be available to help citizens interested in performing genealogical searches for property owned by family members. What a great idea! About 50 people took advantage of the situation.

Records Online

From your home computer you can access deeds from 1955 to the present by going to the website: www.cuyahoga.oh.us/recorder. As an ongoing project, the above date will gradually change as earlier records continue to be added to the database.

---

located in the recorder's office in this building. In the unusual case that you know there is prior information (prior to earliest date given to you at the auditor's office), proceed to the Cuyahoga County Archives and check their records for earlier transfer of property records. Armed with those earlier transfer dates, return to this building and provide that new information to the auditor's office. Then proceed to the recorder's office.

Deeds are kept at:

County Recorder's Office, Room 216
Cuyahoga County Administration Building
1219 Ontario
Cleveland, OH 44113
Phone: 216 443-7300

Armed with the permanent parcel number, the date of transfer, and the names associated with the transfer, proceed to the county recorder's office. Deeds here date from 1810 until the present.

Staff members are available to assist you in this process as well. They will help you retrieve information either from a computer or from ledgers stored in the back of the office. The information is organized according to transfer date and owner's name and will give a deed number. Staff can then find the deed and make a copy of it for you. Copies made from the computer are $.25 per page; copies made from microfiche (records prior to 1946) are $1 per page. Uncertified copies by mail also cost $1 per page.

How Deeds Help in Genealogical Research

Land deeds show the current owner and tell you how long that person has owned the property. They also show previous owners.

By placing your landowner ancestor in a specific time frame and on a specific piece of land, you have opened up new territory.

Plat maps can be extremely helpful tools in researching land ownership as well. These provide the details that can lead us to the name of the landowner and the jurisdiction where those records can be found. Using atlases and county maps, notice names of the surrounding landowners. Do any of them look familiar? They may be relatives or in-laws. Perhaps you'll find a relative with the maiden name of your ancestor's spouse living nearby. Does someone's land ownership keep growing? What happened—has he or she inherited more land, or bought it?

Remember to look at all the deeds of both grantors and grantees with your surname. It's also a good idea to read records a few pages before and a few pages after the one you are interested in—often the same people are mentioned in several documents, and you may glean additional information this way.

Ask as well for copies of state land grants or patents, federal land patents, and especially homestead files. Write down every detail from records cited, including page number and line number. You may just be looking for data on one person, but write down (or photocopy) everything found in the record. It will save you time and answer questions you have not even thought of yet.

No Good Deed Left Unrewarded

You have to be really desperate to do deed research, or so Cynthia thought.

"I was doing some research on a David Robbins who died in Lake County in 1838. The time period has very little in the way of certificates, and I was at a bit of a loss as to what to do to get a good history on this family. I had done research in Geauga County, looking for most of the usual things, but came up pretty empty. There was no actual will. This seemed strange to me, but you never know. I found David Robbins in the 1820 and 1830 census, but there is not much in the way of family information in those years. His obituary gave me a death date, which was before Lake County was organized. I knew from previous research that the church records in Perry would not produce anything so early. I would have to resort to the dreaded deed research!

"It is amazingly easy. I found the old index books, and then the record in the Lake County Recorder's Office in Painesville. And after I remembered to look under "R" for Robbins and then "D" for David, he popped up quite nicely. I found the deed record in the archives, and what a surprise! The record tells of transferring property from David and wife Sally to son Ambrose."

But wait! It excludes an acre that David may choose each and every year for his use. And Ambrose binds himself to "maintain & support . . . David & Sally during their natural lives in sickness & in health to provide a good & sufficient house for David & Sally at or near the dwelling house of David's where he now lives on the ridge road. Also to furnish David & Sally . . . with a good first rate horse, with saddle, bridle, with one good one horse Waggon & harness with one good single sleigh . . . with all necessary clothing suited to their comfort and condition & rank in life. Ambrose further covenants to provide for & support . . . Nancy Robbins a minor child of said David & Sally during her natural life . . . on the premises where David now lives and when Nancy arrives at the age of twenty one years or when she is married to pay to Nancy two hundred & fifty dollars. Ambrose . . . to provide for and support Ferdinand Robbins & Melissa Robbins both minor children of said David & Sally . . . till

they arrive at the age of twenty one years, unless . . . David Robbins should choose to put said Ferdinand to a trade at the age of sixteen or unless Melissa should marry before she arrives at the age of twenty-one years. Ambrose further covenants to pay to Hiram Robbins one hundred dollars . . . at the age of twenty-one years if called for or if called for by said Hiram . . . covenanted and agreed between the parties to this indenture that in case the said Nancy, Ferdinand, Melissa & Hiram should decease before they become possessed of the money ...to be paid by said Ambrose to either of the last named persons then & in that case, the sum so due as aforesaid to each aforesaid shall be paid equally to the surviving heirs at law of said David & Sally."

It goes on to list Milton Robbins, Adaline Merriman, Stillman Robbins, and Harry Robbins, with sums to be paid by a certain date. Ambrose is also to provide a good school education to the minor children. There are other stipulations that protect the estate other than the property for all the heirs, and then, the clincher:

"It is further covenanted . . . that said Ambrose shall never sell or convey . . . any part or parcel of the land this day deeded to him by David and Sally during the lives of either of them but the land is to be held by said David in security for the faithful performance of all . . . covenants aforesaid by Ambrose." It goes on to say the land will be his if everything is complied with, but if not, the deal becomes null and void. This was dated and sealed 15 March 1836.

So you never know what might be included in deed records, and no wonder there was no will. But the story does not end there. A search of court records reminded the researcher that lawsuits are not new to the 21st century. Ambrose appeared quite frequently in the defendant column. After his father's death, a suit was brought by Sally, his mother. She declared that Ambrose did not keep up his part of the bargain; and when his financial difficulties got out of hand, creditors sued for his property. The court considered it to be the property of Ambrose, and believe it or not, his mother lost the suit, and the property was sold at a sheriff's sale.

This research uncovered some good family stories. By using deed research, Cynthia found a list of children, an idea of the lifestyle of the family, an indication that the health of some of the family was not the best, and learned of some of the business dealings of Ambrose. It is indeed amazing what can be found in those old deed records.

MATHER *Famous Families*

Many Cleveland history buffs know that no member of Moses Cleaveland's original surveying party settled in Cleveland. Some family members of the surveyors did settle here and one stockholder's family as well. According to the book, *Cleveland: The Making of a City*, by William Ganson Rose, Samuel Mather, Jr., of Lynn Court was "the only stockholder whose family would be directly and in a large way identified with the history of Cleveland" (page 38).

Yet it was not until about 10 years ago, when Sterling McMillan S. III was asked to give a speech for the dedication of the Mather Pavilion at University Hospitals, that he got personally interested in the Mather family history. "That started me down a path," explains McMillan, to explore the "evolution of the Puritan ethic." While others advised him to write a book, McMillan says he is "working on a life opus" currently consisting of 13 generations spanning 360 years. By the time it's finished it will be 14 generations. In fact, he says he has stopped telling people he is going to publish anything but says he is "still in the research stage." And with a family that has the likes of Cotton and Increase Mather, James Fennimore Cooper, and John Hay on the branches of its tree, it's likely that research can go on for a very long time.

Talking with McMillan about genealogy, and in particular his family history, means getting an in-depth lesson in the history of Puritanism, the founding of Yale, the genesis of the Bay Colonies, and the Puritan ethic then and now. Just look at the corkboard near the kitchen door in his home, and there is a sheet of paper seven feet high that shows the Mather family history to the precolonial period.

He surrounds himself with several books, such as Karen Armstrong's, *History of God* from The Calvin Institute, to *Puritans at Play*, by Bruce C. Daniels. He pores through volumes from 100-year-old histories to current bestsellers. Recently he read *Theodore Rex* by Edmund Morris, in which there are numerous references to John Hay. "John Hay of course was my uncle"–and he played a very major role in Theodore Roosevelt's administration.

McMillan goes on to explain that John Hay and Sam Mather (who were brothers-in-law) "worked together for causes they both cared about. For example, rebuilding the American Red Cross–making it more effective. After the Spanish-American War it became very clear that the Red Cross wasn't up to the job. So John Hay got in touch with Sam Mather and put him on the national committee. Out of that came Cleveland being the showcase for the new forums we have today."

"So here are other ways you learn about family–through other people's writing," continues McMillan.

Theoretically, McMillan devotes from 5 a.m. to 7 a.m. every morning to his family history research. But he is adamant that it is not research just for the sake of adding more names and dates to his family tree. "It's the use of genealogy that I'm interested in–not just understanding names. Names without character and how they acted and interacted are not interesting to me."

"I am not, per se, as interested in genealogy as in one particular topic," he says. And that topic is how Puritanism has been misunderstood and misrepresented. This was the subject of a recent speech entitled "Things We Misunderstand About Puritanism That Are at the Root Cause of Today's Corruption." His whole emphasis is on "trying to learn from the past to create a better future."

McMillan has a family history mystery he is trying to solve. There are three carved medallions on the transom in the library of his parents' home. On one is the likeness of John Hay, his uncle, who was a statesman and author; on the second is the likeness of James Fenimore Cooper, also a relative and an author; the third one is empty. Why?

Why did McMillan's grandparents, who built the home in 1921, have the third medallion put there and then not have anyone on it? Surely there are a number of family members, also authors, who could have been represented–for example, Cotton Mather or his brother, Increase Mather. It is McMillan's theory that at the time the house was built, Puritans were viewed as joyless, frugal, intolerant people, and his grandparents chose not to emphasize those family ties.

And so the research stage continues. And as it does, McMillan will attempt to solve more than just this mystery, and in the process will likely uncover many more.

13 Using Social Security Records

The Social Security Death Index, available online at www.gov/ssdi, can lead to important genealogical information. You can search for a person's Social Security number here. Many genealogical websites have this same death index—no matter what "cyber road" you take to it, the database is the same. Once the Social Security number is known, send for an SS-5 form. This is a copy of the original application for a Social Security number and should have the individual's parents' names on it. This is probably the most valuable information you will receive from Social Security records. Other information is the date of birth of the individual and his or her residence at the time of application.

Fees are charged by the Social Security Administration: $27 for a copy of the original SS-5 application; $29 if you do not know the Social Security number; or $16 for a copy of an abbreviated printout. As long as you are requesting records, I suggest getting a copy of the original application. "Abbreviated" can translate into "something was omitted," and as family history researchers we definitely do not want that. Write to:

Social Security Administration
Office of Earnings Operations
FOIA Workgroup
300 N. Greene St.
P.O. Box 33022
Baltimore, MD 21290

Some of the websites offering the Social Security death index even generate a form letter for your record request. For example, at http://ssdi.rootsweb.com, put in a Social Security Number, and when it comes up in the box on the right it will list "Tools; SS-5 letter"; click on that and a form letter appears on your screen. However, the person you are looking up must have been registered with Social Security and received a pension. Obviously you need the person's name and hopefully the state or county of residence. But you can be creative and still get good results.

What if you are searching for a married woman and know only her given name and maiden name, but are fairly sure in what county and state she resided? Enter her given name, county, and state in the SSDI and view the results. You may get nothing that makes sense to you. Or you may get a surname that you recognize but hadn't considered, or a surname with a variant spelling. Another modification of this would be to enter just the first three or four letters of the given name as well as the rest of the information you have.

To be sure, there is a better chance of success if the given name is uncommon and she is from a relatively small county. But both of these are definitely worth trying. Then, using recognizable surnames plus any other new information gleaned from these searches (such as zip code), plug that into another SSDI search and evaluate those results. Does anything match what you know? Check other resources to verify this information.

Another search method is to use information gleaned from previous searches. Perhaps you found out where one person died. Now search for other members of that same family by their surname and the name of the town or county where the person you already located died. This is especially effective when searching for unusual names or in small towns. You may even locate a living relative in this manner.

That's What Friends Are For

About two years ago, shortly after Feige Stern had become interested in genealogy, a friend of hers asked if she could help him find the paternal side of his family. The man's parents divorced before he was born; he had never met his father and often wondered if he had any siblings.

Feige continues:

"My own research had hit a 'brick wall,' and because I was feeling frustrated at that point I decided to do what I could to help him find out if he had siblings. His stepfather had adopted him. As a result, his surname differed from his father's. He knew his father's surname and found his father's death listed in the Social Security Death Index online. I also found it there and noted that his father had died in California. This was a lucky break, because California has both a birth and death index online that covered the years I was interested in. I postulated that because his father had died in California, any children might have been born there as well. Unfortunately, I was unable to find his father's death certificate in the online index.

"In the meantime, I sent to the Social Security Administration for a copy of the SS-5 form, which is the form that someone fills out when applying for Social Security.

"At the same time I wrote to the Jewishgen Digest (www.jewishgen.org) for suggestions from other readers as to why, if someone died in California, they would not be listed in the online index. Someone suggested I use the soundexed form of the name I was researching. I should have thought of this, of course. I did so and immediately found

that we had been spelling the name incorrectly. Now I found the father listed with a slightly different spelling of his surname and immediately sent away for his death certificate.

"Returning to the SSDI online, I discovered there were two people with the same name, with a spelling difference of one letter. One was the person I previously assumed to be my friend's father. The other one was more likely, however, because Social Security was applied for in Florida, which was my friend's birthplace. I again wrote to SSA for the SS-5 of this second person, who I now assumed was my friend's father.

"While awaiting the arrival of Social Security records, I visited the Western Reserve Historical Society library and was able to find my friend's grandparents listed in the 1920 census, together with some of his father's brothers and his father himself, at one year old. I also wrote to the National Archives and successfully located his grandfather's naturalization record.

"When his father's death certificate arrived, it listed his second wife's name, including her maiden name. With that information, I again accessed the California Birth Index and found two children listed there with the same surname and same mother's maiden name. I assumed these to be a brother and sister. I did an Internet directory search and found a woman with the same name living in New Mexico. I gave this name and phone number to my friend.

"When he called the number, my friend found that indeed this woman was his sister (half-sister, really). She had known about him. Apparently their father always felt bad about having no contact with his son and mentioned this to his children. My friend now has five siblings! Imagine finding out at forty-eight years old that you have five (half) brothers and sisters!"

Casting a Wider Net

Many databases, including the SSDI, have a place to plug in the name of the county as well as the state. Consider entering the names of the counties that surround the one you have been using. Remember that a person might have died in a nursing home, hospital, or friend's home. And since you have searched a wider area, you may get more results and may have a little more analyzing to do to determine appropriate matches.

Know the Number, Not the Name?

If you think you may have found a Social Security number (perhaps a nine-digit number scribbled on the back of a sheet of paper in a box of records) but do not know for whom, go to: www.searchbug.com/peoplefinder/ssn.asp. The site will let you know if this was a validly issued Social Security number, in what year or range of years it was issued, and in what state.

14 Newspaper Research

There are several reasons for our ancestors to have made it into the newspapers. To be sure, life-cycle events were often noted in newspapers of the day—these would include birth, marriage, and death. Articles appear in newspapers depending on several variables: how unique the occasion was; how prominent an individual was; who they knew; and if it was a slow news day so there was more space than usual in the paper. Be certain to search all the newspapers in the area, and check a few days prior to and as long as one week after any event. Remember, it took time for information to be received and then printed in the paper. Also, consider checking milestone dates such as twenty-fifth, fortieth, or fiftieth anniversary parties, and high school reunions.

What to Look For

Newspaper items with a possible genealogical tie-in include:
Marriage—announcements, engagements, anniversaries
Birth—birth notice, birthday celebrations
Death—obituary, funeral notice, burial notice, store closing
Adoption—these were not always secret and were in fact sometimes listed in the newspapers. Often the names of the birth parents were included.

If you do not find an obituary in one paper, check to see if the city or town had more than one newspaper, or perhaps a weekly. Also check the surrounding towns. Especially if your family was from a small town bordering a larger one, there is a strong chance the larger town's newspaper served this need, even that the larger town had more than one newspaper that may have carried this information.

Where to Look

Be sure to check all types of newspapers: daily and weekly, political, ethnic and foreign-language, local and regional, large city and small suburban edition, and religious.

Aside from looking through the microfilm files of all the newspapers, you will want to check the following resources, if the time frames match your search. (Also, if you are researching a Cleveland-area crime, these are good sources.)

Annals of Cleveland—this is an index of items in Cleveland newspapers between 1818 and 1875, and from 1933 to 1938 (can be found at CPL, WRHS, and FPK).

> ### ❗ Burial Permits
> When looking through old newspapers, keep an eye out for small notices in the classified section stating "burial permit issued"—this may offer a clue to an otherwise unpublished death.

Verifying a Family Secret

Local researcher John knew very little about the lives of his maternal great-grandparents other than that they had both emigrated from Germany. He did know that Grandpa Philip was a tailor, that he had married Margaret, and that they had lived on Jay Street in Cleveland. He also knew there were six children who'd lived to adulthood.

After his mother's death, John started doing family history research and talked with a second cousin—a great-granddaughter of Philip. She mentioned that while she was growing up there had been some secrecy about Philip's death; it was rumored that he'd committed suicide. Although John had never heard anything about this, he and his wife began to research it. By locating Philip's probate record, John got the date of death. John and his wife then went to the Cleveland Public Library and looked through Cleveland newspapers for the date in 1867. In a matter of minutes John's wife found the following article in the *Plain Dealer*, 1867:

Suicide from Drowning

Philip ——, a clothing merchant, residing on Jay Street
west side, mysteriously disappeared on Sunday evening
last, and no clue could be discovered to his whereabouts,
till yesterday afternoon, when his lifeless body was
found floating in the river near the Columbus street
bridge. A stone was attached to his neck, and there can
be no doubt that he committed suicide. He leaves a large
family, to whom his untimely end will provide a sad
blow. His financial affairs had become somewhat involved, and this doubtless led him to commit the deed.

Imagine discovering the tale of Philip's death over 130 years later! John speculates that Philip's financial difficulties may have been brought on by the depression that followed the end of the Civil War. He even wonders if Philips the tailor had been making uniforms for the soldiers, and his services were no longer needed.

Cleveland News Index—covers 1976 to the present (found at CPL and FPK).

Cleveland Press Archives—located on the third floor of the library at Cleveland State University, open Mon–Fri 9:30 a.m.–noon and 1–5 p.m.; phone 216-687-2449. The Archives has hard copies of articles from the Cleveland Press, filed by subject. For example, if you have a relative who owned a hotel you'd look under: "hotels, inns."

Newspaper clippings file at the Cleveland Public Library—items are indexed by subject. For example, under the heading "Cleveland—Cemeteries" you will see copies of every article about a Cleveland cemetery that was printed in the Cleveland papers from about 1920 to 1975. This file was created before computers were used, so it is dependent upon someone having made the decision to include a specific category of interest. Although this file covers 1920 to 1975, there are very few items from 1920s.

The weekly suburban Sun newspapers have a regular genealogy column. "Let's Talk Genealogy" started in July 2001. It is written by local genealogist Diana Smith, and the column appears the second and fourth Thursdays each month. Recent columns have covered topics from computer software to passenger lists to family reunions.

Readers can submit subject ideas, comments, or questions to: talkgenealogy@aol.com or by snail mail to: P.O. Box 38314, Olmsted Falls, Ohio 44138. There is always a section listing resources relating to the day's topic as well as notification of special events and local meetings. Ms. Smith is always open to receiving feedback on the column, and although she hears mostly from Northeast Ohio residents, she has heard from folks as far away as the West Coast (with e-mail messages you can't always tell, but sometimes the writers let you know where they're from).

Newspapers in Port Cities

If you know the name, arrival date, and port of entry of the ship your ancestor was on, look for that port of entry in the newspaper. There were often columns about "ships in port"—perhaps written by a reporter looking for an interesting story.

The *New York Times* had a marine intelligence column that often gave a summary of the ship's voyage (weather, problems encountered). Some experts claim the *New York Herald*'s similar columns were better, but these may not be as readily accessible outside of New York, whereas most libraries have back copies of the New York Times on microfilm.

In Canada, papers such as the *Quebec Gazette* and the *Montreal Gazette* had similar columns with details about arrivals and departures. Check other port cities on both coasts for specific newspapers.

And don't forget departure cities. The departure was often a newsworthy event as well, depending upon whatever else may have been happening at the time. So don't neglect to check those newspapers as well.

African-American Research

Look in Civil War–era African-American newspapers for names and information about those serving in the United States Colored Troops.

Copies

As with old photographs, making a copy of old newspaper clippings on a color copier often results in a better, easier-to-read product.

Try searching for newspaper websites for a specific area by putting "Cleveland newspaper microfilm" in a search engine. Change "Cleveland" to any other city you are searching. Try using Google (www.google.com) or other search engines. For newspapers available by state go to: www.neh.gov/projects/usnp.html.

President Lincoln Helps Cleveland Family

Judy B. in Chardon has a family Bible given to her by her father. In the Bible was a silk bookmark with Abraham Lincoln's picture on it and the inscription, "We mourn our country's loss." There was also an old newspaper advertisement for cologne sold at the Lewis A. Heydorn Pharmacy, 582 St. Clair Street, Cleveland.

Judy photocopied the family record page from the Bible, listing names and birth dates, and sent this to a woman named Laurie whom Judy had connected with on the Internet via a posting for the name "Heydorn." Laurie in turn sent Judy a copy of a newspaper article she had received via other Internet connections.

Figure 14-1: Caroline Heydorn. *Courtesy William Edward Vigler and Anita B. Watson*

The article begins, "Lincoln was the most accessible president we ever had"—a quote made by Cleveland resident Caroline Heydorn, who was just over 80 years old at the time of the interview.

The article then recounts Caroline's story of how she met President Lincoln.

During the Civil War, Caroline received a letter telling her that her son Will was wounded and sick in a Washington-area hospital. She took the letter to her husband, who was a dyer at Amasa Stone's woolen works. Mr. Stone was present when Caroline presented the letter to her husband. Stone encouraged Mr. Heydorn to let his wife go to be with "her boy" and even offered to lend the Heydorns money if they needed it for the trip.

Caroline took the train to Washington, was there nine days, but for some reason was not permitted to see her son. To make matters worse, she had to stay in a hotel and pay $4 a day!

She went to the White House but was not permitted to see the president. However, she had heard that the president often drove down Fourteenth Avenue. One day as she saw an open carriage coming toward her, and desperate to see her son, Caroline ran out into the middle of the street. The men riding as escorts in front of the carriage motioned her to move, but she would not. President Lincoln saw the commotion and motioned to the woman to come over to him.

As Caroline recounted in the article: "I couldn't speak when I got there. However, he looked at me very kindly and asked, 'What is it that you want?' My tongue came back. 'I want a few words with you if you will be so kind as to spare me the time.' What do you think he did next? He, the president, held out his hand to me and told me to get into the carriage with him. Indeed he helped me to the seat beside him. Then . . . he laid his hand on my shoulder like this and said, 'You need not be afraid of me. Tell me all.'

"I told him that I have five boys in the army; that all of them enlisted of their own accord. Then he laid his hand on my shoulder again and said, 'Little mother, I am proud to know you. There aren't many women who give five boys to their country. What can I do for you?'

"Then I told him of Will, how they wouldn't let me see my sick boy and that I wanted to take him home with me." He immediately told the driver to 'take us to the hospital.' I had no trouble going in that time. President Lincoln had one of the great doctors come to him and he himself asked all about Will. The doctor said my boy was too sick to be moved, but that he would get well.

Figure 14-2: Photo of Louis Heydorn (standing, right rear) taken after the war.
Courtesy of Judith Bolan

"Then the president turned to me. 'Little mother,' he said, 'rest assured we will do everything we can for your boy. As soon as he gets well enough he shall have his discharge. You yourself shall go to the Secretary of War, Mr. Stanton, and he will give you his papers.'"

Caroline trembled, telling the president she could not do it, she could not go to Stanton. When asked why, Caroline responded: "You see I come from Ohio. We people out there love you and trust you. If you can't help me nobody can." Lincoln, apparently so impressed with the trust of this woman, promised that the trust would "not be misplaced" and that he would attend to her son. If she ever needed a friend, she could come to him again. Next, again according to Caroline's quotes in the newspaper article, the president took out a piece of paper and said, "You know I have so many things on my mind I might forget. This will at any time recall you to my memory."

When asked if this handwritten note from Lincoln still existed, Caroline explained that it was lost. She had brought the paper home and showed it to her husband and Mr. Stone. Stone told Mrs. Heydorn to always keep the paper, that it might be of value to her someday. She gave the paper to her husband for safekeeping. Years later her husband went to work in Baltimore, taking the paper with him. Her husband loaned it to a man and while the man still had it, her husband died, and the family never got the paper back. Although Caroline did not remember Lincoln's exact written message, she said it was something like: "I know this lady, Mrs. Heydorn. She has five boys in the army. I have promised to help her if she ever needs aid. A. Lincoln."

Will recovered, returned to Cleveland, and married Offty Humphrey.

15 Immigrant Ancestors

In tracing immigrant ancestors we have several purposes: to determine exactly where our ancestor was born and raised; to get a better understanding of the journey, how long it took, if he or she came alone or with others, and perhaps even get a picture or description of the ship; to obtain records of birth, death, and marriage, and passenger lists that hopefully will provide more information or confirm what we already have.

Geography

Perhaps you need to know if your ancestor's hometown was in Austria or Hungary or if it was really part of Czechoslovakia at the time of his or her birth. Once you know the hometown (usually obtained from death or birth records) you may need to consult a gazetteer and then an atlas to determine the current jurisdiction (see Chapter 4).

Okay, so you can't find information on the hometown of one of your ancestors. Now what can you do? The individual had to get here somehow, so try checking for the name on a passenger list.

Passenger lists

Finding your ancestor on a passenger list requires a systematic approach, good use of the research log (discussed in Chapter 2), and persistence.

It is easiest to find passenger records if you know the name of the ship, the port of arrival, and the time period during which your immigrant ancestor arrived. These then lead to a passenger list lookup either in a book or on microfilm. You may find the initial information you need in naturalization records or get it from other sources. Most of us, though, are not that lucky. We must try to determine as best we can an approximate date of arrival and perhaps make an educated guess as to port of arrival.

If no naturalization record is available, you can use census records (or other records) to determine the likely port of entry and approximate date. For East Coast and Midwest residents, you can assume the arrival port was New York.

Having made an educated guess as to the port and date, now:

1. Consult books that have passenger lists (see bibliography).
2. Go to the local Family History Center and request the appropriate soundexed films for specific ports (e.g., New York, Baltimore).
3. Go on the Internet and search various sites.
4. Use National Archives and Records Administration (NARA) passenger list records found at the Western Reserve Historical Society or Fairview Park Library, or see below.

Slovenian Ancestors

Parish priests are often in the unique position of maintaining useful genealogical data. Aside from keeping official birth, marriage, and death registers, they also have the Status Animarum—records of sacraments given to parishioners, cataloged according to household and/or address. Often one will find within the Status Animarum information regarding persons who married outside the parish, or later moved away. These records will almost certainly include the birthplace for those who married into the parish. Status Animarum records include the relationship to the head of household for all those residing there and have proved valuable in documenting illegitimate children of daughters within a household.

Chinese immigrants

Due to the 1882 Chinese Exclusion Act there are detailed records for many Chinese immigrants who entered the country through San Francisco in the late 1900s and the first half of the 20th century. These records are kept at the National Archives and Records Administration's San Bruno, California, office.

Cleveland's Early Immigrant Population

In 1900, 40 percent of Clevelanders were either born in Germany or children of German-born parents. Only three other U.S. cities had larger German populations: Milwaukee; Hoboken, New Jersey; and Cincinnati. But during the next 20 years the Cleveland population showed more ethnic diversity. According to the 1920 federal census, the largest group of foreign-born residents of Cleveland were from Poland and represented 14.5 percent of the city's total foreign-born population. Other nationalities with large representations for the same time period were: Hungary, 12.4 percent; Germany, 11 percent; Czechoslovakia, 10 percent; Russia, 9 percent; Italy, 7.6 percent; Yugoslavia, 6.6 percent; and Austria, 6.4 percent. The total population of Cleveland at this time was 806,368, of whom 239,538 were foreign-born (white). That's just over 28 percent of the city's population. (Population History of Eastern U.S. Cities and Towns, 1790–1870, by Riley Moffat; Scarecrow Press, Inc; Metuchen, NJ, & London, 1992.)

Learn More

To read about the Ellis Island Immigrant History Center you can find information at:
http://www.rootsweb.com/ ~rwguide/syft/curcolumn.htm.

NARA Research

The National Archives and Records Administration (NARA) staff can search passenger lists if you can supply the name of immigrant, port of entry, and name of vessel. Also needed are the month and year of arrival, or name of port of embarkation and exact arrival date. If they are given the full names and ages of passengers and accompanying passengers, the port of entry, the ship name, and exact arrival date, they will search passenger lists up to 1954. Put this information on NATF Form 81 and submit it.

Here's how NARA passenger list records are organized:

Port	Arrival Lists	Indexes (cover these time frames)
Baltimore	1820–1948	1820–1952*
Boston	1820–1874	1848–1891
	1883–1943	1902–1920
Galveston	1896–1948	1896–1951*
New Orleans	1820–1954	1820–1946
		1897–1948
Philadelphia	1800–1945	1800–1948
San Francisco	1893–1953	1893–1934
Seattle		1890–1957
Canada	1895–1954	1895–1952
Minor ports	1820–1873	1890–1924
		1893–1954

* How can an index cover a time frame for which there are no NARA films? There may be additional lists that still have not been microfilmed by the NARA but for which there are indexes. So one would have to go to the National Archives and look at the originals.

Ellis Island Website

April 17, 2001, was a big day for family history buffs in the United States. That was when the Ellis Island website went online with a searchable database. Researchers stayed up all night waiting for a chance to "get on it." The site was so mobbed they actually had to close down for a few days and retool. Genealogy websites and many message boards lit up with tips on how to get on the website and use it, as well as tales of long waits and difficult access. Thankfully, most of the bugs have been eliminated, and this valuable tool has celebrated its two-year anniversary.

Records on the Ellis Island website were all compiled from other sources and then entered into a huge computer database. Errors are possible. Perhaps some of the people on lists signed up for a boat but never took it. Others may have died at sea. Use the information on the website as an entrée to get to the original record itself.

The Ellis Island website may prove valuable for you if the port of arrival was New York and Ellis Island was the processing center at the time your ancestor arrived there. Found on the website are records for more than 17 million people arriving in New York between 1892 and 1924. There are several ways to enter the Ellis Island site:

- www.ellisislandrecords.org is the home page.
- www.ellisislandrecords.org/default.asp—this is the page where searches begin.
- http://.stevemorse.org—Dr. Morse offers several different formats for getting information from the website.
- http://sites.netscape.net/stephenpmorse/ellis.html is yet another way to search the site.

Locating Polish Relatives

Lisa writes:"My mom sat down with my great-grandmother in the early 1970s and had her write down family information. She wrote down the names and birth dates of her eight siblings. At the bottom of the paper, she wrote that her mother was born in West Pennard, Somersetshire, England (100 miles south of London). And then there was the note: 'City of Berlin boat sailed Oct 4, 1877.'"

Lisa, in searching for her family's roots, took that information to the Family History Center. There she made a copy of a picture of the ship. At the FHC Lisa found a book that listed cemeteries in countries around the world and directions to these cemeteries.

Lisa also knew a little about her Polish relatives. She entered the name of the city they were from (Krosno, Poland) into a search engine on the Internet. Many websites popped up in response to this, and Lisa started visiting them sporadically. She soon found the Web page of a man from Krosno who was a university professor and spoke English.

"I sent him an e-mail, and after my telling him what I was looking for he decided to mail me a phone book from the Krosno area. I wrote a letter in Polish (with help from www.genealogienetz.de/gene/misc/translation.html—a free Internet translation service, but only for Czech, Dutch, English, French, German, and Polish, and only for genealogical purposes) explaining who I was and what I was looking for. I also included pic-

Figure15-2, 15-3: House in Poland where Lisa's great-grandmother lived—then and now. *Courtesy of Lisa Kubit*

tures of my father, my great-uncle, and myself. I sent 63 letters to people with the same last name as my great-grandfather, and 16 to those with the same last name as the maiden name of my great-grandmother. Also included in the letters were copies of pictures someone had sent my great-grandmother 40 to 50 years ago. (She saved every letter she received!)

"The response was wonderful! I received over 20 letters, mostly in Polish, and a few e-mails. Unfortunately, I received barely any information on my great-grandfather's side. His last name is quite common in the region, and I'd heard there are three different family groups in the area with that surname. I did, however, make one connection—an e-mail from a lady living in New York City, whose parents received my letter in Poland. We became instant friends, and I even traveled to Poland to meet many new family members. I now have my own pictures to add to the family album.

"On my great-grandmother's side I had even better luck. I received a letter from a young girl—the only one in her family who spoke English well enough to write. She went to the church and did some research. She found my great-grandmother's baptism records. She also took pictures of some of the same sites that were in the pictures I'd sent in my letter. She also sent a picture of the home my great-grandmother was born and raised in. It is still in the family. Another woman from Great-gramom's side wrote me and sent me a copy of her/our family tree.

"It is important to note that I was unprepared to handle the many letters I received in reply to my request. I now need a translator to interpret the letters written in Polish."

Address Helps when Spelling of Name Confuses

Frieda Blass (née Neubauer), Matilde Brasch (née Neubauer), and Sofie Adler (née Neubauer) were sisters. Frieda's husband died in World War I. In 1932, Frieda died of breast cancer, leaving her two sons behind as orphans. Their Aunt Matilde stepped in to care for them.

In July 1938, Sofie Adler, along with her three children, Ursula, Ruth, and Manfred (Manny), went to Breslau from Crailsheim to live with Matilde and the two boys. Meanwhile, because there was only one affidavit to emigrate, Manny's father, Albert Adler, left for the United States. The plan was for Albert to obtain more affidavits, thus permitting his wife and children to join him as soon as possible.

As the situation in Europe and particularly Germany worsened, the remaining family made plans to leave the country—all except Matilde. She did not want to leave. By then Matilde's nephews were married. One went with his wife to Sweden; the other went with his wife to Israel.

Unable to convince Matilde to leave and fearing for their own lives, the rest of the family left Germany. Matilde was never heard from again, and Manny never knew what became of Aunt Matilde.

Flash-forward sixty years.

Largely as a result of the disintegration of the Eastern Bloc communist governments, huge amounts of data from the World War II era had suddenly become available. Much of the information consisted of lists of names of those who had been killed in the Holocaust. Certainly by this time most remaining families assumed, and probably knew on one level, that their relatives had perished. Actually confirming this, however, with the finality that entailed, would be difficult work.

Thus we find Manny Adler in 1993 conducting a training workshop with staff of the Greater Cleveland Red Cross. As a psychologist, but more importantly as a Holocaust survivor, he was uniquely qualified for the task of sensitizing the workers' feelings in regard to working with Holocaust survivors.

After working with the local Red Cross for a while, Manny decided to use their tracing service to find out about Aunt Matilde. He filled out tracing papers and sent them to the Cleveland office, which then forwarded them to the Holocaust and War Victims Tracing and Information Center in Baltimore.

On 7 August 1998, Manny received a letter from Baltimore stating that after reviewing his request they sent it to the ITS (International Tracing Service) in Arolsen, Germany (the largest repository of original Nazi documentation in the world). Their response was: "no information available." They also stated the case would be kept open, and that sometimes their office gets requests from others that can help them match information and individuals. (The Cleveland Red Cross chapter had been notified of the above as well, and wrote a similar letter to the Highland Heights family.)

On 27 September 2000, a letter from the Cleveland chapter arrived informing the Adlers that "tracing efforts are continuing through the Polish Red Cross." Because the Adlers had not expected to hear anything anyway, they thought it was nice to receive this response, if nothing else. After all, various family members had tried years ago to obtain information on Matilde, and if they couldn't find out, how could anyone else?

Six months later, in February 2001, a staff member from the Cleveland Red Cross called Manny and said she had received some information but was not certain it was about his family. Both the first and last names were spelled differently than what he had provided. The information forwarded to the Adlers was a reply from the Polish Red Cross regarding the inquiry and giving the following information:

"In the course of our investigation we obtained information that a Mathilda Sara Brasek nee Neubuer, born 18 October 1892 in Farnard Hungary, lived in Roko, formerly Breslau since 1925; she used to live at Sonnenster #32 up to the date of her husband's death; and then at Freiburger Str 27. Since Sept 1939 she lived at #18 Freiburger Str. On 9 April 1942 her property was confiscated by the Nazis."

Manny was not sure this was indeed his aunt. Both her first and last names were spelled incorrectly. But Sheila, Manny's wife, who had been getting more and more involved in genealogy, went directly to her files.

> Nach langen, schweren, mit Geduld ertragene Leiden verschied am Montag, dem 2. Mai, ... 42. Lebensjahre unsere gute, treusorgende Mutter, Tochter, Schwester, Schwägerin und Tante, Frau
>
> # Frieda Blass
> #### geb. Neubauer   [993
>
> Breslau, Freiburger Str. 27, den 3. Mai 1932.
>
> ## Die trauernden Hinterbliebenen
>
> Beerdigung: Dienstag, den 3. Mai 1932, nachmittags 4 Uhr, israelitischer Friedhof, Cosel.

> Für das innige Mitgefühl beim Hinscheiden unserer teuren Frau Blass, danken herzlichst
>
> **Familie Neubauer   Brasch**
>
> **Blass   Adler**
>
> [2

Figure 15-4: These two newspaper notices from Sheila's files provided the clues needed to confirm Mathilda Brasek and Matilde Brasch were the same person.
Courtesy of Manfred and Sheila Adler

Sheila keeps her records according to family groups. She immediately went to the "Blass" file, and in the death notice for Frieda Blass was listed the family residence—the address matched the address in the letter from the Red Cross.

Thus the family was able to confirm that Mathilda Brasek and Matilde Brasch were one and the same.

Navigating the Websites

Try these techniques while visiting the Ellis Island websites:

Register—no fee is involved, it is quick and easy, and your registration is confirmed. After registering, go to bottom of page and hit "continue."

Refresh—keep hitting the refresh button on your browser if you seem "stuck."

Reset—hit this or the "go" button on your browser if you can't seem to actually "get into" the site.

Removed?—if you get kicked off the site, don't exit; hit the "back" button on your browser.

Revisit—names that do not appear one day seem to appear the next, even though spelled exactly the same.

Re-examine—family stories may lead you to discount some of the names you find, but check out all possible matches against the facts before discarding them.

Writing to Another Country

Writing a letter to a non–English-speaking country but don't speak the language?

Contact the International Service Center, 1836 Euclid Avenue (phone 216-781-4560). They will translate for you—either the letter you are sending or the one you receive. A modest fee is charged. (There are websites that offer this service free for genealogical purposes, with varying results. See story at beginning of this chapter.)

What to put in the letter:

Keep it simple. If you are writing to a church or other nonprofit agency, enclosing a check or international money order is often helpful. (Standard donations are usually $20 to $30. In some cases they may prefer cash.)

State what information you are looking for and explain why you believe they may have it.

Using the Site

Once you enter the Ellis Island website, type in the names you are searching.

A yellow screen appears and soon shows hits for the name you've searched; there may be several, and by looking at age, or port of departure, you should be able to determine which one is your ancestor, or at least narrow down the possibilities. (A good reason to keep your family group sheet with you when searching.)

You should be in the " passenger record" by now. You can choose to "add to your Ellis Island file," "view manifest," or "view ship." You will probably want to do all three eventually, but begin by viewing the manifest. Seeing the copy of the manifest page with your ancestor's name on it can really be exciting. Make sure you do not miss this step. At one time, it was possible to make a copy of the manifest from your own computer. Now this seems to be impossible, but you still can see it on your screen and you have the choice of ordering a copy from the Ellis Island website (fee involved). Or, you can make a copy when you track down the actual passenger record, which can be found at the National Archives or at one of the facilities mentioned elsewhere in this book.

Leave a Message

Ever wonder if others are searching this same name and have found the same person you have? If you join the Ellis Island Foundation ($45 for one year), you can actually leave a note for others who may view this record and, perhaps, be related to you. After you have joined the foundation, look on the left side of the passenger record page and choose "create an annotation."

Creative Searching

Whoever said genealogy was dry research? We're thinking up new ways to spell names all the time. So if previous searches have been unsuccessful, try the following at this site, and perhaps others: Type in the surname and just the initial for the given name. Try options such as "close matches" and "alternate spellings." Of course you are casting a wider net here, but it is worth the effort.

Getting the Original Record

Remember that once you've found your ancestor on the passenger list, you are just looking at a copy of a copy. Get the original record or at least a copy of it by requesting film (now that you know the name of the ship and the date and port of its arrival, it's easy) and viewing it at the Family History Center or, as mentioned above, by filing form NATF 82 with the National Archives and Records Administration.

Not all those arriving in New York were processed through Ellis Island (see following table), and there have been errors or difficulties noted with some records provided at the Ellis Island site.

Here are the dates for the different processing sites through which immigrants passed when they arrived in New York:

Dates	Processing Site
1 Aug 1855–18 Aug 1890	Castle Garden
19 Aug 1890–31 Dec 1891	Barge Offices
1 Jan 1892–13 June 1897	Ellis Island

Other Passenger Resources

The Ship's List is an Internet mailing list of people who know a great deal about, or want to know about, vessels bringing people to various parts of the world. You can subscribe for free by sending an e-mail to: TheShipsList-L@rootsweb.com. In the subject line type "subscribe" and you will soon be receiving e-mail about boats and ships going to and from all parts of the world. If you are trying to locate immigrant ancestors and have been unsuccessful, a few weeks on this list will give you a great education. As in so many genealogical circles, the "regulars" on this list know much about the subject and are willing to share it with you.

Portions of the Bremen Emigration Lists have also been placed on the Internet: http://db.genealogy.net/maus/gate/shiplists.cgi. When I last checked (July 2003) the website only covered from 1920 to 1939.

For books with passenger lists see any of the repositories listed in the Appendix.

The American Red Cross

The American Red Cross
3747 Euclid Ave.
Cleveland, OH 44115
Phone: 216-431-3010
Fax: 216-431-3025
Internet: www.crossnet.org

Place of Origin

Just because the "place of origin" on the ship's manifest states "London" do not assume your ancestor was born in London. Read the entire record carefully. In many cases people took one vessel from Eastern Europe to London. They then boarded another ship in London for the trip to the United States. So when asked where they had left from, they said London, because that had, indeed, been their most immediate port of departure.

Bear in mind that persons often made more than one trip to the States. So if information from the ship's manifest does not seem right, search other indexes for the same individual.

The American Red Cross helps out in disasters, conducts blood drives, and distributes needed goods and services to individuals and families who have experienced crises. Its services also include locating relatives through the American Red Cross Holocaust and War Victims Tracing and Information Center. One mission of this agency is reuniting families, but it does not focus on genealogy, per se. Do not describe your request as being for "genealogical purposes" but rather to locate a family member or relative. Individual searches begin at the local Red Cross, where you submit a tracing inquiry.

The Red Cross continues to provide assistance to those requiring tracing services. Their goal is to establish communication between people in the U.S. and their relatives who are citizens and residents of other countries when war, civil disturbance, or natural disaster has caused them to lose contact. The purpose is to help families reconnect. The International Committee of the Red Cross (ICRC) has been providing this service since the Franco-Prussian War in 1870.

Since 1930, a substantial number of requests have come from persons separated during and after World War II. These services are also used to locate persons who have lost contact due to other insurgencies and conflicts such as those in Korea, Vietnam, and Kosovo. Even now, the Greater Cleveland Red Cross is getting "safe and well" messages into Iraq from Iraqi families who live in the Cleveland area.

In 2002, the Red Cross delivered 2,882,000 messages to families around the world, and 1,740 persons were located through the tracing service. In Africa there continue to be thousands of people in refugee camps where normal communication is either nonexistent or extremely difficult, and the Red Cross assists in sending messages and establishing some form of communication between family members in countries such as Liberia with their relatives around the world. During the last 10 years, the Red Cross was active locally in facilitating six reunions/identifications. In June 2003, the Cleveland Area Red Cross had activity on 30 new cases and 24 ongoing cases. These cases "go on" (remain open) until the information requested is found.

Historical Collections of Ohio

Historian Henry Howe published his book Historical Collections of Ohio in 1849 after first visiting each county in the state, talking to many people, and making copious notes and drawings. About 35 years later Howe made a similar trip (by then Ohio had many more counties for him to visit—which he did). He wrote another book, over 1,000 pages in length, also titled Historical Collections of Ohio but with a different subtitle, and it was published in 1888 (see bibliography). This is an excellent book to consult, especially if you had family in Ohio during this time.

Do Some Historical Research

Why should you spend time reading history books or learning about local history? Because knowing the basic history of your immigrant ancestors' countries may help you understand them and their motives. Most people came to the United States for economic, political, or religious reasons. Learning about the socioeconomic climate in their country of origin at the time they migrated may help you appreciate the risks they were willing to take. Knowing more about your ancestors' roots may in turn help explain the ties they kept or did not keep with their homeland, why certain traditions were important to them, and why certain information was passed on—or kept from—family members.

Knowledge of the geographic community in which immigrants first settled may lead to information about their occupation, social life, or religion (perhaps there was no Methodist church in town so they joined whatever church was available).

16 Military Records

M ilitary records have the potential to offer important information that can add to or complete some of the data you have regarding vital statistics (birth and death dates, for example) as well as help flesh out the personalities of your ancestors—where they fought, who their friends were, or if there was a dispute among heirs.

The National Archives and Records Administration (NARA)

The United States government maintains many records of use to genealogists. They are kept either at the National Archives and Records Administration (NARA) in Washington, D.C., (8601 Adelphi Rd., College Park, Maryland 20740; www.archives.gov) or at regional offices throughout the United States and its territories. Chicago is the regional office for Cleveland records. While a visit to the national office can be a worthwhile trip, all, or at least most, of their records are accessible from remote sites via computer, at the local repositories listed in this book, or by requesting information at the Family History Center, as well as by requesting that the Archives send information to you.

But first you need to know what to ask for. There are several books and pamphlets that contain lengthy descriptions of what records are kept at NARA (these are available locally at the Cleveland Public Library, Western Reserve Historical Society, Fairview Park Library, and Family History Centers). Or you can visit their website: www.archives.gov. With the vast amount of records in their keeping, the Archives puts records into "Record Groups" and numbers these groups. So when making a request, you will refer to a NARA Record Group (RG) and then a number.

Common Records Requested from NARA and the Related Fees*:

Type of Record	NATF Form No.	Fee
Ship passenger arrivals	81	$17.25
Census records	82	$17.50
Pension files more than 75 years old (complete file)	85	$37.00
Pension documents packet	85	$14.75
Military service files more than 75 years ago	86	$17.00

*By filling out these forms you are requesting staff to research the specified records for your ancestor, and thus a fee is charged. Fees listed here were current as of July 2003.

For our purposes in this chapter, the area of interest will be military service records (ship passenger lists were discussed in Chapter 15).

Although NARA also has census records, the majority of census schedules that are needed for family history research are available locally. If you need a census or census index that is not owned by one of our local libraries, I suggest going to a Family History Center nearby instead of NARA (see Chapter 7).

Types of Military Records

If your ancestor served in the U.S. military, there is a possibility that records at NARA will be helpful to you. In order to get these records you need to provide the following information on each individual:

- Name
- Age at the time of service
- Birth date (at least the year)
- Residence (when he went into the service, and when he was discharged)
- Spouse (helpful, not required)
- Unit

Military records can provide interesting and helpful information. But you need to know what to ask for. If you request the service record, that's all you will receive—information as to dates of entry and discharge from service, unit and rank, what major battles or engagements fought in, payroll history, and, if your relative was sick, hospital papers.

Draft, or selective service, records will offer information as to occupation, residence, marital status, age, and birthplace.

Some persons who served will have pension or bounty land records (sometimes land was offered instead of money) if the individual or his family qualified for a pension or bounty. (Regulations for qualifying changed, but such things as serving a minimum amount of time, or when a divorce occurred factor into the rules.) Pension records usually include the veteran's application and names of witnesses, details such as the battles participated in, if he was wounded or taken prisoner, and his physical description; the widow's application may have information about where she lived, her financial situation, and verification of the marriage; applications by children/heirs can provide names and married surnames, addresses, and birth dates.

You can request a copy of your ancestor's pension records. There is a fee charged, and the more records copied and sent, the more you are charged. But then, why would you want only the condensed version, if the whole record was available?

Civil War files for Union soldiers are kept at the Archives, and recently some Confederate files have become available. But for Confederate soldiers, you might want to contact state archives as well.

African-American Military Records

African-Americans who served in the Revolutionary War are included in the "List of Black Servicemen Compiled from the War Department Collection of Revolutionary War Records, Special List 36," compiled by Debra L. Newman. For their pension files, get Revolutionary War Pensions and Bounty Land Warrant Application Files (M804). Selections from the files are on roll M805. (M and T indicate the microfilm on which the information is found.)

Ask For Particulars

When writing a letter regarding information from a relative's military pension file, particularly one from the Civil War, add a note to the form mentioning specifically what you are looking for, e.g., "information on marriages and deaths, as well as military service." You have a better chance of getting more information this way, rather than just stating that you are looking for "family information."

Family Records with Regimental Records

Sometimes British families followed the troops, and their vital records were kept in military instead of civilian registers. Thus the Family Records Center in London maintains indexes of Regimental Registers of Births and Baptisms from 1761 to 1924. It also has records of births, baptisms, marriages, and deaths dating back to 1796—a great find for a genealogy researcher.

When the British were defeated, they left New York in 1783, and some slaves left with them. A special list of these former slaves—"Inspection Rolls"—was created and provides rather detailed information. The slave's name and other information can be found on roll 7 of Miscellaneous Papers of the Continental Congress, 1774–1789 (M 332) and roll 66 of Papers of the Continental Congress, 1774–1779 (M247).

The National Archives also has emancipation papers from 1862 and 1863 (M433) and some manumission papers from 1857 to 1863 (M433). The latter are for slaves who were freed by their owners, freed upon the death of the owner, or paid for their freedom.

But My Relative Didn't Serve

Not everyone served in the military. So some of us may feel left out here. But don't forget that once the draft was instituted (1863), all males had to register. And certainly if you had family here by World War I, it is likely the male members between ages 18 and 45 adhered to the law and registered, even if they never entered service.

Draft registration cards are kept at the NARA branch in East Point, Georgia, and you can request a search by filling out a request form and supplying the person's full name and address at the time of registration. While the information on the draft registration varies, it may contain birth date and birthplace, citizenship status, occupation, nearest relative, and a physical description. These cards have also been filmed by the Mormon church and are available by request at any Family History Center.

WPA Records

Works Progress Administration (WPA) workers interviewed thousands of former slaves in the South during the Depression (between 1932 and 1935). Interviews were conducted in Washington, D.C., and in the following states: Alabama, Arizona, Arkansas, Colorado, Florida, Georgia, Indiana, Kansas, Kentucky, Maryland, Minnesota, Mississippi, Missouri, Nebraska, New York, North Carolina, Ohio, Oklahoma, Oregon, Rhode Island, South Carolina, Tennessee, Texas, Virginia, and Washington. More than 3,500 former slaves were interviewed. (Remember: your ancestor might have been living in a different state at interview time from where he lived as a slave.) These interviews eventually were cataloged in the Library of Congress as *Slave Narratives: A Folk History of Slavery*, which is available at WRHS.

The interviews were also compiled in an edited version, *The American Slave: A Composite Autobiography*, George Rawick, editor. The 41-volume set is available at the Cleveland Public Library and the Cuyahoga County Public Library.

William Still wrote *The Underground Rail Road* in 1872, and in it he lists names and descriptions of many African-Americans he helped to freedom. This book does not have an index, but the table of contents lists names for most entries. The book is available through the Cuyahoga County Public Library.

NARA Forms

NARA permits research requests, which requires the filing of various forms. These may be obtained by e-mail from their website: www.archives.gov.

You can e-mail them and put "forms" in the subject line; in the body of the message state the name and number of the forms you need, along with your name and home address. They will be sent via surface mail. Then fill out the forms, pay the required fee, and NARA will attempt to find the information you requested.

To request military service records and pension files, supply the following information to NARA: name of your ancestor, war in which he served or dates of service, and state from which he enlisted or was drafted (mustered in); for Civil War veterans, they will also need to know if your ancestor was a Union or Confederate soldier because those records are kept separately. As always, the more information you provide, the greater likelihood of a complete and speedy response.

Burial Records

The national cemetery system offers some genealogical services, such as burial date and location, to assist next of kin or close friends of the deceased. This is only for individuals buried in one of the nation's 120 national cemeteries. Searches are done only for one individual at a time. No form is required; no fee is charged. Write a letter including: soldier's full name (include alternate spellings); date and place of death; date and place of birth; state from which the person entered active duty; and military service branch. Records are on microfilm, alphabetically and then by death date, so hopefully even if you cannot provide every detail requested the search will still be done. Write to:

> **U. S. Department of Veterans Affairs**
> **National Cemetery Administration (402B)**
> Burial Location Request
> 810 Vermont Ave. NW,
> Washington, DC 20420

Most requests take four weeks for a reply. Be sure to include your return address and, if possible, an e-mail address. I found this information on the website www.cem.va.gov and then followed a link on "locating veterans."

What you will usually receive is: name, birth date, death date, date of interment, date entered and date separated from military, branch of service, rank and unit, cemetery section, and grave number.

Also, check the book series *Roll of Honor: Names of Soldiers Who Died in Defence of the American Union, Interred in the National Cemeteries*. Originally published in 27 volumes, this series now consists of about 10 books, grouped by the state in which a soldier was buried. It was reprinted by the Genealogical Publishing Co. in 1994 and also has a new index and supplement. (I found several listings for this book series on the "World Cat" database at my local Cuyahoga County Public Library as well as a copy of the 1994 edition at Cleveland Public Library.) It is also available on microfilm and can be ordered from any Family History Center.

17 Goldmine or Land Mine?
Using Computers to Your Advantage

Some of us were probably brought reluctantly into the computer age. Others may have embraced the technology like a newfound friend. Learning about genealogy without covering details on the use of computers would be like knowing only half the story. So no matter how you arrived at your level of computer use, let's tune up those skills so the journey can continue

If you do not already have a computer, I am not trying to sell you one. However you should know that the Internet offers family history researchers many benefits:

- A quick and easy way to contact people all over the world
- Access to information any time of the day or night
- Quick transfer of huge amounts of data

And of course if you have a computer, you also have the benefit of using computer software to organize, store, and share your family history information.

Genealogy Software

There are now several software programs from which to choose. Some, such as the Master Genealogist, Family Tree Maker, Ancestral Quest, and Personal Ancestral File, have been around for a long time. Others such as Roots Magic, Family Tree Legends, and My Roots for hand-held computers, are relatively new. There are websites and personal Web pages espousing the benefits or shortcomings of various genealogy software programs. Try going to http://groups.google.com and typing in "genealogy" as a search term. This led me to several newsgroups, one of which was soc.gen.methods, where I read opinions regarding software programs. Another good site for software comparison is www.mumford.ca/reportcard/repcard, which actually has a chart that grades various aspects of the software (such as reports, experience level, convenience).

Choosing which software to use is a personal decision, but I think it helps to see and hear what others are using before making up your mind. Be sure to ask what the person likes and dislikes about the program. Also check out the online sites associated with the software and see if you can try it free for 30 days. This is an excellent way of previewing the software.

Obviously you want to make sure that your software contains features important to you, such as Gedcom capability, chart-making functions, and a way to point out mistakes or missing information.

Not having a computer at your home does not mean you cannot use one. You can ask friends and family and use theirs, and most libraries offer computer use for their patrons either on a walk-in or sign-up basis. And you can learn the basics

The Right Program for You: Software

You may be wondering what computer software has quality genealogy materials. There are several, and most people will gladly share the pros and cons of their favorites with you. I suggest giving yourself a little time before deciding on a particular genealogy program. Although you can switch to a different one, it can be cumbersome. The most popular ones at this time are:

- **PAF Personal Ancestral File**, also called Ancestral Quest (free download from www.familysearch.org)
- **Family Tree Maker**
- **The Master Genealogist**
- **Family Origins/Roots Magic**
- **Brother's Keeper**

of computer use through courses at libraries, adult education classes offered through many communities and school systems, or local community college classes.

There is so much information available on the Internet that it easily overwhelms even the seasoned researcher. I recently heard that genealogy is the second most popular subject covered on the Internet. (The first one, sorry to say, is pornography.)

Let's face it: websites and their accompanying addresses (universal record locators, or URLs) are like rock bands: some, such as the Beatles, Kiss, and Ozzy Osbourne have been around "forever," while others are here today and gone tomorrow. In fact, in a recent newspaper article (the *Plain Dealer*, Sunday Life, Section L, page 7, July 6, 2003), James Billington, Librarian of Congress, states that the average life span for websites is just 44 days. However, many of the websites listed below defy that statistic. Plus I know from experience that though the website may no longer exist, putting the main part of the URL in a search engine may bring up the new and improved website and will often lead you to other websites offering the same or similar information. Some good, dependable search engines are: www.google.com, www.alltheweb.com, and www.hotbot.com.

Websites of Local Interest

Several websites are of particular interest for research on the Cleveland area. These include all of those for the area libraries and repositories described in previous chapters, as well as the following:

www.cpl.org is the home page for the Cleveland Public Library. Although this website is mentioned in Chapter 4, the ability to use the site to find death records is so valuable that I'm including it here, with these specific instructions: scroll down the page until you see "necrology file," click on this, and you will be able to search for death notices in the Cleveland newspapers. (Choose "about database" to get the specifics on what exactly is included.)

http://www.clevelandmemory.org offers over 10,000 images of Cleveland from private collections, newspapers, postcards, etcetera, with a very easy-to-use searchable database.

www.rootsweb.com was started as GenWeb in 1996 by Dale Schneider to help online genealogists. The collection of information on this site grows by leaps and bounds, and you should visit often. Aside from listing great information regarding family history (such as links to websites on Civil War regiments and details on getting vital records), RootsWeb offers ways to communicate with others about your particular genealogy question or problem.

www.rootsweb.com/~cemetery/Ohio/cuyahoga is the site for cemeteries in Cuyahoga County. This will take you to the Tombstone Transcription Project. The page currently consists of two columns: one lists the name of the cemetery or its location; the second lists the recorder or submitter of the information. If a link is in the name/location column, that means a list (usually a partial list) of those buried there is available; if a link is in the recorder/submitter column, you can e-mail the individual with questions.

http://ech.cwru.edu is a way to look up information on people, places, and organizations mentioned in the Encyclopedia of Cleveland History. But it offers much more, such as over 200 digital photos of the Cleveland area as well as a lot of other historical information about the region.

www.Cleveland.com/righttoknow is an interesting site with many helpful links to state agencies, an Ohio telephone directory, and various courts—both state and local.

CPL Website a Big Hit!

When the Cleveland Public Library made its necrology file database available online on 30 March 2001, they received 34,000 hits the first weekend! And they hadn't even announced that it was online.

Reaching Out via the Internet

Vince found out a few years ago that he is a direct descendant of David Weatherly, Sr. He did some Internet research on this family with varying degrees of success. His first online investigations prompted him to subscribe to the Philadelphia list at RootsWeb (Philly-Roots-L).

Vince admits to "engaging in this in a rather intense way, sometimes using a form letter and inquiring of all those who posted 'Weatherly' for Pennsylvania and other states. It was nothing for me to send out a hundred letters at a crack. I became known as one who can write a letter in such a fashion that people would be encouraged to read it. I put touches of humor in my messages and enjoyed writing them almost as much as learning the bits and pieces of information that were revealed to me."

During a visit, Vince's sister showed him a letter she'd found in a grocery bag filled with memorabilia from their parents. The letter discussed the estate of a relative and referenced a Joseph L. Weatherly. It also referred to the burial of J. L.'s wife and children in the family vault in Cleveland, Ohio.

At this point, Vince joined the OHCUYAHO-L mailing list. He sent a query, received no re-

Figure 17-1: J. L. Weatherly. *Courtesy of Vincent Edward Summers*

sponses, and withdrew from the list. After searching other surnames, Vince returned to Weatherly and again to OHCUYAHO-L.

He says, "This time I got a very fine and courteous offer. Another subscriber knew the cemetery where J. L. is buried and offered to take pictures of it for the modest fee of five dollars."

From the list, Vince also learned about websites associated with Cuyahoga County and found a link to an online reference with a search engine he could use—Encyclopedia of Cleveland (the *Encyclopedia of Cleveland History*, compiled and edited by David D. Van Tassel and John J. Grabowski). Accessing the site, Vince found two entries for J. L. Weatherly.

Vince decided to contact Cleveland State University for more information. He first wrote to the archivist. (Sometimes when contacting a university he'll try the alumni association.) CSU sent him a newspaper article about J. L. Weatherly detailing everything from his eating habits to his investment in coffee. The article also mentioned that the family had moved to Buffalo, New York, a lead that sent Vince to NYERIE-L, a RootsWeb mailing list for Erie County, New York (see "Websites of Local Interest" nearby for more about RootsWeb) for a lookup in the city directories.

And so Vince from Virginia was able to successfully complete lengthy family searches incurring only the cost of stamps—and five dollars for photos.

www.cuyahoga.oh.us/common gets you to the home page for Cuyahoga County Common Pleas Court, and www.cuyahoga.oh.us/probate leads you to the probate court home page. Every county will have similar websites. For example, Stark County has a probate court site with marriage records *(www.probate.co.stark.oh.us)* and offers a user-friendly way to search for all types of records.

Newsletters

For example, RootsWeb Review—a biweekly newsletter that arrives via e-mail (called an "e-zine")—contains information on new programs and services available, personal stories of success, and suggestions for how to overcome obstacles, as well as updates on lists of surname websites and much more. To subscribe, send an e-mail to: rootsweb-review-subscribe@rootsweb.com and type "subscribe" in the first line of the body of the e-mail.

Mailing Lists

RootsWeb also has mailing lists—you are placed on a list to receive e-mail that others on the list write regarding a specific location (Medina County) or surname (Arnoff) or special interest (obituaries, adoption). When you sign up, there is always a choice to receive the e-mails in "digest" mode or mail mode. "Digest" means you will get several messages all in one, and "mail mode" means you will receive each e-mail message separately, as it was sent to the list.

To find out what mailing lists exist, go to: http://resources.rootsweb.com/adopt.

To subscribe to the Portage County mailing list, send an e-mail to RootsWeb by typing in: Oh-Portage-L-request@rootsweb.com. If you want to receive it in digest mode, send the e-mail to: Oh-Portage-d-request@rootsweb.com. Or perhaps you have an interest in the Irish in Cleveland. Then your request would be to: Oh-Cleveland-Irish-L-request@rootsweb.com.

Message Boards

Using a message board is like looking at the bulletin board at the local supermarket or coffee shop. People post messages (in this case electronically), and you must go to the message board to see what is posted. If you are interested in the topic or item posted, you can write in and add your ideas, comments, or suggestions. Or just view the replies from others, and learn from fellow researchers in this way as well.

Message boards are organized by surnames, locations (country, state, county), or topic (e.g., naturalization information on Trumbull County). There are also ways you can ask to be notified if a message board contains information on a topic of particular interest to you. When you decide to " post" on a message board, or join a list, you might want to post the same question ("query") in more than one place. In that way, someone searching Italian ancestors who first settled in Warren, Ohio might post a message on the Trumbull County list, as well as on a list for Italians.

User-contributed Databases

Volunteers list information they have found or transcribed on these databases. For example, someone may have a list of all the alumni from Buchtel High School Class of 1966. They make this available to users of RootsWeb in the user-contributed database section, under the heading "high school alumni." These databases can also include a particular batch of census records, cemetery enumerations, or list of schoolteachers employed in Akron during a particular time period.

Remember, before you accept the information you receive from the Internet or by other methods, you must verify it by checking the original source, if possible.

Family trees

Family trees can be posted at: http://worldconnect.rootsweb.com, which offers a free website. You can apply for one at: http://freepages.genealogy.rootsweb.com/. These free Web pages have certain regulations to which you must agree. Be sure to read and adhere to them.

International Internet Connection

Luther O. received an e-mail from Nanna, who lives in Gudbrands-dalen, Norway. She was browsing the guest books on one of the websites for Norwegian genealogy and came across Luther's message regarding the surname Johannesse in relation to certain places in Oyer, where she lived. Because Nanna had the church books for Oyer as well as several censuses, she offered to look up information for Luther. He sent his Gedcom file to Nanna, who wrote back, "I recognized part of your family tree at once, as Ingebjorg T. came from the farm where I live, Kaldor. You can visit the Kaldor farm on the Web." (www.kaldor.no/ged-com/index)

Thus began a long correspondence in which the two discussed Norwegian naming practices, the celebration of Constitution Day—including if Nanna's bunad (a folk dress with a tight bodice, and much ornate stitching) will fit her—and, of course, the weather.

As the e-mail relationship continued, Luther discovered that his second cousin, Jean, was related to him through Nanna's father, who was a cousin of Luther's father. This meant that Jean and Luther were related by two entirely separate lines.

He even learned that a significant battle took place on the farm of his ancestors in about the year 1000.

World GenWeb Project

The World GenWeb Project still exists and is connected with RootsWeb. You can access it at www.worldgenweb.org or through links at RootsWeb. The home page states that GenWeb offers "free research guidance from our worldwide network of volunteer genealogists" and that their goal is for every country in the world to be involved and become "an online resource for international genealogists."

The site is divided into 11 world regions, which are further divided by country, and then state, county, or province. You can learn what records are available and link to websites, including those with databases and repositories. The site is very easy to use; you do not have to guess if the country you are researching is part of Western or Eastern Europe, for example. I found easy links to the Budapest Archives and an excellent chart explaining how to perform advanced searches.

Other Genealogy Websites

Speaking of tombstones, cemetery research is an important part of family history work. More than 40,000 cemeteries in the United States are listed at www.Ceme-teryJunction.com, as well as at least 2,100 in Canada and approximately 495 in Australia. This is a good site to visit because it also has links to transcriptions done by volunteers and to other genealogically relevant websites.

There are many, many genealogy websites that can meet your needs. Take the time to follow links from one website to another. For example, I did this, and it led me to a relatively (pun intended) new website: CousinConnect.com. The expressed purpose of the website is to be a "genealogy query database." The difference between this genealogy website and others is (according to them) that their website is easier to use because it does not have long conversations on message boards, just a query with names and relevant information. As with so many other sites, a free online newsletter is available, and posting instructions are easy to follow. Here are some other websites to check out:

www.findagrave.com—If you are looking for the final resting place of the famous or infamous, visit this site.

www.itd.nps.gov/cwss—Have a Civil War sailor or soldier in your family? Try this site to check for more information on that individual. You can search by surname, regiment, state, or unit number.

www.myfamily.com—allows families to communicate via secure websites. There is a fee involved, although they do offer a free trial for 30 days.

www.ancestry.com—a paid subscription service to thousands of databases, with a locality search section and a series of "research guides." They also offer online genealogy courses for a fee, as well as free access to certain portions of their databases. You can also sign up to receive their e-mail newsletter for free by going to the website and choosing "Learning Center," and then going to "Newsletter Management Center." The historical newspapers available with a paid subscription can be a great source of family history data. At this time they do not have the Cleveland papers (new databases are being added all the time), but newspapers from several nearby towns are available, including Canton, Elyria, Lorain, and Ravenna. These often have Cleveland-related stories that include many lists of people—such as the names of people in attendance at a reunion or 25th wedding anniversary. According to information on the website, nearly half the content on the ancestry.com website is available free to any visitor.

www.familyhistory.com—has a database you can search by subject (marriage, Ohio) as well as surname lists and free message boards. More is available to paid subscribers.

www.cyndislist.com—one of the biggest, most comprehensive genealogy sites and a gateway to many more sites as well. Take the time to become familiar with this site: it will lead you to a lot of excellent and useful information.

Afrigeneas.com—covers African-American genealogy, with some transcriptions of Slave Manifests for the Port of New Orleans, some bills of sale, and slaveowner documentation, and United States Colored Troops service records.

Amberskyline.com/treasuremaps—Robert Ragan publishes a monthly newsletter and sends it to subscribers via e-mail. Although he does not charge, he asks for donations, and I've found the variety and depth of information covered in the newsletter to be well worth a modest donation. He also advertises various "how to" guides on searches, organization of records, and computer techniques. A good place to visit.

www.ccharity.com—Known as Christy's Genealogy Website. Christine Cheryl Charity is the author of this website that focuses on African-American genealogy. The U.S. Internet Genealogical Society (USIGS) designated it as "site of the month" in October 1997. The homepage provides links to searchable databases on the left side and descriptions of noteworthy articles on the right. She accepts contributions from others interested in African-American genealogy. On a recent visit to the site, I found links and an article about oral history and many databases, including one for immigrants sent to Liberia from 1820–1843; tax lists for Surry County, Virginia; and a partial list of African-Americans lynched since 1859.

Veteran Researcher Tries New Trick

Brent recently decided to use one of the popular search engines to look up his relatives. Brent has been involved in researching his family tree for more than 15 years. Although he had done this type of research several years ago, putting in just the last name, this time he went to some of the newer search engines and put in the full name of his Revolutionary War ancestor—and guess what? He got 11 "hits" (responses), of which six were for his ancestor and actually did provide new information.

www.rootsweb.com/~iapottaw/WgnTrnIndx.htm—Looking for a relative who might have headed west during the 1849 California Gold Rush? They might have passed through Council Bluffs, Iowa, where the *Frontier Chronicle* often included the names of men on the wagon trains. Supposedly, more people passed through Council Bluffs than through St. Joseph and Independence, Missouri, combined. The ongoing newspaper extracts can be found here.

www.Familychronicle.com—offers previews and summaries of some of the articles available in the magazine Family Chronicle, and a way to subscribe from the website.

www.genealogy.com—has some good information, including how-to articles, tracing immigrants, and ways to interest and involve children in genealogy. At the site http://GenForum.com, which is hosted by genealogy.com, there are various forums (same as message boards) that one can search or subscribe to; these are organized by surname, state, country, region, and general topic. All, of course, are genealogy related. They also offer many other services with a paid subscription.

www.familyhistory.com/societyhall/main.asp.—Need to locate a genealogical society in an area of interest either by locale or by ethnic or religious group? Go to the website of the Federation of Genealogical Societies (FGS) "Society Hall." Search by location, keyword, or chapter name.

Digital Images; Digital Cameras

The era of digital cameras is well upon us. The advantage of digital pictures is not just the instantaneousness of the medium but its portability and versatility. For example, by using the view mode you can immediately see how the picture will look and decide if it's what you want. You have the choice of printing the picture via your home computer and printer (at a choice of sizes), sending it to a website that will print it for you, or taking it to your local photo shop. You can also e-mail it to friends and family, save it in your genealogy files, or put in up on your website. Another advantage is the ability to enhance the picture, including old pictures found in scrapbooks or other files. For more on digital photos, check magazines such as PC Photo and the May 2003 issue of Consumer Reports (www.consumer-reports.org), which has a digital photo guide in it.

Web-Based Image Searches

Google now has a special image search, which can be found at http://images.google.com. You can use this to search digital images on any Web page—there are thousands, so read some of the advanced searching techniques (link is available on the Google home page) to narrow it down.

Also check out the Ohio and American Memory project at http://memory.loc.gov, as well as one specifically on Cleveland (http://www.clevelandmemory.org), which has over 10,000 images with a searchable database.

Have any old photographs you cannot identify? Visit http://www.familychronicle.com /rootsweb where a new feature explains how to date photos and offers several photos from which to compare.

None of these Internet stories could be successful without the kindness of strangers—the willingness of people who've never met us to go out of their way, take the time, and simply perform a random act of genealogical kindness (raogk). And there is actually a website for just such folks and such requests: www.raokg.org. The site offers ways to volunteer and explains the process for making a request. Typical requests include asking for a picture of a tombstone, or a lookup in a book or local database.

When genealogical research is aided by other people, some researchers believe their ancestors are "showing them the way," and sometimes there may even have

French Connection

In rereading some of his late mother's genealogy research, Jim Jacquet read a sentence written in 1966 by a cousin: "The Jacquet album is with Scheetz." This was the first Jim had heard about a photo album—he had surmised that his mother never pursued it any further.

Jim recognized the surname "Scheetz" from his previous research. Delphine Jacquet married Anthony Myers, lived in Louisville, Ohio, and had three daughters. One of those daughters, Wilda Myers/Meyers, married William Scheetz and moved to Canton, Ohio. And at that point, Jim lost track of the Scheetz line.

Jim posted a query at http://genforum.genealogy.com for the Scheetz name and received an e-mail from a man in Florida who was a Scheetz descendent.

Figure 17-2: Francois and Francoise Jacquet came to the U.S. in 1846 and settled in Stark County, Ohio. *Courtesy of Jim Jacquet*

As a result of that e-mail Jim now is in possession of a family photo album that had been missing for 130 years! His cousin Sam in Florida inherited this album and shared it with him. Jim has a website where he posts the photos, hoping visitors will be able to identify some of the people in them.

Some of the photos are of Albert Ambrose Jacquet. And since posting the pictures, Jim has received help in identifying another individual, Eugene Balizet, in two more of the photos.

Jim Jacquet grew up in Cleveland Heights but now lives in Washington state. From his mother's notes he knows that Albert Ambrose Jacquet and his wife Celestine Balizet moved their family from Louisville, in Stark County, Ohio, to Cleveland because of the panic of 1893/1894.

Random Acts of Genealogical Kindness

Ray Tindira's story is one that demonstrates true "raogk"—random acts of genealogical kindness. Ray sent a letter to the St. Louis Genealogical Society in the mid-1980s asking for information on his Tindira family. The letter got put in a query file at the society's offices.

Several years later, when Ray returned home from a vacation, there was a packet awaiting him. A woman named Brenda, who lived in East St. Louis (across the river from St. Louis), sent pedigree charts for one side of his family. Brenda's son married a girl whose grandmother was a Tindira. Brenda had been going through the query file at the St. Louis Genealogical Society, and because she had done such thorough genealogical research she had included her daughter-in-law Joyce's family. Margaret Tindira was Joyce's grandmother. And John Tindira, Jr., was Ray's grandfather.

Brenda sent Ray postcards of, and brochures about, the lead mine where John Tindira, Sr., (Ray's great-grandfather) had worked. According to the article, visitors (including Jacques Cousteau) came from all over the world to dive at Bonne Terre, Missouri. It is one of the largest scuba-diving facilities in United States because of the great visibility and constant temperatures.

Ray and Brenda began corresponding. She once drove 60 miles and took pictures of the rebuilt church where his grandfather was baptized.

They continued to correspond. One or two years later, Ray went on vacation, and again upon his return there was a large envelope awaiting him. The envelope was not from Brenda, but from her mother. Brenda, who was trying to save money by parking a little farther away from work, had been shot and killed on her way from the parking lot. Brenda's mother sent Ray newspaper articles about the incident and the arrest of the perpetrators.

Ray was stunned, and touched by the kindness of these strangers.

"You contact people who are your direct relatives, and they won't help you. Here's a woman who was not even my relative, and look how much she helped me. She sent me a wealth of information."

been a bit of divine intervention. Whether you attribute it to coincidence or a gentle nudge from above, these stories make the search all the more mysterious and intriguing.

So now you've become more familiar with the woes and wiles of the Web. It's also fun, challenging, massive, and most of all, continually changing. Remember, neither the information nor the people using it are infallible. You may want to develop a more in-depth understanding of how to use the Internet and how to use any information you find to assist you in uncovering your family history. For this I refer you to your local library and bookstore, both of which have many, many books and even audiotapes on genealogy and the Internet (a few are in the bibliography at the end of this book).

You may also need help with keeping up with new websites and search engines—especially those that are "gen friendly." For this, I refer you to friends, genealogy societies, computer-based genealogy groups, genealogy message boards, and the many other networking groups in your personal and virtual community. Good luck, and don't forget to share the wealth with others.

St. Francis to the Rescue

Al writes: "I began my genealogical research on my mother's side. Her maiden name was Wilberscheid. Her parents lived with us when we were growing up, so I knew that part of the history. But her paternal grandfather, my great-grandfather, was more difficult. One uncle remembered great-grandfather's name as Paul, but no one in the family ever mentioned any other Wilberscheids.

"In my research I eventually found a death record for Sybilla Wilberscheid. I had no idea where she fit into the scheme of things.

"I met Paul W. of Nashotah, Wisconsin, through a cousin and developed a relationship with him over the Internet. Paul then sent Ann H. of Wisconsin to me (via the Internet) because she had a Wilberscheid from Cleveland in her line. While Paul had volumes on the Wilberscheids from Wisconsin, he had nothing on any Cleveland Wilberscheids. Ann asked if I knew anything about her grandmother, Pauline G. Wilberscheid, or her great-grandmother, Sybilla Wilberscheid. I sent her the death record and learned that although Ann never lived in Cleveland, the part of her family she was researching attended St. Francis parish at E.79th Street and Superior Avenue. Ann introduced me to her mother, who lived in Medina, and an aunt in Dayton. They told me their relatives never mentioned any other Wilberscheids other than their immediate family. I was fairly certain we were talking about two unconnected, totally nonrelated families, and I began referring to my family as the Schempp Wilberscheids and Ann's as the St. Francis Wilberscheids.

"And so things stayed until I accepted an offer from a friend to judge a speech contest in September 1999. I was asked to participate because my friend broke his hand and needed a driver. The contest was held at St. Francis School, and when we arrived we met Father Thomas F. Martin, the pastor. Out of the blue, I asked if I could see the record books for baptism, marriage, and death. Within minutes I saw 12 Wilberscheid records. One name stood out—it was the baptismal records of my Uncle Victor. This proved that my Schempp Wilberscheids and the St. Francis Wilberscheids belonged to the same parish and surely knew one another. Meanwhile, Paul in Wisconsin sent me a family tree showing that Nicholas, Joseph, and Jacob Wilberscheid were all sons of Johann and Catherine Wilberscheid. All of the Schempp Wilberscheids are related to Nicholas, and all of the St. Francis Wilberscheids are related to Joseph. Paul's Wilberscheids and my Wilberscheids were both from the same small town in the Rhineland. It is now very clear that all these Wilberscheids are members of the same family.

"The clue that the Cleveland Wilberscheids were not separate families came from a chance meeting at St. Francis Church because I agreed to drive my friend to a speech contest."

18 Are We Done Yet?

Well, it's been quite a journey. Have you enjoyed the trip? And did you take time to "smell the roses" as well? Remember those long car trips when you were a kid? The mantra of "Are we there yet?" is just a memory away. And once you arrived at your destination—after stretching your legs, and getting a bite to eat and some rest—didn't you want to hop back in, and take another trip? Just as with that long car ride or airplane flight, we're always relieved to finally arrive at our destination. And so at this point, you must ask yourself if, indeed, you have gone far enough in your research and finally arrived at your destination. And, what do you want to do with the information you've found?

You have already saved, organized, and preserved your findings while doing the research. Now it is time to think about how you might show off a few of your relatives or prized stories.

If your motivation for researching your family was simply getting the answer to a particular question (Why was Uncle Leon afraid to travel out of the country? Answer: his parents died in Europe, and he left there as a child with no papers or passport), preserving that information for the next generation may be as simple as writing down the information and storing it in a safe place. However, if you've done extensive research, you may want to do something more creative, such as:

- Make a scrapbook (there are often adult education classes on this subject)
- Frame some pictures
- Make an audiotape or videotape of your collection
- Display your family history in elaborate family trees, a quilt, or an illustrated family group sheet

Some of us will be happy if we can trace our family back three generations, fill out all the lines on the ancestral chart, and share the information with other family members.

Others may become such good investigators that their goal will be to constantly go further back in the history of their family. In fact, I've met people who can trace their roots to the 16th century and are still pursuing more.

Information can be shared in a variety of ways, too. Some may want to send their Gedcom to the Church of Latter-day Saints, or to various websites and organizations. In this way others who may be related can access it; those doing their own searches can find information on collateral lines, and the original submitter may eventually gain new information. At the very least you have the satisfaction of possibly helping others either now or in the future.

Many family history buffs want future generations to benefit from their long

Black-and-White Movies

Don't dismiss black-and-white movies as "old." The film itself may be less perishable than that on which color movies or prints are made due to the chemicals involved. Check with a professional. Check old home movies (prior to 1951) to see if they were made on nitrate stock (the word "nitrate" or an explosion icon will be on the side of the film). Such films are made of highly combustible material—you really should consult with a professional on how best to preserve them.

◆

hours of painstaking work. You may choose to write a brief family history, put all the personal files in notebooks, and give them to your children and grandchildren. Or, you may even consider publishing a book containing this information.

Writing and Publishing Your Family's Story

As you think about putting together your family history for others to see and read, think about what makes a book or story interesting to you. Recognize that certain aspects of your family history may appeal only to you. Do you want everything written from your point of view? Or do you want to state some facts without comments?

Of course you'll want to present your story so it is easy to read and follow. Putting the information into different segments, using topic headings, and separating information by time periods, individual families, or location may also serve to make the book one that others will read and not just store on their bookshelf.

What to Include

Is this your autobiography or a family history? Should you include interviews? Pictures? Letters?

Of course the answer is very personal. But keep in mind your purpose. And look at what others have done before you commit to your format. Pictures really add another dimension, and with current technology most photographs reproduce well. Do you want to write about people at different times in their lives? Do you want to focus on events such as weddings, holidays, and vacations? Don't forget pets.

Formats

Described below are a variety of formats or designs you can use to present your family history.

The Story Format. You can write about your life as a story with details down to what the kitchen looked like, or what it was like to be in the high school band. Be sure to include information about your family life in an interesting, story-fashion form. In his book, A Complete Guide to Writing Your Family History, Kempthorne calls this "re-creating your family experience."

The Topic Format. You may choose to write about each family member and cover just one or two topics for each person. For this you might want to start with an outline of who to include and what topics to include for each person.

Charts-Plus-Vignettes Format. You may wish to reproduce your five-generation chart and then write vignettes about particular people or events. To prepare for this kind of family history writing, choose one person, say your father, and make a list of things he told you about his life. This will likely lead you to incidents you want to include relating to your mother, or a vignette about a family vacation. You don't want to write about every vacation, just enough so the reader gets a flavor of what those experiences were like and how people interacted in those situations.

Chronological Format. Perhaps you simply want to write what happened year by year. Such a chronological summary can be easy to organize and provides facts for which you may choose to make certain comments or offer more extensive details.

It's a Small, Small World

Lynette Filips's paternal grandparents were divorced when her father was quite young. His only childhood recollection of relatives on that side of the family was of Great Aunt Anna, who lived in New York City and visited the family once in Cleveland. Anna was the widow of Lynette's great-uncle, who was an Orthodox priest.

Knowing of Lynette's interest in genealogy, Lynette's paternal aunt, Virginia, gave her some papers, including the marriage certificate for Lynette's paternal grandparents. These documents stated her grandfather's nationality was Austrian, although Lynette had heard he was Ukrainian. A modest perusal of history books revealed that Ukrainians living in the region of Galicia in 1910 were under the rule of the Austro-Hungarian Empire.

To gain further knowledge of the political situation at the time, Lynette spoke with a Ukrainian neighbor, Irene P. In the course of their conversation Irene asked, "What was your grandfather's surname?"

"Filipowsky," replied Lynette.

"Oh," responded Irene, "my husband Emil had a great aunt Anna Philipovsky/Filipowsky who lived in New York City."

"And Aunt Anna's husband was an Orthodox priest. . . . ," said Lynette. All Irene had to do was nod her head in agreement. Imagine their surprise! They were not only neighbors, but through marriage they shared a great-aunt 500 miles away.

Lynette now realizes that her childhood memory of Great-aunt Anna's visit likely occurred when Anna was in town for the wedding of Irene and Emil.

Sometimes it is indeed a small world.

Picture Format. Another family history record can be an annotated photo album arranged chronologically or by family group with brief typed text naming people and events. Or how about considering a digital photo album? (See Chapter 17.)

Autobiographical Format. Write about yourself and your experiences and bring in information and details regarding the extended family as you see fit.

Specific Purpose Format. Perhaps you want future generations to understand about your ethnic heritage, or the family tradition of military service. You can use your Ancestral Chart as a way to explain how and why your family ended up living in Lorain, Ohio, or why so many men were policemen, or so many women were active in certain clubs or activities.

Entertainment and Information Format. Do you have a specific audience in mind? Are you writing this as a way to finish your family history research and put it all together? Do you intend to give this to your children and grandchildren? Do you want strangers to read this? This type of family history may serve to inspire others to do similar work. Perhaps interspersing anecdotes with factual information and some citations as to where that information was found would be a good combination.

Tough Decisions

What about family secrets? Do you include them, or not? While this is a complicated matter not to be dismissed lightly, in my opinion two things should be considered:

1. Is the secret important to a currently living relative?
2. Is it vitally important to your family's history (for example, an illegitimate birth, or previous marriage)?

If writing about the "secret" would seriously hurt a living relative, I would consider not doing so, and writing an addendum to be included at a later time. If you really feel the information must be included, I suggest letting the affected individuals know first, rather than having them find out from someone else. The goal should be a balanced accounting of the situation or information.

Sources for Graphics

Photographs, animated graphics, special backgrounds, and other nontextual information can make genealogy more interesting and lively. These can be used in a variety of ways: include them in your written family history book, make them part of a newsletter your share with family members, or add them to parts of your genealogy files or records. Sometimes a picture, even though not of your particular family member, may help you say something better than words.

Here are a few websites that offer free graphics or clip art. You will find everything from flags of countries, to old-fashioned cars, holiday images, cemetery art, and religious symbols. The sites explain their rules for use of the materials, which usually include not using images for commercial or for-profit purposes. It is important that you read these policies before using the websites. And then you could add these images to your family newsletter, use them for added interest in a family reunion booklet, or put them in a family history you self-publish. To find more sites, go to a search engine and type in "free clip art" or "free graphics":

- www.aaclipart.com
- www.freegraphics.com/
- www.free-graphics.com
- www.coolgraphics.com
- www.geocities.com/ (type in "genealogy" as a search term)
- www.mayflowerfamilies.com/freebkins/

Starting the Writing

Sometimes the hardest thing about writing something is beginning it. Try these "story starters":

Think of the house (one of many, perhaps) where you grew up. Describe your bedroom. Did you share it with a sibling? Who else lived with you, who were your neighbors, where did you play? This is a good way to begin writing about yourself and also may be good when interviewing older family members.

Look through an old photo album and start writing about the people and events in the pictures.

Pick a year and write about what happened in the world that year, and then connect that to where you lived and what you did, describing how current events affected you and your family.

Publishing Your Story

Unless you or your relative qualify as a famous, or perhaps infamous, individual, most commercial publishing houses will not be interested in publishing your family history. But that shouldn't stop you from getting it into print.

You can publish it yourself right from your computer. Or you can go to any of the commercial copy centers and ask them to print and bind your manuscript into book form.

You can also use a "vanity press" (pay-to-publish company), look at the major genealogical publishing houses (Heritage Quest, Ancestry, Genealogical Publishing Co.), or try looking at some of the family histories available at places like WRHS and see who they used as a publisher.

As important and helpful as the Internet can be, nothing can replace good old-fashioned person-to-person contact. One of the best ways to increase that personal contact while adding to your genealogical repertoire is by belonging to or visiting genealogical groups and historical societies. You will find people with similar interests and varying degrees of expertise who are willing to help, want to learn, and always have a good tale to tell.

Genealogists are Relatively Nice

Ray met Duncan Gardiner, a local researcher, at the Polish Genealogical Society meeting and went up to Gardiner after his talk. As Ray introduced himself, Gardiner commented that "Tindira" was a name he knew. Ray thought, yeah, right. Wouldn't you know, a few weeks later Gardiner called Ray. Gardiner gave Ray the phone number of a woman for whom he'd been doing genealogical research who had a Tindira in her family tree, and who lived about two miles away from Ray. Gardiner had been retained by this woman to help with her genealogical research. Ray called and soon discovered a new relative. When they met, Ray took with him some pictures he had but could not identify. This woman had the same pictures—only she knew exactly who was in them.

You never know from whence your help will come—so network!

Many genealogy groups publish a monthly or quarterly newsletter. Be sure to read it carefully. See the story on the next page for a reason why.

Hiring Help

You cannot, or may not want to, do it all. There are many people who are qualified to do your family research—for a price. Not all of us have the time and patience to do all this work ourselves. Some people prefer to hire a professional to conduct all of the research; others get help at certain points in their research—either when they feel stuck, or perhaps when it involves information needed from other countries.

Cindy writes, "While helping put my genealogy society's newsletter together, I came across a query from a fellow in Australia. What really caught my eye was that he had requested information about my father's family. As I read his query, a strange tingling sensation began. Not only was he asking about my paternal grandfather, William Brandt, but also my great-grandfather and great-grandmother, and he had their address in Cleveland at the turn of the century. This man also listed my great-great-grandfather, but with a different first name than my records indicated.

"Some of the information about my grandfather's children was incorrect—the researcher had connected to the wrong family at that point. That's where having knowledge about the area where someone lives comes in handy. I had come across this same family but knew that none of my immediate family lived on the West Side of Cleveland at the time.

"I wrote to the gentleman in Australia with my family information and he immediately called me. We were definitely connected through my great-great-grandfather and his great-grandfather. My ancestors came to Ohio and his moved from Germany to Serbia.

"One fantastic result of our connection is that he was able to provide me with information to take me back two more generations in Germany, with documentation, no less."

Where to Look

Check for the magazine Everton's Genealogical Helper (available at most large libraries, including the Cleveland Public Library, the Cuyahoga County Public Library, and the Western Reserve Historical Society Library)—it has ads indexed by state and region. You can also go online to www.everton.com, select "genealogy center," and then choose "find a professional," which will allow you to search by name or area of expertise.

Look at websites for such organizations as American Professional Genealogists (www.apgen.org) or Board of Certified Genealogists (www.bcgcertification.org). Both of these allow you to search for a researcher by geographic region and/or specialty.

Inquire at local historical societies or libraries. Sometimes local libraries (especially those with sizable genealogical collections) have bulletin boards that list local researchers for hire. Asking staff at any local library or repository is a good idea.

What to Expect

You are hiring someone to perform a job. As with any other contract, make sure both parties know and understand what they are agreeing to.

As the person requesting the service, make sure you clearly communicate what you expect to the person you are considering hiring. Are there limits to your budget, or to the amount of time you want spent on specific areas of research? What do you expect to get from this? Maybe verification of one or more events, copies of documents, suggestions of what needs to be done next. Do you want a pedigree chart filled out?

It is reasonable to expect a final report from the researcher. If it is a long-term project, regular updates are appropriate.

Your Part

You will need to provide specific, detailed information (probably copies of ancestor charts, family group records, etc.) and state exactly what questions you wish answered.

According to Duncan Gardiner, a professional genealogist in Lakewood, Ohio, most professionals work and charge for their service on an hourly basis. Many have a three-hour minimum. He feels the relationship works best when the person hiring has an idea of what kind of information they want, and perhaps a goal of what specifically they are hoping to find. Other than that, the hired professional needs to be given enough information from the outset to make it possible to collect data and documentation.

Old Houses Really Do Hold More Than Charm

There is a century house at the corner of Prospect and French streets in Berea. Pam X's father used to tell her that he would go there as a child to visit Grandma Siebert and play in the large orchard in the back. That would have been in the 1930s. Pam and her husband, Fred, often wondered if the house was still in the Siebert family but did not want to intrude. A few years ago there were signs of major remodeling activities at the property, and as Fred passed by he decided to introduce himself. The gentleman standing in front of the garage turned out to be Pam's father's first cousin. Just two days before, while pulling off old drywall panels in the bathroom, this man (Stanley B.) found many papers, including a birth certificate for Pam's great-grandfather Adelbert Ludwig Georg Siebert, born in Prussia, as well as pictures of both Adelbert and his wife Susan.

A Trip to the Cemetery

A trip to Woodvale Cemetery was also helpful. Computerized records indicated that five Sieberts were buried at Woodvale. Two separate graves belonged to Adelbert and Susan Siebert, one was for their son Phillip, and two others did not match any names known to Pam and Fred. As they left the cemetery, Fred went to look for Phillip's grave. He found it—an unusually large stone with the inscription "Phillip Siebert, 1905–1939" at the top. As he walked back to his car, Fred turned to have one more look. There on the other side of the headstone were three more names: James McMunn, 1832–1899; Charlott (his wife), 1835–1918, and his sister, Ann, 1881. And at the bottom was the inscription: "Natives of Co. Sligo, Ireland, Erected by Charlott Brett McMunn."

On to the Historical Society

The couple then went to the Berea Historical Society, where they learned that the first owners of the house at Prospect and French streets were James and Charlott McMunn. They also located an obituary in the 1898 Berea Gazette on the death of James McMunn, Berea's "oldest quarry man." More research at the historical society led to the information that Phillip Siebert was a firefighter in Berea and is listed in the book Men of Grit and Greatness.

By checking old subdivision maps, Pam and Fred saw that after the death of Charlott in 1923 the house on Prospect went to Martha Siebert, Pam's great-aunt. Then in 1924 ownership of the house passed to Susan Siebert, Pam's great-grandmother.

And On to the County Archives

The gravestone information from Woodvale sent Pam to the Cuyahoga County Archives looking for obituaries on James, Ann, and Charlott. While helping Pam and Fred, Glenda, one of the staff members at the Archives, casually mentioned that there were probate record numbers for both Charlott and Ann. Glenda told them that probate records are located in the basement of the County Courthouse.

You Guessed It! And Next to—Probate Records

Although checking out probate records was not high on the couple's list, "one day curiosity got the better of me," said Fred, so he went to probate court. He continues, "Ann's probate was just a single-line entry in a ledger, but Charlott from the mystery house had a probate record one can be proud of. We ended up in a room that was narrow but about 40 feet in length, with sheet-metal drawers from floor to ceiling. Using a hook on the end of a long rod, a woman pulled out a box from near the ceiling and handed me a packet of legal papers, 105 pages in all. I was given a desk to work at but soon concluded I was too nervous to determine what was important enough to copy and what not. At 10 cents a page I went for the whole bundle. Among them, we found several pedigrees linking several dozen names. From here we learned that Charlott's sister Fanny Brett married William Irwin, their daughter Ann Irwin married Robert Lawson, and that couple had several children of which one, Susan Jane Lawson, Pam's great-grandmother, married Adelbert Siebert."

Acknowledgments

I would like to thank the following individuals for graciously contributing material for this book:

Sheila and Manfred Adler, Mary Ananea, Mary Bacon Artino, Jo Banks, Oswaldo Bejarano, John Stark Bellamy II, Judith Bolan, Coreen Bush, Rita M. Carfagno, Marie Chesbro, Sandra G. Craighead, Cecilia Eppink, Ann Crile Esselstyn, Lynette E. Filips, Shawn Godwin, Robert D. Gries, Patricia Syverson Hatz, Hazel Head, Kenneth W. Hicks, James Jacquet, Carolyn A. James, Carl L. Johnson, Louise T. Jones, Lisa Kubit, S. Sterling McMillan III, Sandra J. Malitz, Cheryl J. Marone, Manfred Mondt, Brent D. Morgan, Margo Morgan, Sandra Morgan, Murlan Jeremiah Murphy II, Murlan J. (Jerry) Murphy Jr., Ray Murphy, Lucinda Brandt Newton, Betsie Norris, James F. O'Donnell, Luther Olson, Grace M. Phipps, Drew Rolik, Dennis Sherwin, Gary Silverstein, Feige Stern, Marilyn Kerr Sauer, Suzanne Walling Soltess, Albert H. Schempp, Vincent Edward Summers, Bill Takacs, Raymond Tindira, Louise B. Tucker, Cynthia Turk, William Edward Vigler, Carole Villarreal, Daniel Volper, and Anita B. Watson.

These institutions generously cooperated on this project and allowed use of photos or forms: the Cleveland Public Library, the Ohio Historical Society, the Cuyahoga County Archives, the Cuyahoga County Public Library, the Ohio Historical Society, and the Western Reserve Historical Society.

This book is the culmination of the effort, collaboration, and support of many people. While I am indebted to everyone who helped me on this project, the following deserve special recognition:

Thanks to these friends for their guidance, empathy, and steadfast support: Mary Ananea, Judy Eigenfeld, Sharon Goelman, Binnie Gun, Drew Rolik, and Marie Weiss Herlevi.

Thanks are due to my editor Karen Fuller, the entire staff at Gray & Company, and Ted Schwarz, for leading me to Gray & Co. in the first place.

While numerous people helped me with the research for this book, special thanks go to Sandra Malitz, who gave freely of her time and exceptional knowledge.

I am grateful to the many well-informed and highly skilled staff members at the Cleveland Public Library, Cuyahoga County Public Library, Cuyahoga County Archives, Red Cross, and Western Reserve Historical Society—your presence strengthens and energizes this community.

I cannot express adequate thanks to my family for enduring the complaints, frustrations, and excitement of a book "in process" for three years—most especially my children Kiva, Rachel, and Ariana.

To the numerous people who entrusted me with their stories and priceless memorabilia, I value your generosity in sharing with me so I could share with others about your families.

To the personnel at all the courthouses, archives, and libraries I called repeatedly, your patience and tolerance is appreciated.

I am indebted to the Antioch Writers' Workshop for providing a sense of community to writers and would-be writers and lending a hand so many have a chance to fulfill their dreams.

Appendix A:
Where Do I Find It? Records A–Z

One purpose of this book is to make the research easier for the researcher. This section is meant to serve as a point of easy, and hopefully frequent, reference and will come in handy often. Whether you are just beginning your trip back in family history or you are a seasoned genealogist, you are constantly being flooded with facts and details as they pertain to your family. We simply can't remember everything, but by including this as a separate chapter we're making it easier to locate information by subject matter or record type.

Most of these records can be ordered and then viewed at one of the Family History Centers. We suggest calling your local FHC to find out specifically what records they have, or can get, that apply to your research areas. Where "FHC" is listed, we are certain that the materials can be ordered. Where "FHC(K-In)" is listed, this denotes that it is kept in-house at Kirtland (always there, no need to order beforehand).

KEY
CCA Cuyahoga County Archives
CPL Cleveland Public Library
FHC Family History Center
FHC(K-In) Family History Center, Kept In-House
FPK Fairview Park Library
WRHS Western Reserve Historical Society

ACCELERATED INDEXING SYSTEMS INTERNATIONAL (AISI)

The AISI (Accelerated Indexing Systems International) is an index of public records including federal censuses, tax lists, military lists, church records, and land records. Most of the information comes from census records. This is a helpful search if you do not know the state in which an ancestor lived during these times. However, it only lists the head of the household. The information on the AISI refers the researcher to the document, usually a specific census for a specific state and a page number. Most of the information pertains to data from 1850 and earlier. There are nine separate searches:

1. U.S. early colonial records, 1600–1819
2. U.S., 1820–1829
3. U.S., 1830–1839
4. U.S., 1840–1849
5. Southern states, 1850–1860
6. New England and Northern states, 1850
7. Midwestern and Western states, 1850–1906
7A. U.S., 1850–1906
8. U.S. mortality schedules, 1850–1885

AISI for the years 1607–1870 (microfiche): **WRHS**
AISI for the years 1607–1906: **FHC**

AFRICAN-AMERICAN SUBJECT MATTER

Court records listing registration of African-Americans in southern Ohio counties of Green, Miami: **WRHS**

Freedman's Bureau depositor's records: **CPL, FPK, WRHS**

Pennsylvania Abolition Society Records, manumissions @1790s to 1850 (not only from PA): **WRHS**

Records of Antebellum Southern Plantations from the Revolution through the Civil War: **CPL**

Slavery records: **WRHS** (Slave Narratives: stories of 2,300 African-Americans from 26 states compiled by the WPA from 1936 to 1938; on computer disks; searchable by name, state, or territory).

ANNALS OF CLEVELAND—EARLY NEWSPAPER INDEX

1818–1876: **CPL, FPK, WRHS**
1933–1938: **CPL, WRHS**
1837–1875 (court records): **CPL, FPK, WRHS**

ATLASES

Cuyahoga County
For years 1852, 1874, 1892, and 1903: **CCA, CPL, WRHS**

City of Cleveland
For years 1881, 1898: **CCA, CPL, WRHS**
For 1898 suburbs: **CPL, WRHS**

BIRTH RECORDS

Cleveland/Cuyahoga County
1849–1908: **CCA**
1849–1908: probate court in county of birth
1867–1908: **FHC(K-In)**

1909–present: Cleveland City Hall
1909–present: suburbs with separate birth records: Bedford, Berea, Cleveland Heights, East Cleveland, Euclid, Garfield Heights, Lakewood, Maple Heights, Parma, Rocky River, Shaker Heights, South Euclid, University Heights.
Prior to 1952 for Euclid-Glenville Hospital: Cleveland City Hall
Prior to 1936 for Huron Rd. Hospital: Cleveland City Hall
Post 1975 for Southwest General Hospital: Cleveland City Hall

Other Ohio Counties:
Allen: **FHC(K-In)**
Ashtabula, Geauga, Lake, and Portage for 1867–1908: **FHC(K-In)**

BOARD OF COUNTY COMMISSIONERS JOURNALS

1810–1985: **CCA**

BRITISH PARISH REGISTERS: CPL

CEMETERY AND FUNERAL HOME RECORDS

Check cemetery notebook at front desk: **WRHS**
Various books published by cemetery name or locale: **CPL, FPK, WRHS**
Check computer catalog under locality and cemeteries: **FHC**

COAT OF ARMS: CPL

CHURCH RECORDS
Local church histories, prominent churchmen:
CPL, FPK, WRHS

CENSUS—FEDERAL ALL STATES
1790–1930 schedules (microfilm): **WRHS**
1790 (microfilm): **FPK, FHC(K-In)**
1840 (includes Revolutionary War Veterans): **FPK**
1880 and 1900 soundex—all states: **WRHS**
1790–1880 indexes, all states included: **WRHS**
1900 indexes for: AL, OH, IN, IL, KY, MI, WV, NY, NJ:
WRHS
1910 indexes for: OH, WV: **WRHS**
1910 index, **FHC(K-In)**
1920 index: **FHC(K-In)**
1920 indexes for OH, IN, MI, KY, PA, NY: **WRHS**

CENSUS, FEDERAL

Ohio—State
1880, only state index in book form: **WRHS**
1820–1880 printed index (1870—Cleveland only): **CPL**
1910 and 1920 soundex: **WRHS**
1820–1920: **CPL**
1880–1920 soundex: **CPL**
1890, Veterans living in Ohio Counties, **FHC(K-In)**

Ohio—Various Counties
Ashtablula County, 1820–1920: **FPK, FHC(K-In)**
Cuyahoga County, 1820–1920: **FPK, FHC(K-In)**
Geauga, 1820–1920: **FPK, FHC(K-In)**
Huron: **FPK**
Lake County: **FPK, FHC(K-In)**
Lorain: **FPK**
Medina: **FPK**
Portage County: **FPK, FHC(K-In)**
Trumbull County: **FPK, FHC(K-In)**

CLEVELAND CITY DOCUMENTS:
Annual Reports
1855–1914 (not inclusive) CPL branch at City Hall (known as Public Administration Library)
1863–present: **CPL, City Hall Branch**
1950–1955: **WRHS**
City ordinances, 1840s–present: **CPL, City Hall Branch**
Council proceedings, 1837–present: **CPL, City Hall Branch**
Group plan of 1903 and 1907: **CPL, City Hall Branch**
Minutes of Planning Commission, 1915–1941: **CPL, City Hall Branch**
Miscellaneous materials: **CPL, City Hall Branch**
Original articles of incorporation: **CPL, City Hall Branch**
Original township records, 1803–1838: **CPL, City Hall Branch**
Various reports (police, fire, landmarks, recreation): **CPL, City Hall Branch**

CLEVELAND CITY DIRECTORIES
1837–1980 (microfilm): **CPL, WRHS, FPK**
1936–1980 (books): **CPL**
1837–1939 (books or microfilm): **CCA**
1936–present (books): **FPK**
1941–1977 (not inclusive) books (some E-W suburbs): **CCA**

CORONER'S FILES:
Case files, 1833–1900 (not inclusive): **CCA**
Case files, 1901–present: Coroner's Office
Index to Coroner's case files, 1833–1900: **CCA, FPK, WRHS**

DEATH RECORDS

Ohio
1909–1944: Ohio Historical Society, Columbus
1909–1944: Youngstown Historical Center of History and Labor
1909–1944: Akron Summit County Public Library
1913–1922: FHC(K-In)

Cleveland/Cuyahoga County
1840–1908 (originals from Cleveland city): CCA
1867–1908: CCA
1909–1944: Ohio Historical Society, Columbus
1909–1944: Youngstown Historical Center of History and Labor
1909–1944: Akron Summit County Library
*1909–present (index and originals): Cleveland City Hall

Other Ohio Counties
Allen County: FHC(K-In)
Ashtabula County, 1867–1908: FHC(K-In)
Geauga County, 1867–1908: FHC(K-In)
Lake County, 1867–1908: FHC(K-In)
Portage county 1867–1908: FHC(K-In)

Out-of-State
New York City, 1888–1965 (indexes): FHC(K-In)

DEEDS

Cuyahoga County
1810–present: County Recorder's Office
Various: FHC (catalog-subject—land records);
WRHS

Other Ohio Counties
Various Ohio counties, not Cuyahoga: WRHS
Geauga, 1862–1850, 1862–1882: FHC(K-In)
Lake, 1839–1853 (index): FHC(K-In)

DIVORCE
1811–1858: Supreme Court Records: CCA
1837–1925: Juvenile Court and Domestic Relations Court: Cuyahoga County Court
1876–1882, Court of Common Pleas: CCA
1876–1922, Common Pleas Special: CCA
1912–present, index and court records, decrees: Common Pleas Court
Various (specific counties and states): WRHS

INTERNATIONAL GENEALOGICAL INDEX (IGI)
CPL, FHC, FPK, WRHS

LIST OF ELECTORS (CITY OF CLEVELAND)
1893–1982: CCA
1902: WRHS

MANUSCRIPT COLLECTIONS: WRHS

MAPS
Township and ward, 1860, 1870, 1880, 1890: **CCA**
Sanborn fire insurance maps, Cleveland, 1886–1973: **CPL, WRHS**
Plat books, Cleveland and Cuyahoga County, 1912–1968: **CPL, WRHS**
Ward maps, Cleveland and suburbs, 1852–present: **CPL**
World maps/boundary changes: **CPL**

MARRIAGE RECORDS

OHIO

Cuyahoga County
1810–1941, original applications and returns: **CCA**
1810–present: Cuyahoga County Courthouse
1810–1989 (index): **CCA**
1810–1960: **WRHS**
1808–1989 (index): **FPK**
1829–1875 (applications): **CCA**
1942–present (originals): **Cuyahoga County Courthouse**

Cleveland
1818–1876: **WRHS**

Other Ohio Counties
Ashtabula, 1812–1965: **FHC(K-In)**
Geauga, 1806–1920: **FHC(K-In)**
Lake, 1840–1955: **FHC(K-In)**
Portage, 1808–1917: **FHC(K-In)**
Various too numerous to mention: **FPK, WRHS**

OTHER U.S.
Prior to 1700, New England: **FPK, WRHS**
Western PA, eastern OH, 1820–1868: **FPK, WRHS**

MILITARY RECORDS

PENSIONS
Application and bounty land files: **CPL, WRHS**
Application (index): **FPK, WRHS**

REGIMENTAL HISTORIES: WRHS

ROSTERS

Civil War
Index: **WRHS**
Most states (Confederate and Union): **WRHS**

Revolutionary War
Most states: **CPL, WRHS**

Spanish-American War
Ohio: **CPL, FPK, WRHS**

War of 1812
Most states: **WRHS**
Some states: **CPL**

World War I
Ohio: **WRHS**
Roster of Ohio soldiers and index: **CPL, FPK**
Ohio Regimental Histories: **CPL, FPK**
Compiled service records, Union and Confederate
Army Volunteers: **WRHS**
Ancestry.Plus—a subscription to a commercial
company available on the computers at these li-
braries. This subscription permits searching many
databases, several of which have extensive mili-
tary information on them. **(CPL, WRHS, FPK. FHC)**
Records of nearly 50,000 Cuyahoga County veter-
ans: **CPL, WRHS**

NATURALIZATION RECORDS

Cuyahoga County
1818–1971, Common Pleas Court: **CCA**
various dates: **FPK**
1859–1901, probate court: **CCA**
1859–1888, probate court indexes: **WRHS**

Other Ohio counties
Ashtabula County, 1873–1906: **FHC(K-In)**
Geauga County, 1860–1912: **FHC(K-In)**
Portage County, 1860–1912: **FHC(K-In)**
Portage County, 1816–1878: **WRHS**

Pennsylvania
Beaver County, 1804–1840: **WRHS**
Erie County, 1825–1906: **WRHS**
Bucks County, 1802–1905: **WRHS**
Various: **FPK**

NECROLOGY FILES
1833, 1847–1848: **CPL**
1850–1975: **CCA, FPK, WRHS**
1850–present: **CPL**

NEWSPAPERS
Biographical clipping file: **CPL, CCA**
Cleveland Herald, 1819–1886: **CPL, FPK, WRHS**
Cleveland Plain Dealer, 1842–present: **CPL, WRHS**
Cleveland Plain Dealer, 1845–present: **FPK**
Cleveland Press, 1878–1982: **CPL, FPK, WRHS**
Cleveland World, 1890–1905: **CPL, WRHS**
Clipping files, late 1920s–1975: **CPL**

Current dailies from many U.S. states (too many
to list): **CPL**
Historic Cleveland newspapers (selected list, too
many to list): **CPL**
International newspapers (various, too many to
list): **CPL**
U.S. Nationality Newspapers (various—too many
to list): **CPL**

PASSENGER LISTS
Any passenger lists from the ports listed below
can be ordered from a FHC.

New York Ports
1820–1840: **CPL, FPK, WRHS**
1820–1846 (index on microfilm): **WRHS**

Baltimore Port
1820–1879: **CPL, FPK, WRHS**

Philadelphia Port
1800–1819: **CPL, FPK, WRHS**
1800–1906 (index): **WRHS**

San Francisco Port
1850–1875: **CPL WRHS**

Hamburg Passenger Lists
1850–1914: **FPK**
1920–1934: **CPL WRHS**

PERIODICAL RESOURCE INDEX (PERSI)
To 1989, book format: **CPL, FPK, WRHS, FHC**
May 2000 (CD): **CPL, FPK, WRHS, FHC**

TELEPHONE BOOKS
Cleveland, 1880–present: **CPL**
Suburban directories, various years: **CPL**

PHOTOGRAPHIC COLLECTIONS
Both CPL and WRHS permit reprints of some of
the pictures in their collection. Check with staff
for fees and other requirements

Cleveland area
1839–present, subject list available at reference
desk: **WRHS**
African-American Families Collection: **CPL**
Cleveland Picture Collection (bridges, buildings,
churches, etc): **CPL**
City of Cleveland (retrieve by street address/key
word): **CPL**
Hispanic Families Collection: **CPL**
Walker & Weeks Collection (local landmarks): **CPL**
Wright Brothers Collection: **WRHS**

National
Portrait collection: **CPL**
Union and Confederate forces: **WRHS**

PROBATE COURT

Estate Files
1813–1918, cases: **CCA**
1813–1941, indexes: **CCA**

1852–1994: **WRHS**

Cuyahoga County Records
1868–1873: **FHC(K-In)**
1811–1896, index: **WRHS**
1852–1901 (certain dockets only): **WRHS**
1897–1898, wills: **WRHS**

Other Counties
Geauga, 1891–1910: **FHC(K-In)**
Portage, 1819–1853: **FHC(K-In)**
    1817–1874: **WRHS**
Various other Ohio counties: **WRHS**
Some from other states: **WRHS**

RD. RECORDS
1802–1898: **CCA**

SURVEYOR'S RECORDS
Cuyahoga County, 1823–1893: **CCA**
Summit County, 1839–1917: **WRHS**

TAX RECORDS

Ohio: **FPK**
Early Ohio Tax Records index: **WRHS**

Cuyahoga County
1816–1838: **FPK**
1819–1869: **WRHS**
1819–1986 (not inclusive): **CCA**
County Auditor Records, 1899–1901: **WRHS**

Other Ohio Counties
Geauga, 1820–1850: **FHC(K-In)**
Bainbridge, 1822–1931: **WRHS**
Various other counties: **FPK, WRHS**
Other states: **FPK**

VOTES, ABSTRACTS OF

Cuyahoga County
1893–1974, Board of Elections: **CCA**
1907–1908, Board of Elections: **WRHS**
1818–1828, Brooklyn Township: **WRHS**
1896 Cleveland Poll books, wards 24 and 25:
WRHS
1945 Shaker Heights, Precinct C: **WRHS**
Voters, Board of Elections Register of naturalized
citizens 1836–1972: **CCA**

WILLS (CUYAHOGA COUNTY)
1811–1913, index: **CCA**
1811–1896, index: **WRHS**
1810–present, index: **Probate Court**
1810–present: **Probate Court**
1813–1913: **CCA**

Appendix B:
Area Genealogical Groups

Information is organized by county, with the exception of the Ohio Genealogical Society.

OHIO

Ohio Genealogical Society (OGS)
713 South Main St.
Mansfield, OH 44907-1644

Phone: 419-756-7294
E-mail: to office manager at ogs@ogs.org
Website: www.ogs.org
This is the largest state genealogical society in the United States. Yearly membership is $27 and members receive a monthly newsletter and quarterly bulletins. The library in Mansfield has over 15,000 books and is available to members Tues-Sat, 9–5 (except holidays and during the Annual Conference in April). Nonmembers may use the library for $3 per day. The various chapters are listed in each county section.

ASHTABULA COUNTY

Ashtabula County Genealogical Society
Geneva Library
860 Sherman St.
Geneva, OH 44041

Phone: 440-466-4521
Meets: 4th Wednesday of the month at 7 p.m. June–Aug; 1 p.m. other months; no meeting in Dec.
Contact: acgs@ashtabulagen.org
Website: www.ashtabulagen.org

COLUMBIANA COUNTY

Columbiana County Genealogical Society
P.O. Box 861
Salem, OH 44460

COSCHOCTON COUNTY

Coshocton County Chapter OGS
P.O. Box 128
Coshocton, OH 43812

CUYAHOGA COUNTY

African-American Genealogical Society of Cleveland, Ohio
P.O. Box 201476
Cleveland, OH 44120-1476

Meets: 4th Saturday of the month at 9:30 a.m. at Maple Heights Regional Library of Cuyahoga County Public Library

5225 Library Lane
Maple Heights, OH 44139
Phone: 216-475-5000
Contact: scraighead@ssd.com
website: www.aagsclev.org

Brooklyn Genealogical Club
Brooklyn Branch of Cuyahoga County Public Library
4480 Ridge Rd.
Brooklyn, OH 44144

Phone: 216-398-4600
Meets: 3rd Sunday of the month at 2 p.m. (not June-Sept or Dec)
Contact: Sbloom1059@aol.com

Computer-Assisted Genealogy Group (CAGG)
P.O. Box 16794
Rocky River, OH 44116

Meets: 3rd Saturday of the month at 9:30 a.m. (not July/Aug/Dec) at: Fairview Park Regional Library of the Cuyahoga County Public Library
21255 Lorain Rd.
Fairview Park, OH 44126
Phone: 440-333-4700
Contact: Bill Frank 440-734-2021 Website: www.rootsweb.com/~ohcagg

Cuyahoga Valley Chapter, OGS
P.O. Box 41414
Brecksville, OH 44141-0414

Meets: 1st Monday of the month, at 7:30 p.m. at: Independence Civic Center
6363 Selig Boulevard
Independence, OH
Contact: jstojka@juno.com

Cuyahoga West Chapter, OGS
Box 26196
Fairview Park, OH 44126

Meets: 3rd Wednesday of month (not August), 7:30 p.m. at:
Porter Public Library,
27333 Center Ridge Rd.
Westlake, OH 44145
Contact: Jmworkman@att.net

East Cuyahoga Chapter, OGS
P.O. Box 24182
Lyndhurst, OH 44124

Meets: 1st Monday of month, 7:30 p.m. (the next Monday after holidays)
Ross C. DeJohn Community Center

6306 Marsol Rd.
Mayfield Heights, OH 44124
Contact: Morgabd@msn.com

Greater Cleveland Genealogical Society
P.O. Box 40254
Cleveland, OH 44140-0254

Meets: 3rd Monday, 6:30 p.m. (not July or Dec) at: Fairview Park Regional Library of the Cuyahoga County Public Library
21255 Lorain Rd.
Fairview Park, OH 44126
440-333-4700
Contact: mjfc99@core.com

Hungarian Genealogical Society of Greater Cleveland
Meets: 4th Wednesday of the month (3rd Wed, Nov & Dec/no meetings July & Aug) at 6:30 p.m. for dinner; 7:30 p.m. for meeting at:
Marinko's Firehouse Restaurant
2768 Stark Drive
Willoughby Hills, OH 44094
440-943-44983
Contact: johnuray@aol.com
or Dan Corrigan at 4955 South Sedgewick Rd., Lyndhurst, Ohio 44124

Jewish Genealogical Society of Cleveland
Menorah Park Center for Aging
27100 Cedar Rd. (2nd floor, Miller Library)
Beachwood, OH 44122

Meets: 1st Wednesday of the month at 7:30 p.m.
Contact: Arlene Rich, 442-449-2326
Website: ClevelandJGS.org

Northeast Ohio Computer Aided Genealogy (NEOCAG)
St. Bartholomew Church
435 SOM Center Rd.
Mayfield Heights, OH 44124

Meets: 2nd Saturday of the month at 9 a.m.
Contact: lolson@worldnet.att.net
Website: members.tripod.com/~lolson

Polish Genealogical Society of Greater Cleveland
C/o St. Mary's PNC
1901 Wexford Ave.
Parma, OH 44134

Meets: 1st Tuesday of the month (Sept-June) 7:30 p.m. at the church
Contact: EDJMENDYKA@aol.com

Southwest Cuyahoga Chapter, OGS
13305 Pearl Rd.
Strongsville, OH 44136

Meets: 2nd Thursday of the month at 7:30 p.m.
(not June- Aug)at:
Old Town Hall- Strongsville Activity Center
18825 Royalton Rd.
Strongsville, OH
Contact: Carol Williams CNGWILLI@nls.net

GEAUGA COUNTY

Geauga County Chapter, OGS
C/o Chardon Library
110 E. Park St.
Chardon OH 44024-1213

Meets: 2nd Tuesday of the month at 7 p.m. Mar-June; Sept-Nov. Sunday Afternoons at 2 p.m. January & February at the Chardon Library. No meeting July and August.
Contact via e-mail: raccooan@oplin.org

HOLMES COUNTY

Holmes County Chapter, OGS
P.O. Box 136
Millersburg, OH 44654

KNOX COUNTY

Knox County Genealogical Society
P.O. Box 1098
Mount Vernon, OH 43050

LAKE COUNTY

Lake County Genealogical Society Chapter, OGS
c/o Morley Library
184 Phelps
Painesville, OH 44077
Meets: last Thursday of the month at 10 a.m. No meetings in Aug or Dec. Special meeting exceptions are annual potluck luncheon in January and the annual picnic in July. Regular meeting site is Morley Library, but during library construction, meetings are at Mentor Library, 8215 Mentor Ave., Mentor, Ohio.
Contact: To verify meetings, e-mail
mplgen@oplin.lib.oh.us or lcgsohio@juno.com.

LORAIN COUNTY

Black River Genealogists
Lorain Public Library
351 6th St.
Lorain, Ohio 44052

440-244-1192
Meets 1st Thursday of the month at 7 p.m. at
contact: sigsworthj@usa.net

Lorain County Chapter, OGS
Box 865
Elyria, OH 44036

Meets: 2nd Monday of the month at 7 p.m. at:

Oberlin Public Library
South Main St.
Oberlin, OH 44074
Contact: Marge Cheney 440-323-5080
Website: centurytel.net/lorgen

Oberlin African-American Genealogical and Historical group
Meets at first Saturday of each month at 11 a.m. at:
Oberlin Public Library
65 South Main St.
Oberlin, OH 44074
440-475-4790

Wellington Genealogy Workshop
P.O. Box 224
Wellington, OH 44090

Meets: 1st Wednesday of the month at:
Wellington Town Hall
115 Willard Memorial Square
Wellington, OH 44090
Contact via e-mail: jacquejon@aol.com

MAHONING COUNTY

Mahoning County Chapter, OGS
P.O. Box 9333
Boardman, OH 44513

Meets: Third Monday of the month
September–June. No meeting July August, December.

MEDINA COUNTY

The Alliance Genealogical Society (TAGS)
P.O. Box 3630
Alliance, OH 44601

E-mail: tags_ogs@hotmail.com
Meets March–June; Aug–Nov on the third Thursday of the month at 7 p.m. at:
Union Ave. Methodist Church
Alliance, Ohio 44601

Medina County Chapter, OGS
P.O. Box 804
Medina, OH 44258

Meets: 2nd Sunday of the month at 2 pm at:
Medina Library Annex
200 S. Broadway
Medina, OH 44258
Contact: Don Canfield 330-725-8140

PORTAGE COUNTY

Portage County Genealogical Society
Box 821
Ravenna, OH 44266

Meets: 3rd Saturday of the month at 2 p.m. (not June–August; not December) at:
Portage County Historical Society
6549 N. Chestnut St
Ravenna, Oh 44266
Contact: history@config.com

STARK COUNTY

Stark County Chapter, OGS
P.O. Box 9035
Canton, OH 44711

Website: www.stark.lib.oh.us/ohiogen
Meets second Thursday of each month with the exception of picnic in July, annual banquet in Nov, and no meeting in Dec, at 6:30 p.m. at:

Stark County District Library
715 Market St.
Canton, OH 44702

SUMMIT COUNTY

Hudson Genealogical Study Group:
Hudson Library
22 Aurora St. #G
Hudson, OH 44236

330-653-6658
Meets 2nd, 3rd, and 4th Saturday of the month at 10 a.m. at:
e-mail contact: hgsg@bigfoot.com
website: rootsweb.com/~ohhudogs/

Summit County Genealogical Society
Box 2232
Akron, OH 44309

Meets: 3rd Saturday of the month at 1 p.m. at:
Taylor Memorial Library
2015 Third St.
Cuyahoga Falls, OH 44221
330-928-2117
Contact via e-mail: Summitogs@ald.net
Website: www.acorn.net/gen

TRUMBULL COUNTY

Trumbull County Genealogical Society
P.O. Box 309
Warren, OH 44482

TUSCARAWAS COUNTY

Tuscarawas County Genealogy Society
P.O. Box 141
New Philadelphia, OH 44663

WAYNE COUNTY

Wayne County Genealogical Society
P.O. Box 856
Wooster, OH 44691

Meets 1st Saturday of each month at 2 p.m. (not Dec.) at:
Wayne County Public Library
Corner N. Market St. & Larwill St.
Wooster, OH 44691

Appendix C: Area Historical Societies

This book has emphasized the importance of historical information in your genealogical research. The following groups/organizations often are the only repository for local history, including small neighborhood newspapers, details regarding the public schools, and other minutiae that can bring joy and added information to many a genealogist. Often the individuals who work or volunteer with these groups have deep roots in the community and can be extremely helpful. Do not leave out this important resource in your quest for information.

STATEWIDE:

Ohio Historical Society
1982 Velma Ave.
Columbus, OH 43211

REGIONAL

Western Reserve Historical Society
10825 East Boulevard
Cleveland, OH 44106
216-721-5722

Youngstown Historical Center of History and Labor
P.O. Box 533
151 West Wood St.
Youngstown, OH 44501
330-743-5934; 800-262-6137

ASHTABULA COUNTY

Ashtabula County Historical Society
Ashtabula County Historical Society
Route 531 Geneva-on-the-Lake OH 44041
440-466-7337 (call Wednesdays only)
mailing address: P.O. Box 36, Jefferson, OH 44030

Ashtabula Marine Museum
1071 Walnut Blvd.
Ashtabula, OH 44004
440-964-6847

Conneaut Area Historical Society
C/o Bob Blickensderfer
235 Fifield Ave.
Conneaut, OH 44030

COLUMBIANA COUNTY

Lisbon Historical Society
119 East Washington St.
Lisbon, OH 44432
330-424-1861

CUYAHOGA COUNTY

African-American Museum
1765 Crawford Rd.
Cleveland, OH 44106
216-791-1700

Bay Village Historical Society
27715 Lake Rd.
Bay Village, OH 44140
440-871-7338

Bedford Historical Society and Museum
30 S. Park St.
Bedford, OH 44146
440-232-0796

Berea Historical Society
118 E. Bridge St.
Berea, OH 44017
440-243-2541

Brecksville Historical Association
Blossom Hill Complex
Cleveland, OH 44141
440-526-7165

Broadview Heights Historical Society
City Hall
9543 Broadview Rd.
Cleveland, OH 44147
440-237-8122

Brooklyn Historical Society
4442 Ridge Rd.
Cleveland, OH 44144
216-749-2804

Chagrin Falls Historical Society
21 Walnut St.
Chagrin Falls, OH 44022
440-247-4695

Cleveland Police Museum
1300 Ontario St.
Cleveland, OH 44113
216-623-5055

Euclid Historical Society
21129 North St.
Euclid- OH 44123
216-289-8577

Garfield Heights Historical Society
5405 Turney Rd.
Cleveland, OH 44125
216-475-3050

Hungarian Historical Society
1301 East 9th St.
Cleveland, OH 44114
216-523-3900

Lakewood Historical Society
14710 Lake Ave.
Cleveland, OH 44107
216-221-7343

Maple Heights Historical Society
5810 Dunham Rd.
Cleveland, OH 44137
216-662-2851

Mayfield Township Historical Society
505 SOM Center Rd.
Cleveland, OH 44143
440-461-0055

Middleburg Heights Historical Society
P.O. Box 30206
Middleburg Heights, OH 44130

Mill Creek Falls History Center
8404 Webb Terrace
Cleveland, OH 44105
216-271-9300

Moreland Hills Historical Society
4350 SOM Center Rd.
Moreland Hills, OH 44022
440-248-0235

Shaker Historical Museum
16740 South Park Blvd.
Shaker Heights, OH 44122
216-921-1201

Soldiers and Sailors Monument
127 Public Square
Cleveland, OH 44114
216-621-3710

Solon Historical Society
33975 Bainbridge Rd.
Solon, OH 44139
440-248-6419

South Euclid Historical Society
Cuyahoga County Public Library—South Euclid Lyndhurst Branch
4645 Mayfield Rd.
Lyndhurst, OH 44124
216-691-0314

Ukrainian Museum and Archives
1202 Kenilworth Ave.
Cleveland, OH 44113
216-781-4329

Walton Hills Historical Center
Village Hall
Walton/Alexander Rd.s
Walton Hills, OH 44146
440-232-6142

GEAUGA COUNTY

Geauga Historical Society
14653 E. Park
P.O. Box 153
Burton, OH 44021

Russell Historical Society
8450 Kinsman Rd.
Novelty, OH 44072
e-mail: Phetrick@aol.com

KNOX COUNTY

Fredericktown Historical Society
2 East Sandusky St.
Fredericktown, OH 43019

Knox County Historical Society
875 Harcourt Rd.
P.O. Box 522
Mount Vernon, OH 43050
Phone: 740-393-5247

LAKE COUNTY

Croatian Heritage Museum
34900 Lake Shore Blvd.
Willoughby, OH 44095
440-946-2044

Fairport Lighthouse and Marine Museum
129 Second St.
Fairport Harbor, OH 44077
440-354-4825

Lake County Historical Society
8610 King Memorial Rd.
Kirtland Hills, OH 44060
440-255-8979

Perry Historical Society of Lake County
P.O. Box 216
Perry, OH 44081

Wickliffe Historical Society
Wickliffe Civic Center
900 Worden Rd.
Wickliffe, OH 44092
440-943-2644

LORAIN COUNTY

Amherst Historical Society
113 S. Lake St.
Amherst, OH 44001
440-988-255

Black River Historical Society
309 W.5th St.
Lorain, OH 44052
440-245-2563

Litchfield Historical Society
4700 Avon Lake Rd.
Litchfield, OH 44253

Lorain County Historical Society
509 Washington Ave.
Elyria, OH 44035
440-322-3341

Ohio Historical and Improvement Organization
Oberlin Heritage Center
73 Professor St.
Oberlin, OH 44074
440-774-1700

Great Lakes Historical Society
480 Main St.
Vermilion, OH 44089
440-967-3467

MAHONING COUNTY

Austintown Historical Society
3898 Ascot Court
Youngstown, OH 44515
330-792-1129

Berlin Center Historical Society
P.O. Box 175
Berlin Center, OH 44401
330-547-2502

Boardman Historical Society
P.O. Box 2124
Boardman, OH 44513
330-726-7790

Campbell Historical Society
211 Struthers–Liberty Rd.
Campbell, OH 44505
330-755-4406

Poland Township Historical society
4515 Poland Center Rd.
Poland, OH 44514
330-757-2615

MEDINA COUNTY

Brunswick Area Historical Society
Heritage Farm Barn
4613 Laurel Rd.
Brunswick, OH 44212
330-225-3489

Brunswick Historical Society
P.O. Box 714
Brunswick, OH 44212

Granger Historical Society
1261 Granger Rd.
Medina, OH 44256
330-239-1523

Hinckley Historical Society
P.O. Box 471
Hinckley, OH 44233

Medina County Historical Society
John Smart House
206 N. Elm St.
Medina, OH 44256
330-722-1341

Northeast Ohio Military Museum
6807 Boneta Rd.
Medina, OH 44256
330-336-7657

Seville Historical Society
70 West Main St.
Seville, OH 44273

Sharon Heritage Society
P.O. Box 57
Sharon Center, OH 44274

Valley City Historical Society
7060 Center Rd.
Valley City, OH 44280

York Township Historical Society
2862 Abbeyville Rd.
Medina, OH 44256

PORTAGE COUNTY

Portage County Historical Society
Open Tues, Thurs, & Sun 2–4 p.m.
Website: www2.clearlight.com/~pchs/index

STARK COUNTY

Ohio Society of Military History
316 Lincoln Way East
Massillon, OH 44646
330-832-5553

SUMMIT COUNTY

Hudson Historical Society
22 Aurora St.
Hudson, OH 44326

Peninsula Library and Historical Society
1775 Main St.
Boston Township, OH 44264
Phone: 330-657-2291

Summit County Historical Society
550 Copley Rd.
Akron, OH 44320

WAYNE COUNTY

Lodi Historical Society
117 Wooster St.
Lodi, OH 44254

Smithville Historical Society
P.O. Box 12
Smithville, OH 44677

Wayne County Historical Society
546 East Bowman St.
Wooster, OH 44691
330-264-8856

Appendix D: Libraries of Interest

Ohio has many wonderful libraries spread throughout the state. Neither size of the county, nor size of the library, will necessarily determine the amount of excellent genealogical material available. There are also many private libraries in Ohio, most of which are connected to a university or college. Don't overlook them as repositories for genealogical sources.

With the continuing popularity of genealogy, it is a given that every library, large or small, will have some genealogical materials and resources available to patrons. These may include clipping files, historical perspectives, books and articles about local people and places, copies of area newspapers, obituaries, family histories, and books on how to conduct, organize, and share genealogy research. It would be redundant to list every library in all the counties of Northeast Ohio just to include these usual holdings.

Fortunately, The Ohio Public Library Information Network has a wonderful website (www.oplin.lib.oh.us) that easily leads to all the public libraries in the state. Be sure to look at the website for much more than just lists of libraries—the link "Genealogy Gleanings," offers great advice, links, and ideas about genealogy research.

The listing of libraries follows, alphabetically by Northeast Ohio county, with one exception—Allen County Public Library in Indiana.

OUTSIDE OHIO:

Allen County Public Library
200 East Berry St.
Fort Wayne, IN 46802
Phone: 260-421-1200

The Allen County Public Library is the one library outside the state of Ohio that needs to be mentioned here. Located in Fort Wayne, Indiana, the library is the site where genealogical periodicals from around the world are housed. It has far more than just periodicals and is an extremely important resource worthy of your time and attention. Its collection includes:

Census:
All U.S. federal population schedules, 1790–1930
All available statewide indexes and soundexes
All extant mortality schedules, 18500–1880
All extant schedules of Civil War Union veterans and widows, 1890
Agricultural and manufacturing schedules for Indiana, 18500–1880
Family histories:
Compiled genealogies—738,000 volumes on American and European families
Military:
Microfilmed service and pension records from National Archives for conflicts from Revolutionary War—Philippine Insurrection, 18991901
Confederate records from various state archives

Other: Native American records (first-hand accounts), African-American records, and Canadian records.
Periodicals: The largest English-language genealogy and local history periodical collection in the world. Subscriptions to over 3,200 magazines and journals. Use PERSI (see Glossary, p. [insert page number]) to search remotely for relevant material.

ASHTABULA COUNTY

Ashtabula County District Library
335 West 44th St.
Ashtabula, OH 44004
Phone: 440-997-9341
Website: ashtabula.lib.oh.us
Available at the library are:
U.S. Federal Census records 1790-1910
Newspapers: *Ashtabula Star Beacon*, Oct 1900–Feb 2003; Ashtabula Sentinel, Jan 1832–21 Apr 1910; Ashtabula Telegraph, 1 Jan 1874–18 Aug 1911
Obituary index for the Star Beacon, mid 1960s–mid 1990s
Ashtabula county birth and death records from 1867–1908
Ashtabula County marriage records, 1811–1900

Geneva Public Library
860 Sherman St.
Geneva, OH 44041-9101

Phone: 440-466-4521
Archivist on duty, limited hours

Available at this library are: county books, books on townships, census records on film, cemetery readings, family histories, Geneva newspapers, books on rest of U.S.

The Ashtabula Genealogical Society is located at this branch and has a significant collection housed in the archives room. Trained volunteer staff from the genealogical society are available at posted times during the week.

COLUMBIANA COUNTY

Salem Public Library
821 East State St.
Salem, OH 4460
Phone: 330-332-0042
Hours: Mon–Thu 9 a.m.–9 p.m.; Fri–Sat 9 a.m.–6 p.m.; Sun 1–5 p.m. October through May
Copies: photocopy $.20; from microfilm $.50

The Columbiana County Genealogical Society meets at this library. The Ohio Room houses most of the material of interest to family history research. Some of its contents are:
Census—Selected years, but covers only Columbiana County
City/county directories—Columbiana County, 1889-present

County records—Guide to Carroll County births, 1867‑1908; Leetonia births and deaths (no dates given)
Local history
Family histories donated by patrons and others
Cemetery records for the entire county
Military—Rosters of Ohioans who served in the Korean War and Vietnam.
Newspapers—*Anti-Slavery Bugle*, 1836–1861; *Salem News Obituaries*, 1889–present

COSHOCTON COUNTY

Coshocton Public Library
655 Main St.
Coshocton, OH 43812
Phone: 740-622-0956
Web: www.coshocton.lib.oh.us

Their genealogy and local history department has a good collection of genealogy materials and resources. These include:

Census—Early Ohio census records; 1830 and 1870 census indexes for Coshocton County
Church—Grace United Methodist Church records, 1840–1976; History of Presbyterian Church of Coshocton, 1818–1909
County records—Coshocton County marriages, 1811–1930; Coshocton County wills, 1811–1857; Coshocton County birth records, 1867–1875; Obituary card index, 1909–present
County/township history—the complete history of Adams Township; Coshocton County Centennial History, 1811–1911; early history of Linton Township; historical collections of Coshocton County, 1764–1876; postal history of Coshocton County
County/city directories—Coshocton, West Lafayette, Newcomerstown and vicinity, 1925–present
Local history—Indexes to information about Coshocton; historical collections of Coshocton County
Maps/atlases—Atlas of Coshocton County, 1872; Coshocton County "lister" Plat Map: circa 1820–1822; maps of Coshocton County, Ohio ca. 1855
Military—Soldiers' burials in Coshocton County; County veterans from Revolutionary to Spanish American War; Index to Ohio pensioners of 1883
Newspapers—*Abstracts of Coshocton County newspapers* (from 1826–1915); index to newspaper obituaries from Coshocton County 1826–1908 (taken from various newspapers); card file supplement for 1909–1946; 1966–present

GEAUGA COUNTY

Geauga County Public Library, Chardon Library
110 E. Park St.
Chardon, OH 44024

Phone: 440-285-7601
Hours: Mon–Thu 9 a.m.–9 p.m., Fri–Sat 9 a.m.–5 p.m.; Labor Day–Memorial Day same as above except: Fri 9 a.m.–6 p.m., Sun 1-5 p.m.

Computers in the library provide Internet access to databases of Ancestry.com and LDS. This library has a significant genealogical collection, most of it housed in the Anderson Allyn room. This room is opened whenever the library is open. A genealogy specialist is on duty 24 hours a week. Holdings include, but are not limited to, the following:

Census records—population schedule for Geauga County and some other Ohio counties, 1820–1920; 1820–1860 index for Ohio; 1870–1920 index for Geauga County; 1880 every name index, on computer disk, U.S.; 1880 every household, Ohio
County records—birth and death records, 1867–1908; marriage licenses and records, 1806–1919 (transcriptions also on web page); probate records, 1805–1853; index of final records, 1853-1955; wills (indexed), 1853–1923; guardianships, 1867–1886; naturalizations, 1860–1880; aliens and minors, 1880–1893; soldiers and minors, 1894–1903; 1904–1906; Ohio Land office records, 1790–1907; Tax duplicates, 1810–1922
Maps—Lake and Geauga counties, 1820, 1830, and 1878; Geauga County only, 1846, 1857, 1874, 1900
Military Records—"The Raccoon Brigade" (Geauga County soldiers who served in the Revolution); U.S. Soldiers 1784–1811 (records of 21,000 soldiers from 22 states and territories); roster of Ohio Soldiers, 1861–1866; Roll of Honor: Civil War Union Soldiers; official Roster of Ohio Soldiers in War with Spain, 1898–1899; official Roster of Ohioans who served in World War I
Newspapers—*The Geauga Times Leader* 1875–1992 complete. Some from as early as 1830s not complete; Ohio newspapers
Other—family group sheets and family files (thousands of names); manuscript and photographic collection; taped interviews with 450 participants in an oral history project

HOLMES COUNTY

Holmes County District Library
3102 Glen Drive
P.O. Box 111
Millersburg, OH 44654
Phone: 330-674-5972
Hours: Mon–Fri 9 a.m.–8 p.m., Sat 9 a.m.– 5 p.m.
Website: www.holmes.lib.oh.us
Census—Ohio federal, 1820-1920
County records—obituaries from Holmes County papers, 1895–1991; marriage records for Holmes County, 1825–1854, 1854–1875, 1875–1896, 1825–1865; obituaries and marriages, early 1900s, 1879–1885, 1887, 1918–1923, 1924, 1926, 1927, 1929–1931, 1933–1937, 1958–1960; deeds,

1824–1984; Common Pleas Civil court records, 1826–1900; probate estate records, 1854–1900
Local history—Amish Mennonite genealogy; Ohio Amish directories; cemetery records for Holmes and Coshocton County including notes from The Wandering Sexton and Oak Hill
Newspapers; *Holmes County Republican*, 1856–1911, 1923 (partial); *Holmes County Whig*, 1844–1853; *Holmes County Farmer/ Farmer Hub*, 1843–1991; *Laurel Messenger*, 1971–1989

KNOX COUNTY

The Public Library of Mount Vernon and Knox County
201 North Mulberry St.
Mount Vernon, OH 43050
Phone: 740 392-2665
Website: www.knox.net
Census—for Knox county, 1820–1880, 1900–1920
City/county directories—1903–present (some gaps)
Newspapers—*Ohio Register*, 1818–1820; *Democratic Banner*, 1843–1894; *Republic Times*, 1845–1846; *Mount Vernon True Whig*, 1848–1855; *Ohio Times*, 1850–1852; *Ohio State Times*, 1852–1854; *Mount Vernon Republican*, 1880–1938; *Daily Banner*, 1898–1935; *Knox County Republican News*, 1904–1921; *Mount Vernon News*, 1939–present

LAKE COUNTY

Morley Library
184 Phelps St.
Painesville, OH 44077
Phone: 440-352-3383
Website: www.morleylibrary.org/genealogy
Email: mplgen@oplin.lib.oh.us
Hours: Mon–Thu 9 a.m.–9 p.m., Fri 9 a.m.–6 p.m., Sat 9 a.m.–5 p.m., Sun 1–5 p.m. mid-Oct to mid-Apr; phone or check website for Sunday and holiday hours.

At Morley Library the Genealogy and Local History Room is open during regular library hours. The library has a genealogist scheduled at various hours throughout the week. Much of the material can be accessed via the website above. Collection includes:

Census—1790 Connecticut, Maine, Maryland, Massachusetts, New York, North Carolina, New Hampshire, Pennsylvania, Rhode Island, South Carolina, Vermont and Virginia; 1820–1880 Ohio indexes; Ashtabula, 1820–1880, 1900–1920; Cuyahoga, 1820, 1830, 1850, 1880; Geauga, 1820–1880; 1900–1930; Lake, 1840–1880 1900–1930
Church records—baptism records for First Church Congregational, Painesville; St. James Episcopal Church, Painesville

County records—omitted or corrected Lake County births late 1800s from court records, 1941–1954; marriage indexes Ashtabula County, 1811–1900, Cuyahoga County, 1829–1851, Geauga County, 1803–1852 and 1806–1919, Lake County, 1840–1904, Stark County, 1809–1870, Trumbull County, 1800–1900; index to Ohio wills and estates, 1800–1850

County/township histories—individual histories on every county in the state; individual county histories on over twenty-five Pennsylvania counties.

County/City Directories—Painesville 1895, 1902–1903; 1908–1909; 1911–1912; 1923; 1929 1930–31; Cleveland 1837, 1870–71, 1900; many others including: Painesville–Willoughby, Painesville and Rural Routes, and Lake County. Complete list available on website.

Maps/Atlases—Ashtabula County: 1856, 1874; Cuyahoga County 1852; Geauga County: 1857, 1874, 1900; Lake county atlases 1840, 1857, 1874, 1898, and 1915

Military records—roster of Ohio soldiers in war of 1812; roster of Ohio Civil War Soldiers; Ohio World War I Soldiers; Korean War casualties, 1950–1958; Vietnam casualties; index of Revolutionary War pension applications; index to War of 1812 pension files

Newspapers—index of death notices in Painesville Telegraph, 1822–1986; death notices from the News-Herald, March 1986–Present; guide to The Painesville Telegraph, 1822–1986; News Herald, 1986–present

Other—cemetery inscriptions for Lake, Geauga, and Ashtabula counties (but not the cities of Fairport, Ashtabula, Conneaut, and Geneva); high school yearbooks covering several schools and many years; family genealogies donated by visitors; surname file

LORAIN COUNTY

Elyria Public Library
320 Washington Ave.
Elyria, OH 44035
Phone: 440 323-5747

This library has an Ohio Room with much local history about people, places, and events in the city and surrounding towns and cities. Collection includes:

Census—1820–1860 Ohio census indexes; Lorain County indexes, 1830, 1850–1880, and 1900 (9 southern townships only)

Church records—extensive list of church histories as published in Lorain Chronicle-Telegram from 1935–1937.

County records—Cleveland Newspaper Index to marriages and deaths, 1818–1876; marriage applications index to Elyria, Ohio newspapers, 1830–1874; Lorain County marriages, 1822–1830 (extracted from Gateway to the West); Lorain county marriages, 1824–1865; birth records, Apr

1898–May 1908; index to Ohio wills and estates to 1850; Lorain County Courthouse records, 1827

County/township histories—Amherst: Our Town and Ohio Sesquicentennial 18141964; Brownhelm: Brownhelm, Its School and Its People and Country Boy: Growing up in Northern Ohio in the 1820s; Lorain County: Early History of Lorain County and Early Settlements in Lorain County; North Ridgeville: Elm Tree Talks and One Hundred and Fifty Years

County/City directories—Elyria and Lorain counties 1859 to present (incomplete)

Maps/Atlases—map of Lorain County, 1857; atlas of Lorain County, 1874; atlas and directory of Lorain County, 1896; atlas of Lorain County, 1912

Military—Civil War roster index and Civil War roster; WWI selective service draft registration cards for Lorain County, 1917–1918

Newspapers/Periodicals—Crossroad of Our Nation, January 1960–December 1989; Inland Seas (complete); Timeline (includes index), December 1984–present

Other—many cemetery and tombstone records for cemeteries located in Elyria, Carlisle, Sheffield, Wellington, South Amherst, Ridgeville, and Henrietta townships; index to Lorain County 1851 tax maps; Ohio tax records 1800–1810, 1825, 1835, and separate 1810 listing

Herrick Memorial Library
101 Willard Memorial Square
Wellington, OH 44090
Phone: 440-647-2120
Website: www.wellington.lib.oh.us and www.youseemore.com/herrick/about
Collection includes:

Census—1820 for Ohio counties: Clark, Coshocton, Gallia, Hocking, Huron, Knox, Lawrence, Meigs, Monroe, Lorain/Medina, Logan Hardin; 1830 for Ohio counties: Highland, Harrison, Hancock, Holmes, Huron, Lorain, Logan-Meigs; 1840 for Ohio counties Erie, Holmes Huron, Logan, Lorain, Medina; 1850 for Ohio counties: Lorain, Huron, Medina, Summit; 1860 and 1870 for Ohio counties; Erie, Huron, Lorain, Medina; 1880 for Ohio counties: Erie (part), Fayette (part), Huron, Logan, Lorain, Medina–Meigs; 1890 Union veterans and widows of Civil War: Ohio counties of Erie, Holmes, Huron, Lorain, Medina, Richland, Wayne ; 1890 Union veterans and widows of Civil War: Kentucky counties of Boyd, Carter, Elliott, Fleming, Floyd, Greenup, Johnson, Lawrence, Lewis, Macoffin ; 1900 census index of nine southern townships of Lorain County; 1900 census for Logan and Lorain counties

County records—Ashland County obituaries, 1904–1914.; birth records, Lorain County Probate Court, 1867–1897, births, marriages, and deaths, Medina County Gazette 1870, 1872–1875, 1886–1887, 1892–1897

Military records—official rosters of: Soldiers of the American Revolution buried in Ohio; soldiers of Ohio in War of the Rebellion 1861–1865; soldiers from Ohio in War with Mexico, soldiers and Marines in World War I.

Other—Directory of Wellington, 1896; various books on local early settlers and their descendants; church, township, and county histories; various genealogical guides and how-to books; Lorain County Common Pleas Court records, 1824–1839; Lorain County Probate Court marriage applications, 1872–1901

Lorain Public Library

Their website (http://lorain.lib.oh.us/general_guidelines) explains their research policy. The library has a good general collection of circulating books on how to conduct genealogical research.

Census:—Lorain County censuses for selected years; census indexes for other locations; other states

County/township histories—Lorain county histories; histories on counties in New England

Military—D.A.R. lineage books

Maps/Atlases—Lorain County Atlas, 1857

Other—Ohio Historic Inventory: Lorain; published in 1993. This is a unique, two-volume set covering buildings in downtown and south Lorain and it contains an index of owners (compiled by library staff).

Oberlin Public Library
65 South Main St.
Oberlin, OH 44074
Phone: 440-775-4790
Hours: Mon-Thu 10 a.m.–8:30 p.m., Fri–Sat 10 a.m.–6 p.m., Sun 1–5 p.m. from Memorial Day to Labor Day
Website: www.oberlinpl.lib.oh.us

Computers at the library have AncestryPlus subscriptions that allow access to all of the databases of this subscription-only service. Genealogical resources include genealogy CD-ROMs that can be borrowed and used at home. On these computer disks are: census records (indexes of 1840 Ohio census, plus Ohio 1840 and 1870 censuses); FamilyTreemaker archives; Pennsylvania genealogies; and index to Ohio marriages, 1851–1900. Other resources in the collection:

Census:—census film for Lorain county and contiguous counties

Local records—Oberlin history; Oberlin college books

Newspapers—Oberlin News-Tribune, 1900–present; plus some earlier issues, but not complete

Other—history of the Underground Railroad

MAHONING COUNTY

Public Library of Youngstown and Mahoning County
305 Wick Ave.
Youngstown, OH 44503
Phone: 330-744-8636
Census:—Federal census from 1790–1920; 1870 Census index for U.S.; 1910 Miracode for Ohio and Pennsylvania; 1880 census index for United States

County/township histories—Biographical sketches of local families, publication dates generally 1880–1910; with an everyname index
County/city directories—local records; family genealogies; manuscript file; Henry Baldwin genealogical records (8 volumes, typed)
Military—rosters of all wars from Revolutionary War to World War I.; D.A.R. Patriot Index and Lineage books

---

MEDINA COUNTY

Medina County District Library
210 South Broadway
Medina, OH 44256
Phone: 330-725-0588
The collection includes:
Census—Medina County, 1820–1920; Medina County, 1890 (veterans and their widows); Medina county mortality schedules, 1850, 1860; 1790 census for Connecticut, Maine, Maryland, Massachusetts, New Hampshire, Rhode Island, South Carolina, Vermont, and Virginia; 1800 census for Hampshire County, Massachusetts
County records:—marriages, 1818–1965; deaths, 1867–1909; births, 1867–1909; wills, 1820–1901; deeds, 1795–1861; land sales, 1852–1902; tax duplicates, 1819–1838
Newspapers—*Medina Count Gazette*, 1855–present; *Medina County Sentinel*, 1899–1950; *Seville Chronicle*, 1948–1984
Local histories, biographies—Postmasters of Medina, 1880–1890; Phoenix Hall, 1880–1890; Railroads of Medina, 1880–1890; Grand Army of the Republic (GAR) of Medina, 1880–1890; Murder, Mayhem, and Medina; County/township histories for: Brunswick, Chatham, Chippewa Lake, Hinckley, Granger, Seville, Sharon, Wadsworth
Church histories—First Congregational Church of Medina, 1819–1909; History of the York Congregational Church, 1830–1910; The Story of the Mennonites of Medina, 1832–1982
County/City directories:—Medina City, 1948–1989, 1992; Wadsworth City, 1961–1990, 1995; Medina County, 1916, 1949–1989
Maps/Atlases—1857 Medina city; 1897 Medina County; 1925 Medina County plat map
Other—high school yearbooks; newsletters from genealogical and historical societies; landmark files; family genealogies

---

PORTAGE COUNTY

Reed Memorial Library
167 E. Main St.
Ravenna, OH 44266
Phone: 330-296-2827
Hours: Mon–Fri 10 a.m.– 9 p.m., Sat 10 a.m.– 6 p.m.
Website: www.reed.lib.oh.us

Although this library lists "genealogy" as a choice on its website, the information given is about records held by the county (see Chapter 10, Vital Records) and links to websites for genealogy research. Within the library itself, family history sources are cemetery records (transcriptions of local cemeteries); city directories; maps and atlases; newspapers (obituaries as found therein, except for a special group, 1978–2000, indexed by volunteers).

The Portage County Historical Society has about 160 family genealogies, a surname file, and information on townships, churches, organizations, and clubs. Their website is: www.history.portage.oh.us, then look under "library."

STARK COUNTY

Louisville Public Library
700 Lincoln Ave.
Louisville, OH 44641
Phone: 330-875-1696
Website: www.louisville.lib.oh.us/genealogy
Copies: Photocopies of obituaries from the newspapers below are $2. for the first name and $1. each additional name. Limit of five names per request. Mail requests to library and include all pertinent information, as well as the record number associated with each name, and your email address in case clarification is needed.
Also available at this library are:
County records—marriage, engagement, and birth indexes from the *Louisville Herald* from 1984–present is a work in progress and will be online in the near future.
County/township history—cemetery inscriptions in Stark County (seven-volume book published in 1980s)
Local history—Louisville: *The Way it Was*, 1834–1990; Louisville high-school yearbooks
Newspapers—obituary database for *Louisville Herald* 1887–present, available online; obituary database 1998–present; names of Louisville residents or person with a connection to the city printed in the *Canton Repository* but not the *Louisville Herald*.

Massillon Public Library
208 Lincoln Way East
Massillon OH 44646
Phone: 330-832-9831
Hours: Mon–Thu 9 a.m.–9 p.m., Fri 9 a.m.–5 p.m., Sat 9 a.m.–5 p.m.
Website: www.massillon.lib.oh.us

Within the reference department, which has a genealogy specialist on staff, is a Genealogy Corner. There you will find a booklet from the library: *"Your First steps: A Guide to Family Research."* Resources in the Genealogy Corner include:
City/county directories—Massillon City Directories, 1889–1997 (incomplete, but many years represented)
Church/religious groups—St. John's United Church of Christ records 1838–1983

County records
Newspapers—obituary file index of death notices from *The Independent*, 1863–present; microfilm of *The Independent*, 1863–present
Local history—Massillon Cemetery Association records 1846–1983; cemetery inscriptions for Stark County
A variety of "how to" books on genealogy
Computers that allow access to AncestryPlus and many other genealogical websites.

Rodman Public Library
215 East Broadway St.
Alliance, OH 44601
Phone: 330 821-2665
Website: www.rodmanlibrary.com

Rodman Public Library has census records, and an obituary database for the local paper, Alliance Review, 1871–1959 (spotty), and 1961–present.

The major reason for including this library is the "helplist" on their website. Go to: www.rodman.lib.oh.us/rpl/ref/genealogy/genealogy; this will get you to the helplist—a listing of individuals who are willing to do look-ups and take pictures of headstones, or who have access to various databases. The research areas are not limited to Stark County alone. This is a wonderful resource! The collection includes the usual: brochures, clippings and pamphlets about the area and its surrounding environs.

Stark County District Library
715 Market Ave. North
Canton, OH 44702
Phone: 330-452-0665
Website: www.starklib.oh.us/genservs
Email: scdlgen@oplin.lib.oh.us or genealogy@stark.lib.org

This library has an excellent website that offers many genealogy gems. From the website www.stark.lib.oh.us, add "newgensites," and then go to "genealogy links." This leads to more useful information that is not targeted only to Stark County. Also from the library's home page, choose "new sources," which lists recently acquired items.

Staff will accept limited research requests by letter and e-mail for persons living outside the county. Request forms can be found by choosing "Genealogy Request" from the website above. Copies cost $.25 or $.50 per page, plus postage and handling. You may email the library directly if no form exists for your particular request. No more than three requests per week, please. They and the Bierce Library of University of Akron have both been designated repositories for many historically valuable records. Check the website www.probate.co.stark.oh.us/records_main for complete details, or ask the library staff.
Collection includes:
County records—births 1867–1908; marriages 1809–1986 (includes index); court records, 1809–present: births, 1867–1908, deaths: Stark

County, 1867–1908, Ohio, 1908–1944; marriages 1809–1997; land records 1809–1894; wills and estates 1809–1920; guardianships 1809–1920; and naturalizations 1809–1852, 1861–1903

Census records—all of the Ohio federal censuses from 1900–1930; all available federal censuses from 1790–1880 for: Connecticut, District of Columbia, Kentucky, Maryland, New Jersey, New York, Pennsylvania, Virginia, and West Virginia

Newspapers—*Ohio Repository/Canton Repository* death, marriage, and administration notices, indexed 1815–1869; obituaries indexed 1954–present

Cemetery inscriptions—seven-volume set of countywide inscriptions published in mid 1980. Library staff will do look-ups and make copies.

Local history—Snapshots in Time, Stark County History; old photos, letters, journals, and oral history available on-line; a variety of books and journals covering people, places, and events in the county; family histories submitted by patrons and visitors

---

SUMMIT COUNTY

Akron-Summit County Library
Temporary location of Main Library until Fall 2004

1040 E. Tallmadge Ave.
Akron, OH 44310
Hours: Mon–Thu 9 a.m.–9 p.m., Fri 9 a.m.–6 p.m., Sat 9 a.m.–5 p.m., Sun 1–5 p.m. (during school year)
Temporary mailing address until Fall 2004:
Special Collections
Akron-Summit County Library
55 South Main St.
Akron, OH 44326
Location of Main Library (Fall 2004)
60 South High St.
Akron, OH 44326
Phone: 330-643-9030 (special collections reference)
Fax 330-643-9084
Email: special collections@ascpl.lib.oh.us
Website: http://ascpl.lib.oh.us/main-sc

Genealogy resources are part of the special collections division. The library offers genealogy classes, reference service, and an email newsletter, "Past Pursuits." With over 10,000 books, newspaper clippings, microfilmed records, and family histories, I can only highlight the collection. The collection focuses on all of Ohio as well as those states that provided immigrants to Ohio such as Kentucky, Maryland, North Carolina, Pennsylvania, South Carolina, Tennessee, Virginia, and West Virginia. However, the resources are much more extensive. Reference and photocopy requests are accepted via email, fax, mail, and telephone.

Visit in person if you can. Staff will respond to requests by fax, mail, telephone and email (speccollections@ascpl.lib.oh.us), but there can be a wait

of up to two weeks. Check website for actual date of move to new location. Requests for one or two records are most readily filled. Please include your name, address, name of deceased, information from the Ohio Death Certificate Index (if available), or county and approximate date/ year of death. They currently do not charge for this service, but donations are always appreciated. Copies made by patrons at the library are $.05.

Census—census microfilm for many different censuses and many states; complete census for Alabama, Ohio, Pennsylvania, West Virginia, and Kentucky; collection of indexes for Ohio and other states; 1880 census on CD-ROM

County/township—many directories, histories, and transcribed local and vital records for counties in Ohio; over 650 family histories searchable online by title or author; Summit County marriages, 1840–1922, Summit County birth and death indexes, 1869–1908; Summit County estates, 1840–1949

Maps/Atlases—atlases for Ohio, Pennsylvania, Virginia, and many other states, starting in the 1870s; atlases for more than 51 counties in Ohio; atlases of historical county boundaries; 19th-century county atlases for Ohio, Pennsylvania, and selected states

County/city directories—Akron city directories, 1870s–present; Haines Akron City and Suburban Criss-Cross, 1943–present

County records—probate court births, 1869–1908; deaths, 1870–1908; and marriages, 1840–1922

Local history—over 1,000 family histories searchable online by title or author; church histories; over 550 Summit County high school and college yearbooks; Soap Box Derby Collections; history of the rubber and trucking industries

Military—rosters for Ohioans in the Civil War; roster for Ohioans in the Spanish-American War; roster of Ohioans whose served in World War I; genealogical abstracts of Revolutionary War pension files; index to pension files for the War of 1812 and the Mexican War.

Newspapers—*Akron Beacon Journal* indexes 1841–present

Other—Gazetteers; Index of Declarations of Intention and Petitions for Naturalization, 1820–1908, Western District of Pennsylvania; emigration indexes from most European countries; growing collection on Huguenots; Quaker genealogy resources; Ohio 1812 tax list

Hudson Library and Historical Society

22 Aurora St.
Hudson, OH 44236
Phone: 330-653-6658
Website: www.hudsonlibrary.org

Housed in this library are the archives of The Hudson Library and Historical Society. The collection includes:

Census—complete run of all Ohio census
Local history—manuscript collection mostly related to people in Hudson and to the Hudson

community; Grace Goulder Izant's entire collection; large collection on abolitionist John Brown ; history on Ohio Canal; Underground Railroad history, national and local focus; David Hudson

Newspapers—a complete run of Hudson newspapers from late 1827–present; *Ravenna Republican /Portage County Democra*t, 1840s—1900; Summit County Beacon, 1850s–1900s

Of interest—The library is known for having a strong collection pertaining to Connecticut and the New England states.

Stow-Munroe Falls Public Library

3512 Darrow Rd.
Stow, OH 44224
Phone: 330-688-3295
website: www.smfpl.org/LH_archives
The collection includes:

Census—U.S. censuses for Summit County and early Portage County, 1790–1920

Church /religious organizations—Community Church News, 1934–1949 (not just about church members)

County/City directories—city directories from 1940–present

Local history and biographybBiographical sketches of Joshua Stow, William Walker, and William Wetmore; Clippings and pamphlets from 1960s√present; obituaries and news stories of Stow residents; high-school yearbooks and alumni directories; digitized images of Stow School District records, 1830–1855, with a list of names of those included; photographs of school classes, groups, and individuals; oral histories, mostly from 1974. Currently the local history room (located past the magazine section on the ground floor) is open 22 hours a week. For specific dates and times call the above phone number

Other—special collection donated by local groups, individuals, and families: contains scrapbooks, diaries, some daguerreotypes, and more. Index available under "special collections" on computer.

Tallmadge Branch

90 Community Rd.
Tallmadge, OH 44278
Phone: 330-633-4345

Frank E. Lawrence Collection: primarily on the early history of Tallmadge including more than 2500 historic photographs

---

TRUMBULL COUNTY

Warren Trumbull County Public Library (Main Library)

444 Mahoning Ave. NW
Warren OH 44483
Phone: 330-399-8807
Website: www.wtcpl.lib.oh.us/lh&g.htm
Hours: Mon–Thu 9 a.m.–9 p.m. (closes at 8 p.m. from Jun 2–Sep 21), Fri 9 a.m.–6 p.m., Sat 9 a.m.–5 p.m., Sun Sep–May 9 a.m.–5 p.m.

The Local History and Genealogy Center is on the second floor of the Main Library. Staff includes a genealogist and two full-time librarians, as well as volunteers from the Trumbull County chapter of the Ohio Genealogical Association. The Center's hours vary somewhat from those of the library; check the website or call 330-399-8807, ext 120 for details. Requests for brief answers found in indexed materials are accepted. Mail request, including a SASE and prepayment for copying costs ($.25/ for microfilm; $.10 photocopies). No copies are faxed.

Collection includes:

Census Records—U.S. 1820–1880, 1900–1930; all indexes for Ohio; Mercer County, Pennsylvania, 1800-1920; scattered years for other areas

Newspapers—with over 32 newspapers, the complete list is too large to include. The earliest newspaper is *Trump of Fame*, on microfilm from 1812–1816. See website for specific titles. Indexing of obituaries found in these is an on-going project

Military Records—rosters for Ohioans in revolutionary War, War of 1812; Mexican War, Civil War, War with Spain, and WWI; records of Ohio Soldiers' and Sailors' home in Sandusky; library-created notebooks on soldiers who lived or died in Trumbull County, Revolutionary War to current

Other—over 1,000 high school and college year books from the area; manuscript collection by an early genealogist on Trumbull county families 1810–1900; newsletters from most Ohio county genealogical societies, several Pennsylvania counties, and some U.S. publications; Ohio death certificates from 1908–1944

TUSCARAWAS COUNTY

Tuscarawas County Public Library

121 Fair Ave., NW
New Philadelphia, OH 44663
Phone: 330-364-4474
Hours: Mon–Thu, 9 a.m.–8:30 p.m., Fri 9 a.m.–6 p.m., Sat 9 a.m.–5 p.m.

The genealogy and family history resources include the following:

Census—selected census records for Tuscarawas County; index to Ohio for selected dates in 1800s

City directories—1909–present (with just a few missing)

County histories—selective county histories which include the townships

Local history—history of the schools in New Philadelphia; portrait and biographic record of the county; family histories donated by patrons

Maps/atlases—historical atlases, 1871, 1908

Newspapers—*Dover Iron Valley Reporter*, 1872–1900; *Canal Dover Democrat*, Sep 1839–Jan 1841; *New Philadelphia Ohio Democrat*, June 1841–Dec 1842; Jan 1863–Nov 1863; Dec 1865–Dec 1897; *New Philadelphia Ohio Democrat and Times*, Mar 1900–Dec 1925; *Canal Dover Weekly Argus*, Apr 1880–Dec 1882; *New Philadelphia Argus*, Jan 1883–Feb 1886; *New Philadelphia Times*, Jan 1886–Dec 1894; *Dover Daily Reporter*, Nov 1895–Mar 1968; *New Philadelphia Daily Times*, Mar 1903–Mar 1968

WAYNE COUNTY

Wayne County Public Library

304 N. Market St.
Wooster, OH 44691
Phone: 330-262-0916, ext 225
Website; www.wayne,lib.oh.us/newweb/genealogy/resources

Genealogy services include interlibrary loan of Ohio newspapers from the Ohio Historical Society and of census microfilm from 1790–1920 (for a nominal fee). Mail and phone queries are accepted but limited to three per letter or call. Staff will spend up to two hours researching. Copies are $.25 per page plus postage. Send requests to Genealogy Librarian/Genealogy and Local History at the above address.

This library has an extensive collection not only about Wayne County but also surrounding counties of Ashland, Coshocton, Holmes, Medina, Richland, Stark, Summit, and Tuscarawas. They have much information pertaining to Pennsylvania counties such as Philadelphia, Chester, Lancaster, York, Bedford, Bucks, Beaver, Allegheny, Fayette, Somerset, Washington, and Westmoreland.

The genealogy collection has over 2,800 volumes and 661 rolls of microfilm. It is quite extensive, and this list just highlights some of its contents:

Census—1810 for Wayne County; Ohio indexes, 1820–1880; Wayne county indexes, 1820–1900, 1920; Pennsylvania indexes, 1790–1810

County records—birth records, 1800–1908; court records, estates, guardianships, and naturalizations, as early as 1812 until 1934; marriage records, 1813–1934, 1940–1951; land and property records, 1816–1914; will abstracts, estates, and guardianships, 1812–1851; index to probate court records, 1812-1917

City/county directories—Wooster 1859, 1884, 1894, 1900, 1904, 1912; Orrville, 1955, 1958, 1967, 1974-1991; Ashland, 1985–1998

Local history—unbound family Bible records (80+) of Wayne County Historical Society; biographical sketches and historical records of: Kosciusko County, Indiana, Wayne County, and Holmes County; lawyers in Wayne County, 1812–1900; Pennsylvanians settled in Wayne County prior to 1900; over 300 bound histories on families within the county and over 700 unbound (incomplete) family histories.

Military—roster of Ohio Soldiers, 1861–1865; Ohioans who served in World War I; soldiers of the American Revolution buried in Ohio; Revolutionary War pension file abstracts; index to Revolutionary War service records and to War of 1812 pension files; index to soldiers in Indian wars and disturbances 1815–1858; locations of gravesites of veterans buried in the county; soldiers' relief records for World War I; graves registration cards

Newspapers—holdings include 18 newspapers from as early as 1822 and as recent as 1982.

Other—cemetery records for Wayne County and Wooster; Canaan Township records of trustees, 1880–1900; poll books, 1899–1929; obituaries (some on computer, others bound), 1900–present; many school records and yearbooks

Glossary

Ahnentafel—a table of your ancestors, therefore an ancestor chart

Ancestors—people from whom you descended

Ancestor chart—a listing of direct ancestors of an individual (see also pedigree chart, lineage chart)

Bulletin boards—a place on the Internet to leave a message. Responses to messages are then placed next to or underneath the message. These may be associated with specific topics (e.g., Civil War, immigration, or surnames)

Cached—in computer usage, denotes that previous information is stored and therefore available

Certified—certified copies of vital records contain a message or signature attesting to the authenticity of the document and therefore may be used for "official" legal purposes. Consequently they cost more to obtain. See also Uncertified copies.

Chat rooms—forums for online discussion of a topic. All participants have to be online and at the chat room's website at the same time.

City directory—an alphabetical listing for individuals as well as businesses, schools, churches, cemeteries, and hospitals. The individual listings appear after the business listings and usually include the head of household, address, occupation, and perhaps work address. Not everyone had to be included in the directory, but they are a valuable resource for the researcher attempting to locate an individual in a specific time and place.

Collateral lines—a side branch; not direct descendants (e.g., cousins)

Compiled sources—information published from a variety of works (lists, indexes)

Death notice—a brief notice of death, these were more prevalent in urban areas because less space was available in the newspaper.

Decedent—person who died

Deed—a document verifying transfer of property; usually of real estate

Dower—the part of the husband's estate to which his widow is entitled

Emigrant—one who has left his or her native country

Gazetteer—an alphabetical list of names of geographical places and their current location

Gedcom—Genealogical Data Communications. This is a computer file format that permits sharing of computerized genealogical information between genealogy software programs. This allows you to share all or parts of your genealogical data with other genealogists as well as submit your family tree to various sites such as Family Tree of the Jewish People; Rootsweb; LDS, etc.

Genealogy—the study of family history and descendents

Grantee—recipient of land or property

Grantor—person who gives or sells land to another

Host—a designated volunteer who maintains a bulletin board, chat room, or listserv to keep things politically correct and on topic.

Immigrant—one who has come to a new country

Issue—offspring

IGI—The International Genealogical Index is an index to temple work (finding and submitting names of ancestors in order that they can be "saved") done by members of the church of Jesus Christ of Latter Day Saints. The records that make up the index come from two sources:

Extracted records — for many years the church has filmed records (mostly from parish registers) to include in this index. Only registers with entry dates prior to December 31, 1865 were supposed to be indexed.

Personal submissions — Individual church members submit information from their own ancestry research. These records can be from any timeframe and are subject to errors depending on the accuracy and ability of the individual submitter.

Those viewing the CD-ROM version of the IGI will see the source listed as either extracted or submitted, thus indentifying which of the above categories the entry came from. At present extracted records account for about 83% of the IGI entries. Thus the large majority of the information found in the IGI concerns persons and related events that occurred prior to December 31, 1865.

The Church is no longer adding extracted records of temple submissions to the IGI. Still there remain some already extracted records submitted before 1970 but not included on the current IGI, which may appear on future IGI releases.

The IGI does not include every parish because not all permitted the filming of their records and not all records filmed have been extracted. Also since this is an index, original sources should always be checked.

Intestate—dying without leaving a will

Lineage chart—a listing of direct ancestors of an individual (see also ancestor chart, pedigree chart)

Mailing list—a simple online subscription whereby everyone subscribed receives all mail sent to the mailing list (like mass forwarding). Organized according to interest area—Korean War, Great Britain, surnames, passenger ships, etc. You can respond either to the individual submitter if his or her e-mail address is listed, or to the whole mailing list.

Manumission—freedom-granting papers prior to the Thirteenth Amendment and prior to the Emancipation Proclamation

Marriage banns—a public statement of a couple's intention to marry

Miracode—a census coding system using the soundex codes, listing the visitation number assigned by the enumerator instead of the page number and line number. It also has a separate index card per household, with the volume number and enumeration district. There are also index cards for each person in the household who is not a member of the immediate family in that household, or who has a surname different from that of the head of the household.

Mustered in—signed up for service

Née—born; used with maiden name

Newsgroups—maintained by Internet service providers (such as AOL, Yahoo), these are closely connected to e-mail; information shared is not retained indefinitely

Obituary—a lengthy article telling of a person's death and giving details about the deceased's activities during his or her life; also mentions remaining family members.

Pedigree chart—a listing of an individual's direct ancestors (see also ancestor chart, lineage chart)

PERSI (Periodical Source Index)—continuous indexing of names in periodicals, historical publications, ethnic publications, and family and surname publications

SASE—Self-addressed stamped envelope

[Sic]—used to indicate one is quoting or copying something verbatim, including any misspelled or apparently incorrect items

Soundex—a coding system based on how names sound, not how they are spelled. The purpose was to make it easier to find names that were similar, and to account for different spellings of the same surname. All vowels are eliminated and each consonant is assigned a number. The first letter is not coded but kept in letter format. Double consonants are coded only once.

Thread—a computer term: an unfolding conversation between multiple respondents on the same topic

Transcription—word-for-word copying of information

Uncertified copies—these have the same information as certified copies but without the authentication. They are generally used for medical, genealogical, or other nonlegal matters. These copies, when available, cost much less from official agencies.

Medical terminology:

Cholera/ winter fever/summer complaint—disease spread by fecal matter in the water supply

TB/consumption—a bacterial illness that usually affects the lungs and lymph nodes. Also termed phthisis, scrofula, The King's Evil.

Typhoid fever/enteric fever—an infectious disease (persons show fever and inflammation of the intestine) spread through food or drink

Typhus—has no relation to typhoid. Caused by microorganisms often found on lice or fleas.

Bibliography

Civil War– Related

Bates, Samuel P. *History of Pennsylvania Volunteers, 1861–1865*; Prepared in *Compliance with Acts of the Legislature*. Harrisburg, Pa.: B. Singerly, State Printer, 1869–1871.

Dyer, Frederick H. *A Compendium of the War of the Rebellion*. 2 vols. Des Moines, Ia.: Dyer Publishing Co., 1908 (reprint).

Groene, Bertram Hawthorne. *Tracing Your Civil War Ancestor*. New York: Ballantine Books, 1989

McPherson, James M. *Battle Cry of Freedom: The Civil War Era*. New York: Oxford University Press, 1988.

Morebeck, Nancy Justus. *Locating Union & Confederate Records; A Guide to the Most Commonly Used Civil War Records of the National Archives and Family History Library*. North Salt Lake, Ut.: Heritage Quest, 2001.

Reid, Whitelaw. *Ohio in the War*. 2 vols. Cincinnati, Oh.: Moore, Wilstach and Baldwin, 1838.

Schweitzer George Keene. *Civil War Genealogy*. Knoxville, Tn.: G. K. Schweitzer, 1988.

Segars, J. H. *In Search of Confederate Ancestors*: The Guide, ed. John McGlone.

Murfreesboro, Tn.: Southern Heritage Press, 1993.

Family History

Banks, Keith E. *How to Write Your Personal and Family History: A Resource Manual*. Bowie, Md.: Heritage Books, 1989.

Greene, Bob, and D. G. Fulford. *To Our Children's Children—Preserving Family Histories for Generations to Come*. New York: Doubleday, 1993.

Kelly, Ira, and D. S. Kelly. *Kelly Family History*. Shawnee Mission, Kan.: manuscript copy, 1970–71.

Kempthorne, Charley. *For All Time: A Complete Guide to Writing Your Family History*. Portsmouth, N.H.: Boynton/Cook Publishers, 1996.

Reunions

Wagner, Edith. *The Family Reunion Sourcebook*. Los Angeles, Calif.: Lowell House, 1999.

General Genealogy

Carmack, Sharon B. *Organizing Your Family History Search: Efficient and Effective Ways to Gather and Protect Your Genealogical Research*. Cincinnati, Oh.: Betterway Books, 1999.

Crandall, Ralph J. *Shaking Your Family Tree: A Basic Guide to Tracing Your Family's Genealogy*. Boston, Mass.: New England Historic Genealogical Society, 2001.

Croom, Emily Anne. *Unpuzzling Your Past: The Best-selling Basic Guide to Genealogy*. Cincinnati, Oh.: Betterway Books, 2001.

Dollarhide, William, and Ronald A. Bremer. *America's Best Genealogy Resource Centers*. Bountiful, Ut.: Heritage Quest, 1999.

Everton, George B. *The Handybook for Genealogists: United States of America*. Draper, Ut.: Everton Publishers, 2002.

Frisch-Ripley, Karen. *Unlocking the Secrets in Old Photographs*. Salt Lake City, Ut.: Ancestry, 1991.

Greenwood, Val D. *The Researcher's Guide to American Genealogy*. Baltimore, Md.: Genealogical Publishing, 2000.

Melnyk, Marcia Yannizze. *The Weekend Genealogist: Timesaving Techniques for Effective Research*. Cincinnati, Oh.: Betterway Books, 2000.

Pfeiffer, Laura Szucs. *Hidden Sources: Family History in Unlikely Places*. Orem, Ut.: Ancestry, 2000.

Smolenyak, Megan. *In Search of Our Ancestors: 101 Inspiring Stories of Serendipity and Connection in Rediscovering Our Family History*. Holbrook, Mass.: Adams Media Corp., 1999.

Szucs, Loretto Dennis. *The Source: A Guidebook of American Genealogy*, ed. Loretto Dennis Szucs and Sandra Hargreaves Luebking. Salt Lake City, Ut.: Ancestry, 1997.

United States, National Archives and Records Service. *Guide to Genealogical Research in the National Archives*. Washington, D.C.: Published for the National Archives and Records Service by the National Archives Trust Fund Board, 1983.

Immigration

Baxter, Angus. *In Search of Your European Roots: A Complete Guide to Tracing Your Ancestors in Every Country in Europe*. Baltimore, Md.: Genealogical Publishing Company, 2001.

Kemp, Thomas Jay. *International Vital Records Handbook*. Baltimore, Md: Genealogical Publishing Company, 2000.

Newman, John J. *American Naturalization Records, 1790–1990: What They Are and How to Use Them*. Bountiful, Ut.: Heritage Quest, 1998.

Szucs, Loretto Dennis. *They Became Americans: Finding Naturalization Records and Ethnic Origins*. Salt Lake City, Ut.: Ancestry, 1998.

Vital Records and Court Records

Eicholz, Alic, ed. *Ancestry's Red Book: American State, County and Town Sources*, maps by William Dollarhide. Salt Lake City, Ut.: Ancestry Publications, 1992.

Franklin, Charles M. *Keys to the Courthouse.* Indianapolis, In.: Heritage House, 1985.

Hatcher, Patricia Law. *Locating Your Roots: Discover Your Ancestors Using Land Records.* Cincinnati, Oh.: Betterway Books, 2003.

Sankey, Michael L., Carl R. Ernst, and Jimmy Flowers, eds. *The Sourcebook of County Court Records: A National Guide to Civil, Criminal, and Probate Records at the County and Municipal Levels Within the State Court Systems.* Tempe, Az.: BRB Publications, 1998.

Specific to Ohio

Bell, Carol Willsey. *Ohio Genealogical Guide.* Youngstown, Oh.: Bell Books, 1995.

——. *Ohio Wills and Estates to 1850: An Index.* Columbus, Oh.: C. W. Bell, 1981.

Gagel, VanSkiver Diane. *Ohio Courthouse Records.* Mansfield, Oh.: Ohio Genealogical Society, 2002.

Howe, Henry. *Historical Collections of Ohio.* Cincinnati, Oh.: Bradley & Anthony, 1849.

——. *Historical Collections of Ohio* (1888). Published by State of Ohio, 1908.

Knepper, Dr. George W. *The Official Ohio Lands Book.* Columbus, Oh.: Auditor of State, 2002. (free by request)

Lentz, Andrea D., ed. *A Guide to Manuscripts at the Ohio Historical Society.* Sara S. Fuller, assistant ed. Columbus, Oh.: Ohio Historical Society, 1972.

Ohio Genealogical Society Chapter Directory and Publications Lists. Mansfield, Oh.: The Ohio Genealogical Society, 2003.

Ohio Research Outline. Salt Lake City, Ut.: Church of the Latter-day Saints. n.d.

Schweitzer, George Keene. *Ohio Genealogical Research.* Knoxville, Tn.,1994.

Sperry, Kip. *Genealogical Research in Ohio.* Baltimore, Md.: Genealogical Publishing, 1997. [2nd ed. scheduled 2003/04]

Abstracts of Wills, Estates, and Guardianships; Cuyahoga County, Ohio Common Pleas Court, 1811-1852. Apollo, Pa.: Closson Press, 2003.

Wickham, Gertrude Van Rensselaer. *The Pioneer Families of Cleveland 1796-1840.* Woman's Department of the Cleveland Centennial Commission (1896). Cleveland, Oh.: Evangelical Publishing House, 1914.

Workman, Jeanne B., ed. *Cuyahoga County, Ohio, Genealogical Research Guide.* Fairview Park, Oh.: Cuyahoga West Chapter of the Ohio Genealogical Society, 1993.

Adoption

Rillera, Mary Jo. *The Adoption Search Book*, 3rd ed. Westminster, Calif.: Triadoption Publications, 1991.

Sorosky, Arthur D. *The Adoption Triangle: The Effects of the Sealed Record on Adoptees, Birth Parents, and Adoptive Parents.* New York: Anchor Press, 1978.

Klunder, Virgil L. *Lifeline: The Action Guide to Adoption Search.* Cape Coral, Fla.: Caradium Publications, 1991.

Specific to Ethnic or Religious Group, National Origin, or Gender

Anderson, S. Chris, and Ernest Thode. *A Genealogist's Guide to Discovering Your Germanic Ancestors: How to Find and Record Your Unique Heritage.* Cincinnati, Oh.: Betterway Books, 2000.

Bowen, Jeff. Native *American Wills and Probate Records, 1911-1921.* Signal Mountain, Tn.: Mountain Press, 1997.

Byers, Paula K. *Asian American Genealogical Sourcebook.* Detroit, Mi: Gale Research, 1995.

Carmack, Sharon DeBartolo. *A Genealogist's Guide to Discovering Your Female Ancestors: Special Strategies for Uncovering Hard-to-Find Information About Your Female Lineage.* Cincinnati, Oh.: Betterway Books, 1998.

——. *Italian-American Family History: A Guide to Researching and Writing About Your Heritage.* Baltimore, Md.: Genealogical Publishing, 1997.

Gingerich, Hugh F., with Rachel W. Kreider. *Amish and Amish Mennonite Genealogies.* Gordonville, Pa.: Pequea Publishers, 1986.

Goldie, Douglas Bruce. *In Search of Hamish McBagpipes: A Concise Guide to Scottish Genealogy.* Bowie, Md.: Heritage Books, 1992.

Johnson, Arta. *Aids for Research in Germany.* Columbus Oh.: A. F. Johnson, 1988.

Kavasch, E. Barrie. *A Student's Guide to Native American Genealogy.* Phoenix, Az. Oryx Press, 1996.

Kurzweil, Arthur, and Miriam Weiner, eds. *The Encyclopedia of Jewish Genealogy.* Northvale, N. J.: J. Aronson, 1991.

Mokotoff, Gary, and Warren Blatt. *Getting Started in Jewish Genealogy.* Bergenfield, N.J.: Avotaynu, 2000.

Palatines to America Society. *Palatines to America. Columbus, Oh.: Palatines to America,* 1978.

Platt, Lyman D. *Hispanic Surnames and Family History.* Baltimore, Md.: Genealogical Publishing, 1996.

Rowlands, John, ed. *Welsh Family History: A Guide to Research.* Baltimore Md.: Genealogical Publishing,1999.

Ryskamp, George R. *A Student's Guide to Mexican American Genealogy.* Phoenix, Az.: Oryx Press, 1996.

Sack, Sallyann Amdur, and the Israel Genealogical Society. *A Guide to Jewish Genealogical Research in Israel.* Teaneck, N.J.: Avotaynu, 1995.

Schaefer, Christina K. *The Hidden Half of the Family: A Sourcebook for Women's Genealogy.* Baltimore, Md.: Genealogical Publishing, 1999.

Schleifer, Jay. *A Student's Guide to Jewish American Genealogy*. Phoenix, Az.: Oryx Press, 1996.

African-American

Burroughs, Tony. *Black Roots: A Beginner's Guide to Tracing the African American Family Tree*. New York: Fireside Books, 2001.

Rawick, George, ed. *The American Slave: A Composite Autobiography*. Westport, Ct.: Greenwood Publishing, 1972.

Still, William. *The Underground Railroad*. Philadelphia, Pa.: Porter & Coates, 1872.

Streets, David H. *Slave Genealogy: A Research Guide with Case Studies*. Bowie, Md.: Heritage Books, 1986.

Smith, Franklin Carter, and Emily Anne Croom. *A Genealogist's Guide to Discovering Your African-American Ancestors: How to Find and Record Your Unique Heritage*. Cincinnati, Oh.: Betterway Books, 2003.

Thackery, David T. *Finding Your African American Ancestors: A Beginner's Guide*. Orem, Ut.: Ancestry, 2000.

Witcher, Curt Bryan. *African American Genealogy: A Bibliography and Guide to Sources*. Fort Wayne, In.: Round Tower Books, 2000.

Passenger Records

Coletta, John P. *They Came in Ships: A Guide to Finding Your Immigrant Ancestor's Arrival Record*. Salt Lake City, Ut.: Ancestry, 1993.

Glazier, Ira A., and P. William Filby, eds. Germans to America: Lists of Passengers Arriving at U.S. Ports. Wilmington, Del.: Scholarly Resources, 1988.

Morton Allan Directory of European Passenger Steamship Arrivals for the Years 1890 to 1930 at the Port of New York and for the Years 1904 to 1926 at the Ports of New York, Philadelphia, Boston and Baltimore. Baltimore, Md.: Genealogical Publishing, 1931.

Tepper, Michael. *American Passenger Arrival Records: A Guide to the Records of Immigrants Arriving at American Ports by Sail and Steam*. Baltimore, Md.: Genealogical Publishing, 1993.

Census

Dollarhide, William. *The Census Book: A Genealogist's Guide to Federal Census Facts, Schedules, and Indexes, with Master Extraction Forms for Federal Census Schedules, 1790–1930*. Bountiful, Ut.: Heritage Quest, 1990.

Thorndale, William, and William Dollarhide. *Map Guide to the U.S. Federal Censuses*. Bellingham, Wa.: Dollarhide Systems,1983.

———. *Map Guide to the U.S. Federal Censuses, 1790–1920*. Baltimore, Md.: Genealogical Publishing, 1987.

Jay, Thomas, ed. *The 1930 Census: A Reference and Research Guide*. North Salt Lake, Ut.: ProQuest, 2002.

Computers and Genealogy

Helm, Matthew, and April Leigh Helm. *Genealogy Online for Dummies*. Foster City, Calif.: IDG Books Worldwide, 2001.

McClure, Rhonda. *The Complete Idiot's Guide to Online Genealogy*. Indianapolis, In.: Macmillan, 2000.

Forms

ANCESTOR CHART

Compiled By:

Name
Address
City
State, Zip

Date

YOUR NAME

1

Born
Place
Married
Place
Died
Place

FATHER

2

Born
Place
Married
Place
Died
Place

3

Born
Place
Died
Place

YOUR SPOUSE

MOTHER

PATERNAL GRANDPARENTS

4

Born
Place
Married
Place
Died
Place

5

Born
Place
Died
Place

MATERNAL GRANDPARENTS

6

Born
Place
Married
Place
Died
Place

7

Born
Place
Died
Place

PATERNAL GR. GRANDPARENTS

8

Born   Place
Married   Place
Died   Place

9

Born   Place
Died   Place

10

Born   Place
Married   Place
Died   Place

11

Born   Place
Died   Place

MATERNAL GR. GRANDPARENTS

12

Born   Place
Married   Place
Died   Place

13

Born   Place
Died   Place

14

Born   Place
Married   Place
Died   Place

15

Born   Place
Died   Place

Form courtesy of Sandy Malitz.

FAMILY GROUP RECORD

Page _____ of _____

HUSBAND'S FULL NAME

	Day ~ Month ~ Year	City ~ Town ~ Township	County	State ~ Province	Country
Born					
Christened					
Married					
Died					

Burial Date	Cemetery		Section	Lot

Occupation	Religious Affiliation	Military Service

Other Wives (if any): No. 1, 2, etc.

Father's Full Name

Mother's Full Maiden Name

WIFE'S FULL MAIDEN NAME

Born					
Christened					
Died					

Burial Date	Cemetery		Section	Lot

Occupation	Religious Affiliation	Military Service

Other Husbands (if any): No. 1, 2, etc.

Father's Full Name

Mother's Full Maiden Name

CHILDREN   List each child in order of birth.

1 Full Name   Spouse's Full Name

Sex					
Born					
Christened					
Married					
Died					

2 Full Name   Spouse's Full Name

Sex					
Born					
Christened					
Married					
Died					

3 Full Name   Spouse's Full Name

Sex					
Born					
Christened					
Married					
Died					

Record the sources of your information.

Write Dates - 3 Dec 1946   **Write Places** - Lafayette, Tippecanoe Co., IN (city, county, state or province, country)

Tomsan Publication ~ 1091 Dorsh Rd. ~ South Euclid, OH 44121

Form courtesy of Sandy Malitz.

CHILDREN

4	Full Name	Spouse's Full Name			
Sex	Born				
	Christened				
	Married				
	Died				

5	Full Name	Spouse's Full Name			
Sex	Born				
	Christened				
	Married				
	Died				

6	Full Name	Spouse's Full Name			
Sex	Born				
	Christened				
	Married				
	Died				

7	Full Name	Spouse's Full Name			
Sex	Born				
	Christened				
	Married				
	Died				

8	Full Name	Spouse's Full Name			
Sex	Born				
	Christened				
	Married				
	Died				

DOCUMENTATION

Attach another sheet of paper if necessary.

Compiled By: (date, name, address, phone)

Form courtesy of Sandy Malitz.

HAVE YOU CHECKED THESE SOURCES ?

___ Adoption Records
___ Address Book/Calendar
___ African-American & Slave
    Estate Records
    Freedmen's Bureau
    Mortgage Records
    Plantation Records
___ *American State Papers*
___ Biographical Sketches
___ Bureau of Vital Statistics
___ Cemetery Records
    Cemetery Office
    Plot Owner's Records
    Sexton's Records
    Tombstone
___ Censuses
    Federal
    Indian
    State
    Special - Mortality,
        Agricultural, etc.
    Territorial
___ Church Records
    Baptism/Confirmation
    Denominational Archives
    Membership
    Pastor's Personal Records
___ Coroner's Files
___ Court Records
    Civil & Criminal
___ Delayed Birth Registration
___ Directories
    City/County
    Organizations
___ Divorce Records
___ Election Records
    Enumerations
    Voter Registration
___ Employment Records
    Applications/Resumes
    Pay Stubs
    Pension
    Personnel Files
    Union Records
___ Estate Papers
___ Ethnic Societies
___ Family Associations
___ *FamilySearch*
___ Funeral Home Records
___ Genealogical Societies
___ Health Department
    Burial Permit
    County Vital Records
___ Historians
    City/County/Town
    Family
    Local
___ Historical Societies
___ Home
    Airline Ticket Stubs
    Albums

Home (continued)
    Autograph Book
    Baby Book
    Christmas Card List
    Family Bible
    Household Budget
    Jewelry - Inscriptions
    Letters/Diaries/Journals
    Recital Program
    Scrapbook
___ Hospital Records
___ Immigration/Emigration
    Naturalization
    Passenger Lists
    Passports
___ Institutional Records
    County Infirmary
    Mental
    Orphanage
    Poor Farm
    Prisons/Jails - Incl. Youth
    Sanitoria
___ Internet
    On-line Magazines
    Searchable Databases
___ Land Records
    Bureau of Land Mgt.
    Deeds
    Homestead
    Leases
    Mortgages
___ Libraries
    Academic/Public/Special
    Genealogical
___ Licenses
    Business
    Driver's
    Professional i.e. Nurse
___ Lineage Societies
___ Marriage Records
    Banns/Bonds/Consents
    Licenses
___ Medical Records
___ Military Records
    Draft/Service/Pension
    National Cemetery Service
    Soldier's Homes
    State Adjutant General's
        Office
___ *National Union Catalog of*
    Manuscript Collections
___ Native American
    Enrollments
    Census
    School
___ Newsletters
    Company
    Organizations
___ Newspapers
    Advertisements
    Gossip Column

Newspapers (continued)
    Legal Notices
    Vital Statistics
___ Obituaries
    Newspapers
    Trade Magazines
    Newsletters
    Periodicals
    Death Notices
    Thank Yous
___ OCLC/FirstSearch
    Ask Your Public Librarian
___ Oral Histories
___ Organization Records
    Membership Lists
    Meeting Minutes
    Applications
    Fraternal, Military,
        Service, Social, Sorori-
        ties, Fraternities, etc.
___ *Periodical Source Index*
___ Periodicals
    Trade
    Fraternal
    Genealogical
___ Plat Maps
___ Postcards
___ Powers of Attorney
___ Probate Court
    Adoptions
    Estates
    Guardianship
    Insanity Inquest
___ Recorder's Office
    Brands
    Grave Registrations
    Military Discharges
    Patents
___ Reunion Minutes
___ School Records
    Alumni Association
    Awards
    Permanent Record Card
    Diplomas
    Yearbooks
___ Social Security Death Index
___ State Treasurer's Office
    Military Bonus
    Custom's Records
___ Tax Records
    Personal
    Poll
    Real estate
___ Territorial Records (Before
    Statehood)
___ WPA County Record Surveys

Compiled By: Teeter Grosvenor
& Sandy Malitz, 2001

Form courtesy of Sandy Malitz.

RESEARCH LOG

Ancestor's Name		Date	Soundex Code
Time Period		Facility	
General Locality		Address	

Description of Source (author, title, year, pages, roll #, etc.)	Results (names & years searched, positive & negative results)	

Call # Microfilm #		Copied Yes No
Call # Microfilm #		Copied Yes No
Call # Microfilm #		Copied Yes No
Call # Microfilm #		Copied Yes No
Call # Microfilm #		Copied Yes No
Call # Microfilm #		Copied Yes No
Call # Microfilm #		Copied Yes No
Call # Microfilm #		Copied Yes No

Tomsan Publications ~ 1091 Dorsh Rd. ~ South Euclid, OH 44121

Form courtesy of Sandy Malitz.

Researcher: _____

Address: _____

City/State/Zip: _____

Ohio Historical Society
Research Services Department
1982 Velma Avenue
Columbus, OH 43211-2497
(614) 297-2510

Ohio Death Certificate Request Form

COPY CHARGES:

The base fee is **$6.00 per request/name**, which covers up to **4 pages of copies and postage**. The charge for each additional page is 25 cents. Copy requests must be **PREPAID** with check or money order payable to the Ohio Historical Society. **DO NOT SEND CASH.** No refund will be provided for records that are searched but not found.

The Ohio Historical Society holds Ohio death certificates for the period December 20, 1908, through 1944. An index to certificates filed from 1913 to 1937 is maintained on the Ohio Historical Society website at http://dbs.ohiohistory.org/dindex/. The Ohio Department of Health, Vital Statistics Unit, PO Box 15098, Columbus, OH 43215-0098, holds death certificates filed from 1945 to the present.

For the above copy charge to apply, each request **MUST** include **full name of decedent**, **year of death**, and **at least ONE** of the following: month/day of death, place of death, or certificate number.

Full Name of Decedent: _____

Year of Death _____ (month and day if known): _____

County/City (if known): _____

Certificate Number (if known): _____

****

RESEARCH REQUESTS: (Complete fields ONLY if paying RESEARCH FEE)

A death certificate copy request that does not provide the above information will be treated as a research request, the filling of which is governed by separate policies and procedures of the Ohio Historical Society. Death certificate research by staff of the historical society includes the following:

- searching multiple years of the death certificate index for one name

- matching specific information provided by researcher with multiple certificates to find an exact match

The fee is **$20.00** for each name searched. Requests must be **PREPAID** with check or money order payable to the Ohio Historical Society. For that fee, staff will search up to two of the eight index groupings. The individual index groupings and the years they cover are as follows:

1908-12   1913-17   1918-22   1923-27   1928-32   1933-37   1938-40   1941-44

Circle one or two of the above groupings to be searched.

Name to be searched: _____
　　　　　　　　　　　first　　　　　　　　middle　　　　　　　last
One variant spelling: _____

Parents/maiden name: _____

Date/year of birth: _____   Date/year of death: _____

Place of death/burial: _____

Rev. 10/21/03

Researcher: _____

Address: _____

City/State/Zip: _____

Ohio Death Certificate Multiple Requests Form

PLEASE USE THIS FORM FOR REQUESTS OF 2 OR MORE NAMES/CERTIFICATES.

COPY CHARGES:

The base fee is **$6.00 per request/name**, which covers **copies and postage**. Copy requests must be **PREPAID** with check or money order payable to the Ohio Historical Society. **DO NOT SEND CASH.** No refund will be provided for records that are searched but not found.

The Ohio Historical Society holds Ohio death certificates for the period December 20, 1908, through 1944. An index to certificates filed from 1913 to 1937 is maintained on the Ohio Historical Society website at http://dbs.ohiohistory.org/dindex/. **OHS DOES NOT HOLD CERTIFICATES FILED AFTER 1944.** The **Ohio Department of Health**, Vital Statistics Unit, PO Box 15098, Columbus, OH 43215-0098, holds death certificates filed from **1945 to the present.** DO NOT send requests for death certificates from 1945 to the present to the Ohio Historical Society. We will not forward requests to Ohio Department of Health.

For the above copy charge to apply, each request **MUST** include **full name of decedent, year of death**, and **AT LEAST ONE** of the following: **month/day of death, place of death, or certificate number**. No refund will be provided for records that are searched but not found.

NAMES MUST BE LISTED IN CHRONOLOGICAL (DATE) ORDER, EARLIEST TO LATEST. MULTIPLE PAGE REQUESTS MUST BE IN CONTINUOUS DATE ORDER.

	Full Name	County/city	Month/ day	Year of Death (list in order by year)	Certificate #
1					
2					
3					
4					
5					
6					
7					
8					
9					
10					

Rev. 10/21/03

1840 CENSUS - Abstract Form & Worksheet

STATE   COUNTY   TOWN-TOWNSHIP   DATE

Head of Family	Free White Males Including Heads of Families												Possible Names	Free White Females Including Heads of Families												Possible Names
	Under 5	5 - 10	10 - 15	15 - 20	20 - 30	30 - 40	40 - 50	50 - 60	60 - 70	70 +			Under 5	5 - 10	10 - 15	15 - 20	20 - 30	30 - 40	40 - 50	50 - 60	60 - 70	70 +	

Notes	Free Colored Males						Possible Names	Free Colored Females						Possible Names
	Under 10	10 - 24	24 - 36	36 - 55	55 - 100	100 +		Under 10	10 - 24	24 - 36	36 - 55	55 - 100	100 +	

Page

Tomsan Publications ~ 1091 Dorsh Rd. ~ South Euclid, OH 44121   1993, Revised 1998

Form courtesy of Sandy Malitz.

STATE   COUNTY   TOWN-TOWNSHIP   DATE

Page

Head of Family | Notes

Slaves - Males

Under 10	10 - 24	24 - 36	36 - 55	55 - 100	100 +

Possible Names

Slaves - Females

Under 10	10 - 24	24 - 36	36 - 55	55 - 100	100 +

Possible Names

Number of Persons Employed In

Mining	Agriculture	Commerce	Manufacturing and Trades	Navigation of Ocean	Navigation of Canals, Lakes, etc.	Engineers, etc.

Possible Names

Pensioners In Revolutionary or Military Services

Names and Ages

Possible Names

White Persons

Deaf and Dumb Under 14	Deaf and Dumb 14 - 25	Deaf and Dumb 25 +	Blind	Insane and Public Charge	Insane and Private Charge

Possible Names

Colored Persons

Deaf and Dumb	Blind	Insane and Private Charge	Insane and Public Charge

Possible Names

Tomsan Publications ~ 1091 Dorsh Rd. ~ South Euclid, OH 44121   1993, Revised 1998

Form courtesy of Sandy Malitz.

1850 CENSUS

State _____ County _____ Town-Township _____

Post Office _____ Enumeration Date _____ Handwritten Page # _____ Printed Page # _____

Line #	Dwelling #	Family #	Names	Age	Sex	Color	Occupation	Real Estate Value	Birth Place	Married Within the Year	School	Can't Read or Write	Deaf, dumb, etc.

Tomsan Publications ~ 1091 Dorsh Rd. ~ South Euclid, OH 44121   1993, Revised 1998

Form courtesy of Sandy Malitz.

1860 CENSUS

OFFICIAL CENSUS DAY
June 1, 1860

State _____

Post Office _____

County _____

Enumeration Date _____

Town-Township _____

Handwritten Page # _____

Printed Page # _____

Line #	Dwelling #	Family #	Names	Age	Sex	Color	Occupation	Real Estate Value	Personal Property	Birth Place	Married Within the Year	School	Can't Read or Write	Deaf, dumb, etc.

Tomsan Publications ~ 1091 Dorsh Rd. ~ South Euclid, OH 44121   1993, Revised 1998

Form courtesy of Sandy Malitz.

1870 CENSUS

OFFICIAL CENSUS DAY
June 1, 1870

State ———
County ———
Post Office ———
Town-Township ———
Enumeration Date ———
Printed Page # ———
Handwritten Page # ———

Line #	House # and Street Name	Dwelling #	Family #	Names	Age	Sex	Color	Occupation	Real Estate Value	Personal Property	Birth Place	Father Foreign Born	Mother Foreign Born	Month Born	Month Married	School	Can't Read or Write	Deaf, dumb, etc.	Eligible to Vote

Tomsan Publications ~ 1091 Dorsh Rd. ~ South Euclid, OH 44121   1993, Revised 1998

Form courtesy of Sandy Malitz.

1880 CENSUS

OFFICIAL CENSUS DAY
June 1, 1880

State _____

Enumeration Date _____

County _____

Supervisor's District _____

Town-Township _____

Enumeration District _____

Handwritten Page # _____

Printed Page # _____

Line #	House # and Street Name	Dwelling #	Family #	Names	Color	Sex	Age	Month Born	Relationship to Head of Family	Marital Status	Month Married	Occupation	Deaf, dumb, etc.	School	Can't Read or Write	Birth Place of This Person	Father's Birth Place	Mother's Birth Place

Tomsan Publications ~ 1091 Dorsh Rd. ~ South Euclid, OH 44121   1993, Revised 1998

Form courtesy of Sandy Malitz.

1900 CENSUS

State _____   County _____   Township _____   City _____   Ward # _____

Institution _____   Date _____   Supervisor's District _____   Enumeration Dictrict _____   Sheet # _____

Line #	Street Name	House #	Dwelling #	Family #	Name	Relationship to Head of Family	Color or Race	Sex	Month Born	Year Born	Age	Marital Status	# Year Married	# Children Born	# Children Living	Birth Place	Father's Birth Place

Tomsan Publications ~ 1091 Dorsh Rd. ~ South Euclid, OH 44121   1993, Revised 1998

Form courtesy of Sandy Malitz.

1900 CENSUS - continued

State ——— County ——— Township ——— City ——— Ward # ———

Institution ——— Date ——— Supervisor's District ——— Enumeration District ——— Sheet # ———

Line #	Name	Mother's Birth Place	Year of Immigration	# Years in U.S.	Naturalization	Occupation, Trade, Profession	# Months Unemployed	Attend School	Read and Write	Speak Englsh	Own or Rent	Own Free or Mortgaged	Farm or House	Farm Schedule #

Tomsan Publications ~ 1091 Dorsh Rd. ~ South Euclid, OH 44121   1993. Revised 1998

Form courtesy of Sandy Malitz.

1910 CENSUS

State _____   County _____   Township _____   Date _____   City _____   Supervisor's District _____   Enumeration District _____   Ward # _____   Sheet # _____

Institution _____

Line #	Street Name	House #	Dwelling #	Family #	Name	Relationship to Head of Family	Sex	Color or Race	Age	Marital Status	# Years Married	# Children Born	# Children Living	Birth Place	Father's Birth Place	Mother's Birth Place

Tomsan Publications ~ 1091 Dorsh Rd. ~ South Euclid, OH 44121   1993, Revised 1998

Form courtesy of Sandy Malitz.

State ———

County ———

Institution ———

Date ———

Township ———

Supervisor's District ———

City ———

Enumeration Dictrict ———

Ward # ———

Sheet # ———

Line #
Name
Year of Immigration
Naturalized or Alien
Speak English If No, What Language
Trade, Profession or Particular Kind of Work Done
Industry, Business, or Establishment in Which at Work
Employer-Wage or Salary Worker - Work on Own Account
Unemployed
Weeks Unemployed
Read and Write
Attend School
Own or Rent
Own Free or Mortgaged
Farm or House
Farm Schedule #
Union or Confederate Vet.
Deaf, dumb, etc.

Tomsan Publications ~ 1091 Dorsh Rd. ~ South Euclid, OH 44121   1993, Revised 1998

1920 CENSUS

State _____ County _____ Township _____ Date _____ Institution _____

City _____ Supervisor's District _____ Enumeration District _____ Ward # _____ Sheet # _____

Line #	Street Name	House #	Dwelling #	Family #	Name	Relationship to Head of Family	Home - Owned or Rented	Owned Free or Mortgaged	Sex	Color or Race	Age	Marital Status	Year of Immigration	Naturalized or Alien	Year Naturalized	Attend School	Able to Read	Able to Write

Form courtesy of Sandy Malitz.

Tomsan Publications ~ 1091 Dorsh Rd. ~ South Euclid, OH 44121   1993, Revised 1998

Line #	Name	Birth Place	Mother Tongue	Father's Birth Place	Father's Mother Tongue	Mother's Birth Place	Mother's Mother Tongue	Speak English	Trade, Profession or Particular Kind of Work Done	Industry, Business, or Establishment in Which at Work	Employer - Wage or Salary Worker - Work on Own Account	Farm Schedule #

State ———   County ———   Township ———   City ———   Ward # ———
Institution ———   Date ———   Supervisor's District ———   Enumeration District ———   Sheet # ———

Tomsan Publications ~ 1091 Dorsh Rd. ~ South Euclid, OH 44121   1993, Revised 1998

Form courtesy of Sandy Malitz.

1930 CENSUS

State ____ County ____ Township ____ City ____ Ward # ____

Institution ____ Date ____ Supervisor's District ____ Enumeration District ____ Sheet # ____

Line #	Street Name	House #	Dwelling #	Family #	Name	Relationship to Head of Family	Home - Owned or Rented	Value If Owned or Monthly Rental	Own Radio Set	Live On Farm	Sex	Color or Race	Age	Marital Status	Age at 1st Marriage	Attend School	Able to Read & Write	Birth Place	Father's Birth Place

2002

Tomsan Publications ~ 1091 Dorsh Rd. ~ South Euclid, OH 44121

Form courtesy of Sandy Malitz.

1930 CENSUS - continued

State _____ County _____ Date _____ Township _____ Supervisor's District _____ City _____ Enumeration District _____ Ward # _____ Sheet # _____

Institution _____

Line #	Name	Mother's Birth Place	Language Spoken Before Coming to U.S.	Year of Immigration	Naturalized or Alien	Speak English	Trade, Profession or Particular Kind of Work Done	Industry, Business, or Establishment in Which at Work	Employer - Wage or Salary Worker - Work on Own Account	Actually At Work	Line # For Unemployment	Veteran of Military	War or Expedition	Farm Schedule #

Tomsan Publications ~ 1091 Dorsh Rd. ~ South Euclid, OH 44121   2002

AFRICAN-AMERICAN RESEARCH
WHERE TO FIND INFORMATION Selected List

Including Enslaved Persons & Free People of Color Prior to the Civil War
As Well As All People During the Late 19ᵗʰ Century & 20ᵗʰ Century

TYPE OF INFORMATION	TYPE OF RECORD	RECORD LOCATION
name - slaves & free people of color	census - state & Federal *Southern Claim's Commission* Native American Rolls i.e. *Dawes Rolls, Guion Miller Rolls, etc.* military records *Freedman's Bureau*	National Archives, Family History Centers, other libraries
	registers of free person of color deeds marriage contract court records guardianship estate records apprenticeship records slave register voter registration birth, marriage, death records	county courthouse, Family History Centers
	county history tombstones city directories slave narratives *Records of Ante-Bellum Southern Plantations....* Plantation records	public, regional libraries, Family History Centers
birth date	birth, marriage, death records	health or vital records dept. county & state, Family History Centers, *FamilySearch*
	family Bible baptismal records tombstones	church records
	Native American Rolls i.e. *Dawes Rolls, Guion Miller Rolls, etc.* *Freedman's Bureau* plantation records	National Archives & Family History Centers, other libraries
death date	death records	health or vital records dept. county & state
	Social Security Death Index	http://www.rootsweb.com, public & regional libraries
	cemetery records funeral home records tombstones plantation records	public & regional libraries
marriage records - former slaves	post Civil War cohabitation records "delayed" marriage registers	state archives
	Freedman's Bureau Native American Rolls i.e. *Dawes Rolls, Guion Miller Rolls, etc.*	National Archives
	church records	local churches, libraries, church archives
migrations	court records registers of Negroes estate records	county courthouse
migrations (continued)	voter registration	

Form courtesy of Sandy Malitz.

TYPE OF INFORMATION	TYPE OF RECORD	RECORD LOCATION
	deeds census records Native American Rolls i.e. *Dawes Rolls, Guion Miller Rolls, etc.* *Freedman's Bureau* slave narratives	National Archives & other libraries libraries
manumission records	abolition societies court records estate records deeds	regional libraries, state archives county courthouse
names of parents	education census state census federal census *Freedman's Bureau* Native American Rolls i.e. *Dawes Rolls, Guion Miller Rolls, etc.* birth, marriage, death records estate records tombstones	state archives National Archives Family History Centers & other libraries county courthouse cemeteries, libraries
plantation owner	newspapers - runaway slaves *Freedman's Bureau* - depositors, marriages Native American Rolls i.e. *Dawes Rolls, Guion Miller Rolls, etc.* post Civil War land owner - tenant farmer estate records apprenticeship records court records deeds marriage contracts birth & death records *Records of Ante-Bellum Southern Plantations...* slave narratives plantation records	state archives National Archives, Family History Centers & other libraries county courthouses regional libraries
military service	service & pension records WW I Draft Registration Records *Roll of Honor* census records tombstones	National Archives, Family History Centers & other libraries cemeteries, libraries
property	tax records deeds	county courthouse
education	school census federal census alumni records & periodicals	state archives National Archives, Family History Centers, & other libraries alumni associations

Form courtesy of Sandy Malitz.

Index